THE COUNTRY OF

BALOCHISTAN

ITS

GEOGRAPHY, TOPOGRAPHY, ETHNOLOGY, AND HISTORY

THE COUNTRY OF
BALOCHISTAN

ITS

GEOGRAPHY, TOPOGRAPHY, ETHNOLOGY, AND HISTORY

BY
A. W. HUGHES

GYAN

Published by

GYAN

Gyan Publishing House
5, Ansari Road
Daryaganj, New Delhi-110002
Phone: 011-47034999, 9811692060
E-mail: books@gyanbooks.com

Distribution Network
gyanbooks.com
India, USA, Canada, UK, Australia

ISBN: 978-93-6433-416-7 (HB)
First Published, 1877

2nd Impression 2024

Printed at: Gyan Press, Delhi.

THE COUNTRY OF BALOCHISTAN ITS GEOGRAPHY, TOPOGRAPHY, ETHNOLOGY, AND HISTORY
Author: A. W. HUGHES

KALĀT, THE CAPITAL OF BALOCHISTAN.

Frontispiece.

THE COUNTRY OF

BALOCHISTAN,

ITS

GEOGRAPHY, TOPOGRAPHY, ETHNOLOGY, AND HISTORY;

WITH A MAP, PHOTOGRAPHIC ILLUSTRATIONS, AND APPENDICES CONTAINING A SHORT VOCABULARY OF THE PRINCIPAL DIALECTS IN USE AMONG THE BALOCHIS, AND A LIST OF AUTHENTICATED ROAD ROUTES.

By A. W. HUGHES, F.R.G.S., F.S.S.,

BOM. UNCOV. CIVIL SERVICE.

LONDON: GEORGE BELL & SONS, YORK STREET,
COVENT GARDEN.
1877.

TO

COLONEL SIR WILLIAM LOCKYER MEREWETHER,

K.C.S.I., AND C.B., BOMBAY STAFF CORPS,

AND COMMISSIONER IN SINDH,

WHOSE EXTENSIVE AND INTIMATE KNOWLEDGE

OF THE BORDER BÅLOCH TRIBES, AND OF ALL MATTERS

CONNECTED WITH THE KALĀT STATE,

ACQUIRED DURING A LONG SERVICE OF MANY

YEARS ON THE SINDH FRONTIER, IN

VARIOUS POLITICAL CHARGES,

IS SO WELL KNOWN AND APPRECIATED,

This Volume

IS SINCERELY AND GRATEFULLY INSCRIBED.

TO

COLONEL SIR WILLIAM LOCKYER MEREWETHER,

K.C.S.I., AND C.B., BOMBAY STAFF CORPS,

AND COMMISSIONER IN SINDH,

WHOSE EXTENSIVE AND INTIMATE KNOWLEDGE

OF THE BORDER BÅLOCH TRIBES, AND OF ALL MATTERS

CONNECTED WITH THE KALĀT STATE,

ACQUIRED DURING A LONG SERVICE OF MANY

YEARS ON THE SINDH FRONTIER, IN

VARIOUS POLITICAL CHARGES,

IS SO WELL KNOWN AND APPRECIATED,

This Volume

IS SINCERELY AND GRATEFULLY INSCRIBED.

PREFACE.

THE publication of this single volume on the very extensive, though as yet imperfectly known country, called Balochistan, had been determined upon for a two-fold reason. First, because all information concerning this immense tract has hitherto been contained, not alone in a few books of history and travel of a somewhat old date, but in numerous Government reports and pamphlets, either printed or in manuscript, which have appeared at various times during the past forty years. The information contained in each of these is no doubt valuable, and it was thought, that if the whole of these *disjecta membra* were collated with some amount of care and diligence into one volume, and arranged in such a manner as might be deemed most acceptable to the general reader, its value as a work of reference upon matters connected with Balochistan would be at once appreciated.

The second reason adduced for the publication of the book is the growing interest in that particular part of Balochistan bordering upon Afghanistan and Sindh, which is more especially under the sovereignty of the Brahui Khān of Kalāt, and the attention which has of late been drawn to what may be called the "Kalāt question," in special reference to the necessity for a good understanding between the Baloch ruler and the British Government so far as regards the safe conduct of Central-Asian trade into

British India, and to the better and more effectual observance of the treaties previously entered into between the two Governments.

The authorities consulted in the preparation of this volume (which, it may be as well to remark, is to be regarded more as a compilation than an original work,) are the following, and it is hoped that they may be considered a sufficient guarantee for its general accuracy and trustworthiness :—

ALLEN, Rev. J. N., Bombay Ecclesiastical Establishment (1843).
ARRIAN, (Expeditio Alexandri).
BELLEW, Dr., Bengal Medical Service (1872).
BROWN, Capt. Lewis, Bombay Army (1841).
BRUCE, Mr. R. B. J., Bengal Civil Service (1871).
CARLESS, Lieut. T. G., Indian Navy (1838).
CHRISTIE, Captain, Bombay Army (1816).
COOK, Dr. H., Bombay Medical Service (1860).
GLADSTONE, Mr. C. E., Bengal Civil Service (1874).
GOLDSMID (present Sir F. J.), Madras Army (1863).
GORDON, Lieut. M. F., Bombay Army (1841-42).
GREEN, Sir H. R., Bombay Army.
HART, Capt. S. V. W., Bombay Army (1840).
JACOB, General John, Bombay Army (1854).
LE MESSURIER, Major P., Bombay Army (1841).
MASSON, Mr. Ch., Traveller (1844).
MEREWETHER, Sir W. L., Bombay Army.
MONTRIOU, Lieut. C. W., Indian Navy (1842).
OUTRAM, Major James, Bombay Army (1840).
PIERCE, Mr. E., Indo-European Telegraph Dept. (1874).
POTTINGER, Lieut. H., Bombay Army (1816).
PREEDY, Major H. W., Bombay Army (1854).
ROBINSON, Lieut. G. H., Bombay Army (1841).
THORNTON, Mr. E., Indian Gazetteer Compiler (1844).
ROSS, Lieut.-Col., Bombay Staff Corps.
ST. JOHN, Major, R.E.
etc. etc. etc.

A. W. H.

KARĀCHI, *August, 1876.*

CONTENTS.

LIST OF ILLUSTRATIONS.

BALOCHISTAN.

CHAPTER I.

A GEOGRAPHICAL SKETCH OF BOTH PERSIAN AND KALĀTI BALOCHISTAN.

THERE are but few countries in the vast continent of Asia of which, as regards their general geography, so little was, till within a comparatively recent period, really known as that extensive region shown in modern maps under the name of Balochistan, or the country of the Baloch tribe. Much greater, indeed, and possibly more accurate, it may be said, is the knowledge at this present time of that immense territory vaguely designated as "Central Asia," the land of terrible deserts and fertile oases, that, thirty or forty years ago, was a veritable *terra incognita* to geographers, but which the slow yet sure tide of Russian conquest has successfully opened out to scientific exploration and research.

With perhaps the single exception of the interior of Arabia, concerning which geographers of the present day as yet know hardly more than of Equatorial Africa itself, Balochistan, taken as a whole, might, till within the last ten or twelve years, have fairly laid claim to the second place in this maze of geographical ignorance and doubt, while even the latest compiled map of the country, prepared in 1875, shows vast tracts of land as still unexplored and unknown. Nor are the reasons of this state of things at all strange or difficult of explanation, as will be seen when treating of the hydrography and climate of this peculiar region.

Balochistan, in the modern acceptation of the term, may be said, in a general sense, to include all that tract of country which has for its northern and north-eastern boundary the large kingdom of Afghānistan, its eastern frontier being limited by the British province of Sindh, and its western by the Persian State, while the Arabian Sea washes its southern base for a distance of nearly six hundred miles. Since, however, this can only be regarded as a very general description of the boundaries of Balochistan, it will be necessary for a better elucidation of this part of the subject to enter into more minute particulars as to both the natural and political limits of the country, giving the best and latest information possible on these points. In that portion of Balochistan extending to the eastward and comprising the provinces of Las and Jhalawān, the frontier from the sea-coast near Cape Monze (Rās Muāri), in about lat. 24° 53′ N. and long. 66° 41′ E., is, in a northerly direction, well demarcated for a considerable distance, first, by the Habb river, and afterwards by the Brahuik range of mountains separating it from the British province of Sindh up to within a few miles of the 28th parallel of north latitude. Thence the boundary line, following the southern portion of the Gandāva district, runs in an easterly direction, and is conterminous with the Sindh frontier as far as a point 20 miles or so north-east of the Lehni tower. From this, skirting the Panjāb frontier, it pursues a similar direction, passing the Gendāri mountain, and at last reaches a spot near Harrand, where the British, Baloch, and Afghān boundaries meet. Thence it runs nearly due west for a distance of upwards of 160 miles, till it strikes the Lalleji range of hills near the Bolān pass, and from this point makes an abrupt turn to the north-west, and so proceeds till within a few miles north of the Tokātu mountain in the Shāl district of Kalāt, where, in this particular locality the Lora rivulet marks the true boundary between Balochistan and Afghānistan. Here it attains its most northerly limit, and afterwards pursues a south-westerly course, skirting the Kalāti districts of Shāl, Nushki, and Kharān, all of which, in the newly compiled map of Balochistan, are shown as a part of the great Sarawān Province. At the southern extremity of the Kharān tract it meets the mountain range of the Washati, or, as it is also called, the *Mach* which, it is presumed, may possibly mark this portion of its northern boundary; but, unfortunately, nothing *definite* seems to be known of this part of the frontier line. St. John states that the highlands of Sarhad undoubtedly form a portion of Balochistan, while the neighbouring plain district of Zirreh, when inhabited, belonged to Sistān. He believes that the 29th parallel of latitude, between the 59th and 64th meridians of longitude, may be taken as the approximate limit in this direction. Bellew, however, in his record of the mission to Sistān in 1872, considers that the southern (or desert) portion of that province of Afghānistan, as bordering upon Balochistan, is separated from it by a range of hills known as the Mushti, which may possibly be the same as the Mach or Washati, but he agrees in the view taken that the Sarhad (or boundary) mountains divide the Zirreh basin of the same Afghān district from the Baloch province of Makrān. But while this state of uncertainty prevails regarding the northern frontier of Balochistan, the western boundary, or that separating it from Persia, does not appear to be quite so ambiguous. According to the first authority (St. John) previously quoted, the most westerly limit in that direction is a pillar, or cairn, of stones, a few miles from the sea-coast, and not far from lat. 25° 47′ N., and long. 58° 35′ E. This boundary mark is called "Malik Chadar," or the king's monument, and is probably one of a very ancient date. It points out, in fact, the westernmost portion of the Baloch district of Makrān, and the frontier line thence runs to the Saif-u-Din pass, near a swamp called the Dag-i-Farhad, on the road between the towns of Ban and Banpur, in lat. 28° 14′ N., and long. 59° 5′ E., which marks the limit of the Karmān district of Narmashir. South of this, Jar-Moriān, where the Rudbar and Banpur rivers meet, is *probably* the point of division.

Area.—In area Balochistan had long been supposed to cover in its entirety quite 160,000 square miles, but the latest estimates do not raise it higher than 140,000 square miles, of which 60,000 are said to belong to what is termed Persian Balochistan, and the remaining 80,000 to Kalāti Balochistan, or that portion which is more or less directly under the rule of the Brāhui Khān of Kalāt.

Physical Aspect.—The natural aspect of so large a country as Balochistan must of a necessity be both varied and peculiar. It is decidedly a mountainous region, but yet possesses many plains and valleys, some so sandy and desert as to be utterly useless for any agricultural purpose, while others are fertile, and capable of high cultivation when sufficiently irrigated. Among the many mountain ranges of Balochistan, the most extensive, and, so far as is at present known, the loftiest, is the Brahuik—so called by Pottinger—and which is in some sense a continuation of the Afghān mountains north of Quetta. It extends from the Shāl district of Sarawān in a southerly direction through the Jhalawān and Las Provinces down to Cape Monze, a distance of quite 340 miles. The tract varies in breadth, being about 150 miles from the Kachh Gandāva border on the east to Nushki on the west; but it is said to be widest about the centre, gradually narrowing as it approaches the sea-coast of Las. Though this extensive mountain mass may well pass under the general name of the Brahuik plateau, it has locally other names in the several districts through which its chains extend. Thus, that portion which separates the highlands of Sarawān from the low country of Kachh Gandāva is known as the Takāri; further south, and down to the 26th parallel of latitude, this same chain is called the Kirthar, and thence to the ocean it obtains the name of the Pabb hills. Similarly other offshoots west of these are known as the Harbui, the Dauwaru, and the Hāra mountains. These last form a line of demarcation between the Las and Makrān Provinces. It is the Brahuik range in which the two mountains said to be the loftiest yet known in Balochistan are situate. One of these is the two-forked hill of Tokātu in the Shāl district, about 14 miles north of Quetta, having an elevation of between 11,000 and 12,000 feet above the level of the sea. The other is that of Chehel-Tan, near Mastung, which in height is believed, if anything, to exceed that of Tokātu. Another high mountain is the "Kuh-i-Māran," or hill of snakes, which Cook* thought was not much inferior in height to Chehel-Tan. It bounds the Mangachar valley, in the province of Sarawān, to the east-north-east. Along the Kirthar range are also peaks having an altitude of between 7000 and 8000 feet above sea level.

The table-land of the Brahuik range, which covers a very large portion of the provinces of Sarawān, Jhalawān, and Las, in Kalāti Balochistan, would appear to attain its greatest elevation, about 6800 feet, at Kalāt, whence, to the northward, it gradually decreases, being but 6000 feet at Mastung, and 5600 feet at Quetta. Southward from Kalāt

* Surgeon-Major Henry Cook, formerly in medical charge of the Kalāt Agency.

the height rapidly diminishes, till at length, in the Pabb hills, in the southernmost part of Las, it is but a few hundred feet. It is in that portion of the Brahuik range locally called the Takāri, separating the low plains of Kachhi from the elevated table-land of Sarawān, that the two great gaps, or rents, leading from the upper to the lower country, and known as the Bolān and Mula passes, occur. At these two places the mountain mass is broken through in a very distorted manner, and down the cuts so formed flow the Bolān and Mula rivers, or what might, more correctly speaking, be termed "mountain torrents."

Next in importance to the Brahuik range of mountains are two lofty plateaus, one situate partly in Persian and partly in Kalāti Balochistan, the other wholly in the former division of the country. The first, or "Baloch plateau," as it is called by St. John, who personally visited several of the districts over which this plateau extends, runs—to use his own words—parallel to the coast, *i.e.*, east and west from the 59th to the 66th meridians of longitude. Its extension is limited on the east by the trans-Indus system (the Brahuik) running from east of north in a south or south-west direction, and on the west by three distinct chains from the mountain system of Persia, which, south of the Elburz, has, with rare exceptions, a north-west and south-east direction. For sixty or seventy miles from the sea the general level rises, at first very gradually, but afterwards more rapidly, to an altitude of 500 feet. Beyond this there is an abrupt scarp of 1500 to 2000 feet, behind which is a gradual ascent of 500 feet more to the foot of a second scarp of about the same altitude as the last, but occasionally, as south of Panjgur, much lower. The summit of this last scarp forms the water-parting between the basin of the Halmand and the Arabian Sea. Its northern slope is gentle, falling to a long and wide valley, over 3000 feet in altitude, drained by a single outlet through the lofty hills which bound it on the north into the Kharān desert. This vast plain, 2500 feet above the sea, at the foot of the hills, appears to slope gradually to half that height towards the Halmand and the Sistān lake. The outward appearance taken by the Baloch hills to the eye is curious and perhaps unique. The geological components are chiefly sandstone and shale, almost unfossiliferous, with a dip approaching more or less to the vertical, and a strike generally at a small angle to the axis of the ranges. The result is a sea of parallel ridges, separated by ravines generally narrow and of small depth, and almost bare of vegetation. Bold masses of mountain are entirely wanting, except in the hills bounding the Kharān deserts. Even the faces of the scarps, which at a distance have a precipitous aspect, are found on approach to be made up of the same insignificant ridges set on a slope steeper than usual. One consequence of this configuration is that though Balochistan is a thoroughly mountainous country, its least accessible parts are comparatively easy of approach. Art has done nothing to improve the paths, but camels, the most clumsy of beasts, traverse them in every direction.

The Baloch plateau would seem to present but few features of interest, and the only range of any considerable altitude belonging to it is the Siāneh Kuh in Persian Balochistan, which bounds it on the north; and the highest summit of this chain is but 7000 feet above the sea, an elevation very much below that of either Tokātu or Chehel-Tan in the Brahuik mountains.

The other plateau—the Sarhad—which lies wholly within Persian Balochistan, and is, in fact, but the southern prolongation of the great elevated mass that forms the highlands of Khorasān, consisting—to quote again the previous authority, St. John—" of numerous parallel ridges of various altitudes, separating valleys level in transverse section, but having a rapid slope to the south-east, *i.e.*, in the direction of the axes of the dividing ranges. Each is drained by a river or torrent bed. The parallel streams thus formed, abutting on the Baloch plateau, turn eastwards to unite in a single stream, the Māshkid, which bursts through the Siāneh mountains into the Kharān desert. It is remarkable that the entire plateau is drained to the eastward, the water-parting being on the extreme edge of the western scarp. Of the dividing ranges of the Sarhad plateau, the Kuh-i-Birg, an abrupt ridge of limestone rock, is the most prominent, rising 4000 feet above the Magas valley, itself 4000 feet above the sea. Further east and north, the Kuh-i-Safēd, a range probably metamorphic, towers to an equal altitude above the Kharān desert. Lofty crags of limestone, similar to those which overhang the Dizak valley, are found on the line of prolongation of Kuh-i-Birg, near the villages of Kant and Molatan, and the same limestone reappears on the same line further south in the peaks of Shairas, the highest summits of the southern scarp of the Baloch plateau."

In comparison with the three mountain systems just described, there are no others of any note in either Persian or Kalāti Balochistan. The chains of hills found in the province of Makrān are small and of inconsiderable altitude, and of these the Jambki hills, lying between the Dasht and Sarbāz, would appear to be the most important. Some few ranges there are in the same province which, though small both in extent and elevation, are nevertheless prominent objects when viewed from the sea-coast; these will, however, be considered in a future chapter, when the Makrān district comes more directly under review.

Hydrography.—Of the water system of Balochistan, both Persian and Kalāti, there is but little to be said. No large river—like the Indus, for instance—charged with fertilizing matter, flows through any part of this immense territory, and to this circumstance is, in all probability, due the slight knowledge at present possessed of the interior, where arid, sandy deserts, dangerous alike to the native of the country and to the traveller, are the rule and not the exception, and cover generally those large open spaces shown upon the maps as "*unexplored.*" Of lakes there are none throughout the entire area of Balochistan. In the hilly districts of Sarawān and Jhalawān, large as are their respective areas, there is not a single river of any magnitude. The Bolān and Mula streams in Sarawān and Kachh Gandāva are simply mountain torrents on a large scale, fierce and turbulent after a heavy rainfall, but almost dry at other times. The Urnach, Nāl, and Purāli rivers, so-called in the Jhalawān and Las districts (the last presumed to be the *Arabis* of the Greeks), are of a similar nature; and, notwithstanding the great width of the bed of the Purāli in many places in the Las Province, it has no regular *embouchure* into the sea, but its water, when in flood from rainfall, seems to lose itself in the level plains in a chain of temporary swamps and marshes. The Habb river, dividing Las from the British province of Sindh, is another instance in point. It possesses, certainly, permanent banks, is fed from the Pabb chain of mountains, and after heavy rains in those hills a large body of water is generated, which rushes down towards the sea with tremendous force and velocity. But at other times water is to be found only in a few small pools in its rocky bed. It is, in short, but another mountain torrent on a large scale. So also with the greater number of the streams in the western districts, though a few of these have more of the semblance of rivers than can be found elsewhere in Balochistan. Among these are the Nihing (or Dasht), with a course of about 170 miles in Kalāti Makrān, the Sarbāz (or Bahu) river, and the Kāju (or Dashtiyāri), in Persian Makrān. All three, after circuitous routes, fall into the sea at Gwattar Bay. The bed of the upper part of the Nihing is, however, mostly dry during the year, and in other places has only occasional pools of water. It drains, in conjunction with the Kēj river and other streams, not only the southern slopes of the Baloch plateau, but a large area also in the western portion of Kalāti Balochistan. The Sarbāz (or Bahu) river has its rise in a range of hills of some considerable elevation about 20 miles north of the town of the same name, and flows entirely through Persian Balochistan, meeting the Kāju a short distance from the sea, into which, at Gwattar Bay, the two combined ultimately fall. The Kaju rises in the same range of hills as the Sarbāz, meeting it as has just been stated. In the latter part of its course this stream is known as the Dashtiyāri. The Hingol (or Aghor, or Paho) river, for it bears all three names in different parts of its course, for some distance separates the province of Makrān from that of Las. It is said to take its rise somewhere near Kalāt, but this is doubtful; still, like the majority of the streams in Balochistan, it is an impassable torrent after a rainfall, but dry during the rest of the year. The singular phenomena of mud volcanoes, as existing in various parts of Makrān and Las, will be mentioned when describing those provinces. One other stream still requires to be noticed as occurring in Persian Balochistan, and this is the Māshkid, which takes its rise in the northern portion of the Baloch plateau. This river (the *Boodoor* of Pottinger), which it is now ascertained flows in a north-westerly direction, is largely fed, it is supposed, by streams coming down from the Sarhad plateau, but ultimately loses itself in the Kharān desert, though St. John believes that it no doubt eventually assists to form the Zirreh swamp, lying mostly in Afghān territory, between the 29th and 30th parallels of north latitude.

Soil and geological formation.—The soil of a country like Balochistan, so peculiar in its physical aspects, must necessarily be very varied, more especially when its vast extent of table-land, its numerous scattered valleys, and its arid deserts come to be considered. In the Brahuik plateau, covering the Sarawān, Jhalawān, and a portion of the Las Provinces of Kalāti Balochistan, the soil in the valleys is said to be light and rather sandy, in places exceedingly soft and yielding, and only requiring a proper system of irrigation to make it highly productive. Where so great an area is covered with hilly land, there must needs be much stony ground, and scattered over portions of it are found numerous small boulders of nummulitic limestone, the main ingredient, it may be remarked, of the Brahuik range generally. This plateau, according to Cook, who examined much of it personally during his tours in the Sarawān and Jhalawān Provinces, is composed essentially of nummulitic limestone, with lines of disruption, apparently running from east to west, in several places. Among this mountainous mass are situate valleys of different degrees of elevation and of various extent as regards area.

The limestones examined in these hills have been found to be of several kinds, such as arenaceous, silicious, argillaceous, and shaly; some of them are exceedingly hard, compact, and fine-grained, with a variety of colours, such as white, red and white, orange, purple, chocolate, blue, bluish-grey, and dark-grey; some containing fossils, others altogether destitute of them. Cook also discovered that the white limestone was minutely veined throughout its substance, that solitary sandstone strata in some places cropped out containing pebbles of grey limestone and flint arranged in parallel layers, while in others this formation was so close as to become a conglomerate. In parts, too, of the Jhalawān Province, trap-rock, black, purple, green, bright red, and white in colour, was found capped by limestone, in places of a crystalline character, with or without fossils. This trap-rock, according to the same authority, differed much in different places. In some spots it is composed of serpentine, and in others of diorite, in the former occasionally veined with carbonate of copper. At times, also, masses of clear white marble were seen. The trap-rock prevails in the middle, north-western, and south-western portions of the Jhalawān Province. That part of the Brahuik plateau known as the Harbui mountains, and extending eastward from Kalāt, consists, according to Cook, of a nummulitic series composed of a compact white or reddish-white limestone, and contains nummulites, orbitolites, orbitoides, operculina, assilina, alveolina, and fossils of this series; the thickness is unknown, but is supposed to be probably over a thousand feet. The subnummulitic series, consisting of limestone strata differing in character, but compact, subcrystalline, saccharoid, at times cretaceous, he found to occur in the north-western parts of Jhalawān, and he estimates its thickness at from 200 to 500 feet. These strata contained assilina, alveolina, occasionally orbitolina, and minute indistinct foraminifera.

Another group, which he terms "the lower cretaceous," some two thousand feet or thereabouts in thickness, was found by him also in Jhalawān, in the Nograma valley, and very generally in other portions of the same large province. It consisted of a more or less compact, fine-grained red and white limestone, interleaved with slabs of flint or chert, the limestone generally containing fine microscopic specks, and the upper part one or two massive strata of an exceedingly hard limestone, abounding in orbitoides, orbitolina, and operculina. The lower strata were argillaceous and shaly, and contained, though rarely, *ammonites*. Another group of the "lower cretaceous" of the same series—the subnummulitic—comprising dark-blue fossiliferous underlying limestone, and containing strata yielding *lead-ore* with a probable thickness of 2000 feet, he found in other parts of the Jhalawān district. He also refers to a fifth group, consisting of clay slate, some 2500 feet thick, and granite, and further mentions that the valley of Mushki, in north-eastern Makrān, was bounded on the west by hill-ranges of clay slate.

In the Kachh Gandāva province of Kalāti Balochistan, the soil and geological formation are essentially different from that just described. This extensive district, owing to its peculiarly low situation, is, as has been well observed, a boundless, treeless, level plain of indurated clay of a dull, dry, earthy colour, and showing signs of being sometimes under water. The soil is, in general, a hard-baked clay, quite flat, probably deposited by the numerous torrents holding their transitory but violent courses over the surface—parched up in the intensely hot summer season, when water is scarce, but highly productive when a careful system of irrigation can be brought to bear on it.

Turning to Central and Southern Balochistan, namely, to the Las and Makrān Provinces, it may be stated that, excepting the hilly land which on three sides borders the first-mentioned district, the soil is everywhere alluvial; and composed of a light, loose clay mixed with more or less fine sand. The level plains commence a short distance from the sea, and where the soil admits of being irrigated it is capable of cultivation. So also with the province of Makrān; wherever irrigation can be resorted to, the soil in the valleys at least will repay to some extent the labour of tillage, but there are in this large district numerous deserts and inhospitable wastes, where nothing is to be seen but sand or hard black gravel. Much of the northern part of the Makrān Province, between the 63rd and 65th meridians of longitude, is to this day, comparatively speaking, unknown, and, indeed, in the latest compiled maps of the country, a large area is marked as "unexplored." It partakes, no doubt, of the character of the great desert lying within the Afghān border, immediately north of this unknown tract, and is very probably of a similar nature as regards formation. The mountains of both Kalāti and Persian Makrān have to some slight extent been already described, but little or nothing seems to be known of their geological features.

Climate.—The climate of Balochistan, owing to the great inequality of the surface existing in it, must be considered as presenting extraordinary varieties. Thus, at Kalāt and other elevated towns and villages on the Brahuik plateau, the summer season, which includes the months of May, June, July, and a part, or perhaps the whole, of August, may be hotter than that of the British Islands—that is, the intensity of the sun's rays may be greater; still, the weather itself is decidedly less changeable, and, as Cook remarks, "is seldom or ever broken up into short seasons of heat and cold by the occurrence of rains and cold winds, as is so often the case in England." During the months of June, July, and August—the hottest in the year—the extreme *maximum* heat recorded at Kalāt, which is about 6800 feet above sea-level, was but 103°, while the extreme *minimum* was as low as 48°. It is the same relatively at other towns and villages seated on this lofty plateau, though in point of position it must be observed that Kalāt is the highest in elevation of them all. The prevailing winds are westerly, but they blow from other quarters occasionally. The exciting cause producing this westerly wind is believed to be the great heat arising from the sultry plains of Kachh Gandāva, which induces a steady current of air to blow from the west so long as this cause is in action. Heavy storms occur at times in the hill country, but the regular annual rainfall appears to be connected with the south-west monsoon, as the steady down-pour generally takes place about the latter end of July, which may be considered to be the height of that season. The winds, however, which bring it up do not, on this plateau, come direct from the south-west, but, crossing the easternmost range of the Brahuik mass, reach it from the *east*. The fall of rain on this plateau has been noticed to be considerable in a short time, that is to say, it is very heavy, but for a short period only. During the winter season, the cold on the elevated portions of this plateau is intense, and its keenness is increased by strong north-easterly winds which generally blow about that time. That the cold is exceedingly severe on the Brahuik plateau is evident from the joint testimony of those European travellers who have at various times visited these highlands during that season. Thus, Pottinger states that on the 7th February, 1810, when at Baghwāna in the Jhalawān Province, five or six marches from Kalāt, his water-bags were frozen into a mass of ice, and seven days afterwards, when at Kalāt, he found the frost so intense that water froze *instantly* when thrown upon the ground. Masson, too, bears testimony to the extreme cold met with in parts of the Shāl district in Sarawān, where he saw the roads sheeted with ice, and heard that snow remained on the ground during winter for about *two* months in that valley. Cook speaks also of the bitter cold he experienced even in the early part of November when at Kapote, a march or so south of Kalāt. "The air," he said, "was intensely cold before the sun rose, the thermometer standing at 28° Fahr. with a sharp cutting *southerly* wind blowing. The next morning the mercury stood at sunrise at 26°, and water spilt on a table froze instantaneously." Bellew—another witness—in the month of January, 1872, found the temperature to be even lower than this, as when at Rodinjo, thirteen miles or so south of Kalāt, the thermometer at seven a.m. stood at 14°; the next night, when at Kalāt, it fell to 8° Fahr. The weather, he at the same time mentions, was clear, sharp, and cold; the ground about Kalāt was frozen hard all day, and snow wreaths lay in the shelter of the walls, whilst a cutting north wind blew down the valley with unmitigated severity. The most southern known limit of snow-fall on this plateau is said to be the Bāran Lak (or pass), near Wadd, in the Jhalawān Province; but, generally speaking, it barely extends so far south as even Khozdār and Baghwāna. Such is the severity of a climate which, so far as latitude is concerned, is in the same parallel as that of Delhi. But it is far different in Kachh Gandāva (or Kachhi), the eastern low-lying province of Kalāti Balochistan. Here the climate during the summer season is excessively hot, and even during the winter it is warm, as in the month of February the thermometer has been known to register a temperature of 98° Fahr. The *juloh*, or scorching hot wind of the desert, is not only frequent in this district, but fatal also in its effects upon animal and human life. The low situation of this tract—the fact of its being bordered on the west as well as on the north-east by bare and lofty hills, and the general want of forest and water, are considered to be the chief causes of its exceedingly high temperature.

In respect to the other provinces, Las and Makrān, the climate of the former is reported to be subject to considerable variation, the atmosphere in the winter season being clear, dry, and cool, but in the summer months intensely hot and disagreeable, and this notwithstanding the occurrence at times of refreshing showers of rain. Its position greatly conduces to this state of things, since it is out of the range of the south-west monsoon, and surrounded on three sides by high and barren mountains. The climate of the large district of Makrān, both Kalāti and Persian, must also, from its peculiar physical features, present a great variety. Like its neighbour, Las, it does not receive any benefit in the shape of rain from the south-west monsoon, neither does it come within the limits of that from Persia. Situate as it is midway between these two rainfalls, its water supply is naturally scant and precarious, but the fall of rain, such as it is, occurs generally in the winter months. This applies for the most part to the coast districts, where pleasant breezes are said to blow almost continuously, and thus prevent that excessive heat which is so commonly felt in the valleys in the interior of this province. No doubt the climate of the Baloch and Sarhad plateaus is, owing to their elevation, of a similar character, though somewhat milder perhaps than that prevailing in the Kalāti provinces of Sarawān and Jhalawān, but no record of this is as yet available.

The hot season in the low-lying valleys and on the coast begins, it is reported, in March, and lasts till October, and the heat about the beginning of August, during what is there called the *khurma-paz*, or date-ripening, is so intense as to prevent even the inhabitants themselves from venturing abroad at such a time. Pottinger also refers to the effect of the blowing for eight months together of the hot winds inland, which he states destroys every symptom of vegetation, and scorches the skin in a most painful manner. The climate of Makrān is, on the whole, admitted to be unhealthy, except directly on the coast, where the sea-breezes moderate the heat to some extent. In the sandy deserts bordering upon Southern Afghānistan, where the summer heat is greater than is experienced in any other part of Balochistan, the *juloh*, or hot scorching wind, is said to prevail, and Pottinger maintains that it is deadly in its effects upon anything, either vegetable or animal, that may be exposed to its action.

Productions.—Of the various productions, animal, vegetable, and mineral, of Balochistan, the first may be said to comprise among its wild animals, the leopard (*palang*), the hyæna (*kaftār*), the bear (in Makrān), the wolf (*gurges*), jackal, tiger-cat, wild dog, wild goat and sheep (*gad*), wild ass (*gurkhar*), antelope, ibex, deer (*khasm*), and hares. Of birds there are eagles (in Jhalāwān and Sarawān), kites, vultures (*khālmālak*), magpies, crows, herons, flamingoes, bustards, hawks, swallows, owls, partridge, quail, pigeons, wild geese and ducks (near Sohrāb and Kharān), king-fishers (*mitu*), and paroquets in Las. Vermin and venomous animals are, Pottinger observes, not so common as in Hindustan; but Masson especially calls attention to a loathsome bug called *mangur*, which he found infested the houses at Kalāt. There is a large kind of guano known as the *shushmar*, and a smaller one called *chēlpassa*. The field-rat is very numerous, and particularly destructive at times to the crops. The wild dogs hunt in packs of twenty and thirty, and will, it is said, seize a bullock and kill him in a few minutes.

Of the domestic animals the most important is the camel, or, to speak more correctly, the dromedary. It is used as a beast of burden, being heavy in make, strong, and incredibly patient of hunger, thirst, fatigue, and the extremes of temperature; in form and appearance it varies considerably. It is trained to travel at a great speed for a consecutive number of days; and on this account it is much used by the predatory tribes in their *chupaos*, or marauding expeditions. Those of Makrān and Las are slender, light in colour, and, generally speaking, beautifully proportioned. The horses of Balochistan are, says Pottinger, strong, well-boned and large, but usually extremely vicious. They are bred, it seems, mostly southward of Kalāt and in Kachh Gandāva. In Las and Makrān the horse is, according to the same authority, both undersized and deficient in spirit; but Ross affirms that a small though hardy breed of ponies is common in the western districts of the latter province. Neat cattle and buffaloes are by no means numerous; indeed, they may be said to be rare on the Brahuik plateau. The sheep are chiefly of the fat-tailed variety known as the *dumba*, and the goats have rough black hair. These two last-mentioned animals are common throughout Balochistan, and immense flocks of them are often met with in different parts of the country. Shepherds' dogs and greyhounds are greatly prized, and their pedigree is as carefully attended to by the Balochis as is that of valuable dogs in Great Britain. Greyhounds of a good breed are said by Ross to be procurable in the Makrān province at Panjgur, and again in the Kharān district.

Fish of numerous kinds abound on the sea-coast, and some varieties are excellent, but from the rivers little or none are obtainable. Fish, to this day, is the staple article of food for those of the inhabitants living on the sea-board, and in this respect they fully bear out the name of *ichthyophagi* given to their ancestors by ancient writers.

Of the vegetable productions of Balochistan it may safely be stated that, so far as forest and other large trees are concerned, the country is on the whole but sparsely covered, and the mountains are in many places singularly bare of wood. The forest trees rarely attain a greater height than 20 or 25 feet. On the Brahuik plateau, and in its valleys, the principal trees and shrubs are the "apurs," or "hapurs" (*arbor vitæ*), known as the juniper-cedar; the blackwood (*siah-chob*), the wild olive (*khat* or *zaitun*), the "gwan," or "ghwen" (*pistacia kabulica*), the tamarind (*ambli*), the "nim" (*melia azadirachta*), the "chinār" (*platanus orientalis*), the mulberry, some varieties of the willow, and the fig-tree. Among shrubs there are the "mazmuk," low and bushy, but useful for its gum, the common tamarisk (*gaz*), the oleander (*gandeli*), the "banti," or "tarkha" (*artemisia Indica*), having a strong aromatic smell, the "kar-shutar," or camel-thorn (*hedysarium alhagi*), called "shinz" in the Kharān district; the "shinalak," the "panirband" (*withiana coagulans*), the "jau," and the "pis," or "pish," a kind of fan-palm.

In Kachh Gandāva there are no trees of any size or importance; stunted mimosas, that is to say, the "bābul" tree, the "ber" (*zyziphus*), and the "karil," or wild caper, only are found. In Makrān and Las those most frequently met with are the "bābul," pipal (*doguri*), the tamarisk, oleander, pish, the kenàtti, or *palma Christi*, the date, and camel-thorn bush. In some few parts of Las the cypress is met with. Of the different kinds of forest trees growing upon the Baloch and Sarhad plateaus, little or nothing seems to be known; but both these elevated tracts are presumed to be as barren and devoid of foliage as is the Brahuik plateau. Of plants and herbal growth generally, there is a fair variety in Balochistan. Cotton is grown in both Makrān and Kachh Gandāva, but to no great extent. Asafœtida, or "hing," is largely obtained from the hill districts in Sarawān. There is also the "gugal," producing the gum called bdellium; and several plants used medicinally are to be found on the Brahuik plateau. The "lani," or "lana," a species of *salsola*, a small bush, covers the plains of Las, and is common in the Kachh Gandāva Province; it is a camel-fodder plant, and is much relished by those animals. Flowering plants with bulbous roots are very common to the Jhalawān and Sarawān hills, and a thorny bush called the "shinalak," found in the same locality, is used for fuel. The fruit-trees are numerous in their variety, especially in the more favoured districts of the Brahuik plateau, but these will be more minutely referred to hereafter in the description of the several provinces and districts in which they are found. They comprise chiefly the apricot (*zardalu*), pear, apple, quince, plum, peach, pomegranate, grape, almond, mango, date, pistachio (*pista*), mulberry, walnut, and fig, and Pottinger even adds the cherry. The principal crops raised in Balochistan are wheat of two kinds, white and red, grown mostly in what are known as "khushkāwah," or rain-lands; barley, rice, "juār" (*sorghum vulgare*), "bājri" (*pencillaria vulgaris*), maize, madder (*manjit*), "nakod," "mung" (*phaseolus mungo*), "gāl," tobacco, lucerne (*aspust*), cotton, mangel-wurzel (*lab-lab*), and melons of various kinds.

The vegetables raised are not very numerous, but still comprise a fair variety. They are the turnip, cabbage, carrot, lettuce, radish, pea, bean, onion, beet-root, egg-fruit, celery, parsley, cucumber, mustard, spinach, *kaddu*, a kind of gourd, fenu-greek, *rawash*, or native rhubarb, and a few others. The flowers found in various parts of the country are the rose, jasmine, narcissus, the red, white, and yellow varieties of the *gulabās*, or Marvel of Peru, stock, sun-flower, prince's feather, marigold, Indian pink, holly-hock, China-aster, and tulip (*lāla*); but in such a climate, for instance, as that of the Brahuik plateau, all the flowers of temperate regions might no doubt be cultivated with every chance of success. Of the grasses, there are several kinds found on the plains of the Brahuik plateau, such as clover, hawk-weed, mallows, thyme, horse-mint, docks, camomile, and many others. The *aspusht*, or camel-grass, a kind of clover, is very prolific in yield; the true furze also is found on this plateau. The *khushe-pat*, or desert-grass, abounds in the western part of Sarawān, where it grows in bunches or tufts, with thick coarse stalks, the leaves being long and sawn at the edges. This grass is very sweet and nutritious.

Of the mineral kingdom of Balochistan, but little is at present known, though from the mountainous nature of the country it may not unnaturally be expected to be of some importance. Pottinger has stated that both gold and silver have been found, but only in the working of iron and lead, at mines near the town of Nāl, on the Brahuik plateau. The mines here referred to are no doubt those of Sekrān, twelve miles or so west of Khozdār; but Cook, who visited them in 1860, makes no mention whatever of any find of either gold or silver, but merely speaks of them as having been worked for the extraction of *lead*-ore. That lead is a mineral found in the Brahuik plateau there can be no doubt, since Masson states it to be abundant in the hills of Central Balochistan, and that the lead mines were situate at Kappar (or Sekrān), where alone any regular system of mining was carried on. He observed that the hill whence the lead was extracted seemed to be entirely composed of that metal; but Cook does not corroborate this. Copper is reputed to have been found in large quantities in the Las district, between the towns of Liyāri and Bela, and Captain Hart (Bombay Army), who wrote on this province in 1840, mentions the fact of a Hindu merchant having loaded twenty camels with copper ore, from which he is said to have extracted as many maunds of good metal; but he was deterred from repeating the experiment, owing to the jealousy of the ruling authorities, and it was declared to be as much as his life was worth if he renewed the attempt. Other minerals also are found in Balochistan, such as antimony, sulphur, and alum. A fine porcelain clay is said to be obtainable in the Brahuik plateau, and Masson mentions that coal occurs not only in a part of the Bolān pass, but in the Gurghina hills as well. This fact Cook, who in his tour made geological notes on the former locality, bears out to some extent, as he speaks in the course of his survey of having found at one place a "seam of coal, much decomposed," and at another in the same pass, near Sir-i-Bolān, "some thin seams of coal strata" in a bed of clay. Common salt unfortunately abounds too frequently in several parts of

Balochistan, and this, by the streams and springs, destroys much of the vegetation, which would otherwise be luxurious.

Agriculture.—The system of agriculture, as generally pursued by the natives of Balochistan, is very simple, and, to a certain extent, effective. The fields are divided off, says Cook, referring to the Sarawān Province, by ridges of earth and raised embankments to an accurate level. They are then further subdivided longitudinally by ridges which are thrown up about seven paces apart. All this is with reference to the irrigation, which is conducted in a very efficient manner. The soil is then ploughed and manured, the former operation being generally carried on by means of bullocks. Tracts of land not irrigated by streams, but which are dependent on rain and the rivulets which come down from the hill-sides after rain, are called "*kushkāwah*," and are found scattered about the valleys here and there near the *tumāns*, or tent encampments, of wandering tribes, who plough a piece of land, sow it, and return to gather in the crop when it is matured. The implements of husbandry in general use are the following:—(1) A very light wooden plough of simple construction, consisting of a vertical piece, bent forward at the bottom, and covered with an iron point, and a long horizontal beam, which passes forward between the pair of bullocks that draw it, and is fastened to the yoke. This instrument seems to answer the purpose sufficiently, as the soil is very soft and yielding. (2) The harrow, which is only a wooden board, about six feet long by two wide. This is dragged over the ploughed land by being attached to the yoke with iron chains. If not heavy enough in itself, the driver stands upon it to make it more effective. There is also a spade or shovel, exactly like its English counterpart, and used in the same way, and a reaping-hook, or sickle, having its cutting edge furnished with minute teeth. The Balochis have, it is said, to some extent a knowledge of the proper rotation of crops. The irrigation of lands is effected mostly by "*karēzes*," or subterranean aqueducts, supplied from hill-streams or springs. In the Sarawān Province these aqueducts are very numerous, and convey water in streams of from two to four feet in breadth, and one to one and a half in depth. Some are two or even three miles in length, having shafts about every one hundred yards. They are situate at various depths from the surface, commencing near the base of the hills at a depth of 15 to 20 or more feet; they gradually near the surface and issue in the neighbourhood of the town, but where they pass under low hills their depth is of course proportionately increased. They are rarely bricked, and pass through either sandy clay or gravel. In Makrān, artificial means of irrigation, where possible, are also resorted to; *bandhs*, or dams, are constructed in many places, while in others advantage is taken of natural slopes to conduct the water to the surface by means of wells connected by subterranean passages (*karēzes*). The water is then conveyed in suitable channels to irrigate the neighbouring fields.

CHAPTER II.

A TOPOGRAPHICAL AND ETHNOLOGICAL SKETCH OF BOTH PERSIAN AND KALĀTI BALOCHISTAN.

Towns and Villages.—Owing to the nomadic nature of the great majority of the inhabitants of Balochistan, the general barrenness of the country, and the consequent absence of any valuable commerce and manufactures, towns and villages are comparatively speaking few, and but of little importance. The chief towns, such as they are, comprise Kalāt, the capital of Balochistan, Shāl (or Quetta), Mastung, Rodinjo, Khānak, Pargawad, and Tiri, all in the Sarawān Province; Khozdār and Baghwāna in that of Jhalawān; Bagh, Gandāva, Dādar, and Kotri, in the Kachh Gandāva (or Kachhi) district; Bēla and Sonmiāni in Las; and Gwādar, Chāhbār, Kēj, Pasni, Panjgur, Pishin, Bahu-Kalāt, Gwattar, and Sarbāz, in Kalāti and Persian Makrān. Of these Las and Makrāni towns, Gwādar, Sonmiāni, Pasni, Gwattar, and Chāhbār, are ports on the Arabian Sea. The forts are numerous, and are found scattered about different parts of the country; they would seem to be very necessary, owing to the generally disturbed state at times of many of the districts.

Inhabitants.—Balochistan may be said to be inhabited chiefly by the Baloch tribe, the most numerous in the country, and this name was given to the tract they occupy by the great Persian monarch, Nādir Shāh, who, as St. John remarks, after driving the Afghān invaders from Persia, made himself master in his turn of the whole country west of the Indus, and placed a native chief over the new province, formed out of the districts bounded on the north and south by the Halmand valley and the sea, and stretching from Karmān on the west to Sindh on the east. This newly-formed province he called Balochistan, or, the country of the Baloch, from the name of the most widely spread and numerous, though not the dominant, tribe. According to Masson, who, it must be admitted, had more ample opportunities of obtaining correct information on this subject than any other European, the Balochis are divided into three great classes, viz., (1) the Brahuis; (2) the Rinds; and (3) the Lumris (or Numris); but this must be taken more in the sense of inhabitants of Balochistan than as divisions of a tribe, since the Brahuis are of a different race and language and call the true Balochis "Nhāruis," in contradistinction to themselves as "Brahuis." These, again, resolve themselves into numerous subdivisions, some of the names of which will be given in a tabular statement further on.

The origin of the word "Baloch" is evidently involved in some obscurity, and has given rise to many different interpretations. Professor Rawlinson supposes it to be derived from Belūs, king of Babylon, the Nimrod of Holy Writ, and that from "Kush," the father of Nimrod, comes the name of the Kalāti eastern district, "Kachh." Pottinger believes the Balochis to be of Turkoman lineage, and this from a similarity in their institutions, habits, religion—in short, in everything but their language, for which latter anomaly, however, he has an explanation to offer. But be this as it may, the very tribe themselves ascribe their origin to the earliest Muhammadan invaders of Persia, and are extremely desirous of being supposed to be of Arab extraction. They reject with scorn all idea of being of the same stock as the Afghān. They may possibly be of Iranian descent, and the affinity of their language, the Balochki, to the Persian, bears out this supposition; but the proper derivation of the word "Baloch" still remains an open question.

The original settlement of the Baloch tribe in the country is thus referred to by Pottinger:—"Ninety-two years after the epoch of the Hijri (A.D. 677), the Kalifahs of Baghdad, incited by the combined motives of zeal for the Muhammadan faith and desire to avenge the insult that had been offered to their dignity by the idolaters of Sindh, despatched an army against that kingdom by the same route that the Macedonian hero had selected on his return to Babylon nearly a thousand years before. This force is expressly stated to have kept close to the sea-shore, that it might be certain of a supply of water, which is always procurable by digging a foot or two deep on the sandy beach; it consequently knew nothing of the inland regions, nor was any attempt made, so far as can be learnt, during the administration of the Kalifahs of the houses of Ummia and Abbas, to explore them. When Muhammad, the successor of Subaktaji, the first Sultan of the Ghaznavide dynasty, turned his arms towards India, he subjugated the whole of the level district west of the Indus to the very foot of the Brahui mountains. His son Musāud extended these conquests still more westerly into Makrān; he adhered, however, to his father's plan of not ascending the lofty ranges, and all subsequent invaders of Sindh seem to have been guided by their example. The former was so well ascertained at an early date that the compiler of the Chachh-Nāma states that those infidels who would not conform to the doctrine of the Kurān were driven to the mountains, there to perish by famine and cold. Wilds thus spoken of, it is presumed, were void of people, and from this epoch will hereafter be fixed the first regular settlements to the provinces of Jhalawān and Sarawān, or at least their most elevated districts. We now arrive at a period when some indistinct memory of the historical events of Balochistan begins to be orally preserved."

Bruce states that, according to their own traditions, the Balochis believe that their country was formerly Aleppo; that they are descended from Mir Hamra, son of Abdul Mahtab, who lived in the time of Hāzrat Imām Husain (Hijri 61), about A.D. 646. They seem to have left Arabia owing to internal strife and contention, and to have gone in the direction of Persia, arriving in the hill country of Kermān, in Persia. Thence they came into Makrān, where they are said to have remained for about 500 years. They would appear to have been, during their long sojourn in Makrān, under one Amir, or head; and, prior to their leaving that province for Kalāt and Khorasān, their chief was Jalāl Khan, who had four sons and one daughter, named respectively—Rind, Hōt, Lashāri, Korai, and Massamat Jatoi. From Rind was descended Mir Chakar Khān, and from Lashāri, Mir Raman Khān; and at the time of their appearance in Kalāt and Kachhi (about A.D. 1540) they were in two sections, Rind and Lashāri (so-called after the sons of Jalāl Khān), and under the leadership of Mir Chakar and Mir Raman. The Hōt and Korai also became known as distinctive tribes, and from the daughter, Massamat Jatoi, is said to have sprung the Jatoi tribe. After their settlement in Kalāt and Kachhi, quarrels appear to have arisen between the Rinds and Lashāris, resulting ultimately in the defeat of the latter, who fled towards Sindh, where they subsequently settled. The Rinds were in the first instance unsuccessful in their encounters with the Lashāris, but, obtaining the assistance of the King of Persia, they were enabled in the end to conquer their adversaries. After this, Mir Chakar and his Rinds are said to have received a grant of land in the Bari Doāb, in the Panjab, from Humayun Shāh, the Mogul Emperor of Hindustan, to whom he had rendered assistance at a time when that monarch was an exile, and seeking to recover his lost throne. From this period the tribe seems to have become divided, and to have spread throughout Kalāt, Sindh, and the Dērajāt frontier, driving out the inhabitants where they were able, and taking possession of their lands.

The Brahuis, who, as a race, are very numerous in Balochistan, Pottinger considers to be a nation of Tartar mountaineers, who settled at a very early period in the southern parts of Asia, where they led an ambulatory life in *Khels*, or societies, headed and governed by their own chiefs and laws for many centuries, till at length they became incorporated and attained their present footing at Kalāt and throughout Balochistan generally.

Masson supposes that the word "Brahui" is a corruption of Ba-roh-i, meaning, literally, *of the waste;* and that that race entered Balochistan originally from the west. The Nhāruis, mentioned by Pottinger as one of the three principal tribes into which the Balochis are divided, would appear to inhabit the district *west* of the Kharān desert. The meaning of the word "Nhārui" being *not a hill man*, i.e., a dweller in the plains, they may be considered to hold the same place with reference to the Brahuis that "lowlanders" do to "highlanders." These Nhāruis have the character of being the most savage and predatory class throughout Balochistan, and in appearance and physique are said to be a tall, handsome, and active race. The Brahuis believe that they are the aborigines of the country. Their language, which is known as Brahuiki, is, strange to say, altogether void of affinity to that of the Balochis—it is, in fact, a

Dravidian tongue, while the Balochki is as decidedly Indo-Germanic; and this difference in language is presumed by some writers to prove the fact of the Brahui being an older inhabitant of the country than the Balochi.

Besides those mentioned, there is another of the principal divisions of the Balochi which requires especial notice, though reference has already been made to it in the previously quoted extract from Bruce. This is the Rind tribe, who have a tradition that they originally came from Aleppo; but Masson remarks that they may in all probability have found their way into Kachh Gandāva from the *eastward.* The word "Rind" means "brave man," and the tribe are mostly found in Kachh Gandāva, and the hills north-east of Sarawān, as also in portions of Kalāti Makrān. Their language is the Jatki, and they themselves are broken up into numerous sub-divisions (about forty-four branches), but as a tribe they are considered highly respectable, though noted for their marauding propensities. In person they resemble the Nhāruis, but have darker features. The Maghzis are another Baloch tribe, distinct according to Pottinger, but merely an offshoot from the Rinds according to Masson. They reside at Jhal at the foot of the western hills in Kachh Gandāva, but are now few in number; at one time they were able, it is said, to muster a force of two thousand men. The Lumris (or Numris) of Las are pretty numerous, and are said to claim a close affinity with the Bulfat (or Burfat) tribe. They are believed to be descendants of the ancient Samma and Sumra Rājputs, whose chiefs formerly ruled in Sindh. In appearance the Lumri is neither robust nor good-looking, and is both physically and morally inferior to the tribes inhabiting the provinces north of Las. The Jokias are a branch of the Lumris. The Afghān inhabitants of Balochistan are few in number, and are chiefly found in the Shāl district and at Kalāt, at which latter place they are known as Bābis, or Abābis, their business there being trade. These Bābis are considered to be a wealthy people, and in person are stout, well-made men, with good features. The Jats are numerous in Kachh Gandāva, where they form the principal portion of the agricultural population. They are presumed to be the descendants of the ancient Getæ, who once peopled those tracts of country situate east and west of the river Indus. The sub-divisions of this tribe are numerous, and their language, which is known as the Jatki, is closely allied to Sindhi and Panjābi. The only other Muhammadan race requiring notice are the Dehwars, not on account of their number, which is small and unimportant, but because they are, as Pottinger says, *distinct* from all other natives of Balochistan in both manners and appearance. They are found only in and about Kalāt, so far as the country of Balochistan is concerned. They are believed, however, to be of the same stock as the Tajiks of Afghānistan and Turkistan, both classes being somewhat undersized, with blunt features and high cheek-bones. They are agricultural in habit, and, as their name imports, dwellers in *dehs*, or villages, and not nomadic, like the greater number of the Baloch tribes. Their language is a fairly pure Persian, and in religion they are Suni Muhammadans.

The Hindu portion of the population of Balochistan is small, and found only in the large towns and sea-ports, where, as merchants or bankers, they carry on the greater part of the trade and commerce of the country, such as it is. Their numbers are said to be greater in Kalāt than elsewhere, and Pottinger mentions that in his time (A.D. 1810) they were principally mercantile speculators from the cities of Multān and Shikārpur, who were, however, as in Sindh, by no means strict in their observance of the Brahmanical laws, since they ate every kind of flesh-meat, except beef, though killed by a Musalmān, drank water out of leathern bags, and wore caps made of Bokhāra skins. Hindus are to be found at the ports of Sonmiāni and Gwādar, on the Las and Makrān coast, but rarely, except at Kalāt, in the towns of the interior.

In order to give, to some extent, the names of several of the principal sub-tribes of the Balochis, and in what part of Balochistan they are chiefly to be found, the following table, drawn up mostly on the authority of Masson, Jacob, and Ross, is here appended, and has been made as full as the data supplied will admit of :—

Name of Sub-tribe.	Province.	In what district residing.	No. of armed men.	Remarks.
1. Gitchki ...	Kalāti Makrān.	Panjgur and Kēj	...	Settled in Makrān about the 17th century.
2. Gujar ...		Malān and Batt	...	
3. Hallada ...		Jau	...	
4. Homarāri ...		Kolwah	...	
5. Hōt		Central Makrān	...	Is the most numerous in Makrān.
6. Kalmatti ...		Kalamat and Pasni	...	Claim affinity with the Rind tribe.
7. Kaudai ...		Kolwah and Dasht	...	
8. Mehmasani ...		Mushki	...	
9. Nurwāri ...		Mushki, Jau, and Kolwah	...	
10. Mirshirvāni		Panjgur and Kolwah	...	Kharān is the head-quarters of this tribe.
11. Rodahi ...		Kolwah	...	
12. Saka		Greshar, in Mushki	...	Are supposed to be descendants of the ancient Sacæ.
13. Sangur ...		Malān and Batt	...	
1. Bizanju ...	Jhalawān.	Hills north of Las, and west of the Minghal tribe	...	Have 2 important branches, the Amalāri and Tambarāri.
2. Jataks ...		Hills east of Zehri	...	Are nomadic in habit.
3. Kaidrāni ...		Hills near Khozdār	...	
4. Lutianis ...		Zehri	...	
5. Minghal ...		Hills north of Las	18000	Have two great divisions, the Shāhizai, and the Pahlawānzai.
6. Saholi ...		Hills near Khozdār	...	
7. Zehri		Zehri	...	Numerous and generally respected.

Name of Sub-tribe.	Province.	In what district residing.	No. of armed men.	Remarks.
1. Bangalzai ...	Sarawān.	Mastung	2000	
2. Ghazghi ...		At Ghazg	400	
3. Kurd ...		Dasht-i-Bidaulat and Merv	500	Presumed to have come originally from Kurdistan; have numerous subdivisions.
4. Langhau ...		Mangachar	1500	Said to have been formerly slaves of the Rinds, but enfranchised by the famous Mir Chakar.
5. Lari ...		Mastung	1500	
6. Mahmudshāhi		"	1500	
7. Raisāni ...		Mastung and Shāl	500	
8. Rakshāni ...		Nushki	...	
9. Rodāni ...		Ashi Khān and Puden	400	A branch of the Sirperra.
10. Samalāri ...		Hills west of Khānak	500	
11. Shēkh Husaini		"	300	
12. Shirwāni ...		Mastung	2000	Say their forefathers came from Shirwān, near the Caspian Sea.
13. Sirperra ...		Gurghina	1000	Literal meaning of Sirperra, "Cutters off of heads." Ancestors supposed to have been the Saraparæ mentioned by Pliny.
14. Sunāri ...		Dasht Gurān	200	
15. Zigar Minghal		Nushki	...	
16. Kallui ...		Lup	...	These tribes are found in the north-eastern hills of Sarawān, known as the Kirta district.
17. Kuchik ...		Kirta	...	
18. Pugh ...		Kajuri	...	
19. Mandarāri ...		Rodbar	...	
20. Puzh ...		Johān	...	
1. Bughtis ...	Kachhi (or Kachh Gandāva).	Hills east of Lehri, at Sing Saloh and Teriki	...	Are of the Rind tribe, and have strong predatory propensities.
2. Dumbkis ...		Lehri	...	Rind tribe.
3. Homarāri ...		Tambu	...	"
4. Jakrānis ...		Lehri	...	"
5. Jallui ...		Sanni	...	"
6. Jamāli ...		Rojān	...	"
7. Lashāri ...		Gajān	...	"
8. Maghzis ...		At Jhal	2000	Had but four families.
9. Marris (Doda Marris)		Eastern hills	...	Are Rinds, and are noted for lawlessness.
10. Utanzai ...		Suran	...	

Dress.—The dress of the natives of Balochistan is much the same all over the country, but is, as Masson remarks, not an elegant costume. The men wear a *khuss*, or long loose upper garment, a kind of tunic, in fact, extending nearly to the feet, and trousers, or *paijāmas*, narrow at the bottom. The cap worn is of different varieties of chintz, cotton-stuffed and close-fitting. The national head-dress is the peculiar cylindrical cap worn in Sindh. The Brahuis, as also the Lumris of Las, wear a small tuft or button affixed to the centre of the crown. Turbans of white muslin and of a preposterously large size are also worn by the higher classes, together with *lungis*, or scarves, which they are said to put on in exactly the same way a Scotchman does his plaid. Shoes are only worn by the inhabitants of towns, the pastoral tribes using sandals, made generally from the leaves of the *pīsh*, or fan-palm. In winter the lower classes wear a tunic of a warm material, made up from goats' hair and sheep's wool, and the wealthy have their chintz coats lined and stuffed with cotton. The equipment is complete when the wearer is provided with the usual arms, such as a sword, matchlock, shield, dagger, and small pouch, which are often handsomely mounted in silver.

The women wear long loose robes or gowns, usually of a red colour, the part covering the bust, as also the seams and portions of the skirts and long sleeves, being at times elaborately embroidered in silk. Their trousers, when worn, are very wide. A *chadar*, or large piece of cotton-cloth, is universally put on over the head and allowed to trail along the ground. The hair is tied up in a knot behind, and is kept there by a species of fixature. The trinkets consist of armlets, ear and nose rings; besides the puncture for this latter ornament, the cartilage of the nose is usually perforated, and made to serve, in the absence of any ornament, as a receptacle for bodkins, needles, etc. It is not, it would seem, the custom for women to hide their faces on the appearance of a stranger when at home, but both young and old muffle up their faces so as not to be seen when they go abroad. It may also be mentioned that the Balochis are as a rule universally filthy in their persons and garments, hardly ever changing the latter, but allowing them to fall off their bodies from age and dirt.

Food.—The food of the greater portion of the people consists of cakes or bread made of inferior grain with buttermilk. The preparations made from ewes' and goats' milk are numerous, and are held in great estimation by the Balochi. *Māss*, or curd-butter, one of these, is made by boiling the milk and then inserting a portion of buttermilk, which imparts, says Masson, a tendency to coagulation and a slightly acidulated taste. It is eaten as a relish, or accompaniment, with bread and rice. *Roghan*, or clarified butter, is another of these preparations, and is very much used. It is made by simply boiling the substance until its water is absorbed, or till it shows a disposition to granulate. There is yet another of these milk foods, known among the Brahuis as *shalanch*, called also *krut* by the Afghāns, the manufacture of which is thus described by Masson:—" It is made by boiling buttermilk till the original quantity is reduced one-half. The thickened fluid is then placed in a woollen or hair bag, and allowed to drain exposed to the sun. When the draining ceases, the mass in the bag is formed into small dumps, which are dried into hardness in the sun's rays. When required for use, these dumps are pounded and placed in warm water, where they are worked by the hands until dissolved. The thickened fluid is then boiled with some *roghan*, and this, saturated with bread, makes a meal. It is a convenient food for travellers. In the Mastung and Shāl districts a very nutritious winter meal is composed of dried mulberries and apricots. A dish called *chamari*, in the same part of the country, is made by beating dried apricots in water and boiling them with a certain proportion of *roghan*, adding spices. In Makrān and Las, camels' milk is obtainable in large quantities, and this, with *juāri* bread, rice, dates, and salt fish, forms the chief article of food in that part of Balochistan. Meat is rarely indulged in.

Among all classes of the people asafœtida, or *hing*, a plant so repugnant to European taste, is largely employed in flavouring dishes, and so much is it liked by the Balochis, that it goes by the name of *khush-khorak*, or pleasant food. The Brahuis roast and eat the stem of this plant, or stew it in butter; at Kalāt it is pickled, and is said to be not unpalatable. The leaf and stalk of a kind of rhubarb, known as *rawash*, found in large quantities in Nushki and Gurghina, is also used as food. In some districts mutton is cured in much the same way that bacon is in Europe, and is then called *khaddit* by the Brahuis; it is the same as the "*landi*" of the Afghāns, and serves as stock during the winter. The Baloch is given to smoking, and he chews opium and *bhang*, but is not, says Pottinger, addicted to spirituous liquors or wine; which however may be in part attributed to their scarcity, as well as to the inhibition of his creed.

Language.—There appear to be two languages of current use in Balochistan generally. These are Balochki and Brahuiki, both differing essentially from each other. The first has a decided affinity with modern Persian, but the dialect spoken in the province of Makrān would seem to differ very considerably from that used by the Balochis of northern Balochistan. The Makrān Balochki is reported to be a dialect or *patois* of the Persian, but deteriorates from this latter tongue the further one travels eastward. The sound is rough and harsh-toned, and, to use Pottinger's words, is greatly disguised under a corrupt and unaccountable system of pronunciation. It is supposed to be derived from the Persian of a former age. Mr. E. Pierce, of the Government Telegraph Department, in a paper sent by him in 1874 to the Bombay branch of the

Royal Asiatic Society, thus speaks of the Makrān Balochki tongue:—"The Makrāni Balochki is the dialect spoken by the people living in the eastern and southern parts of Balochistan. Its limits on the sea-coast are the Malān mountains on the east, and a line drawn about fifty miles west of Chāhbār on the west. Inland it is spoken generally over the large divisions of Kēj, Kolānch, and Kolwah, with their adjacent districts." He considers that the Makrān Balochki is a dialect of Persian, mixed up with a great many words of Indian origin, which have probably been introduced by the Jadgāls (Sindhi tribes settled in Makrān), and that in the districts of Bahu and Dashtiyāri, north-west of Gwādar, where these tribes are found, a dialect of Sindhi generally prevails. The coast dialect, as spoken by the Mēds, or fishing classes, seems to differ but slightly from that spoken by the people living in the jungle. Another authority (Bruce) who treats of the Baloch tongue as spoken on the north-western frontier of India, and in parts of the Panjāb, says that it is there composed to such a large extent of *corrupted* Persian, that it would hardly be worthy of the name of a distinct language, were it not that the corruptions are so gross, that from no knowledge of the one, however perfect, could the other be understood. The many differences which exist between Persian and Balochki have been mainly brought about, it is said, from the habit that Balochis have of transposing letters in words, and so changing them as to be scarcely recognizable in their original form. The Balochki dialect is spoken among several of the Jhalawān tribes, such as the Minghals and Bizanjus, and it is used also by a portion of the Rind tribes; it is, moreover, spoken exclusively by the Brahui Khān of Kalāt and his Sardārs, who consider Brahuiki as *vulgar*.

This latter tongue, called also Kur-Gālli (the *patois*), is peculiar to the tribes of Sarawān and Jhalawān, and belongs to the Tamulian family, that is, it is a Dravidian language. How this came to pass is open to several interpretations, but the most credible seems to be that the ancestors of the present Brahuis were no doubt driven out of India by the invading Arians, though, as Cook believes, not before they had adopted the Hindu religion, which they subsequently exchanged, most probably on *compulsion*, for the Muhammadan. The distinctive character, habits, and language of the people, he thinks, bear out this theory, which is further strengthened by the fact of the Brahuis being confined to the mountain districts, amidst the fastnesses of which they had fled when dispossessed of the plain country. He does not, however, suppose that they, as at present existing, are all traceable to *one* class, or that all belonged originally to the same family, but that they are undoubtedly composed of many races, which have been added to the community from time to time, and have, so to speak, become incorporated with the Brahui tribes. The Brahuiki dialect, as spoken in Sarawān and Jhalawān, contains a fair amount of both Balochki and Persian, but has very little Pashtu mixed up with it. Persian is spoken by the Dehwars of Kalāt, and Pashtu by the Afghān inhabitants of Shāl, (or Quetta). The Jats of Kachh Gandāva speak what is called Jatki, which is closely allied to the Sindhi, and the Lumri (or Numri) tribes of Las use the dialect common to the kindred tribes of Jokias and Burfats in the west of Sindh. The Balochki cannot be called a written language, and such written correspondence as is necessary is carried on in Persian, but not by the Baloch chiefs themselves, who, as a rule, know nothing of this latter language, but are dependent upon their *munshis*, who do all the correspondence. Among the hill Balochis, on the Sindh and Panjāb borders, every tribe is said to have its own difference of dialect. There cannot, therefore, be any literature among the Balochis, but popular ballads brought down by oral tradition for many generations supply its place to some extent, and these are sung by wandering bards and minstrels. The subject selected is generally an account of the exploits of some tribe, or of an individual of it, or, it may be, the valiant deeds of former heroes. These bards, says Cook, carry about with them a rudely-shaped lute, and keep time with their voices to the music. The metre of many of their lays is very peculiar, the verses being generally composed in three lines, the last of which is occasionally repeated twice or thrice.

Habitations.—As the great majority of the population are *nomadic* in their habits, permanent places of abode, except in the large towns, which are very few in number, are rarely met with. The houses in these towns are usually constructed of mud, or of half-burnt brick on wooden frames, and plastered over with mud or *chunam.* The dwellings of the pastoral tribes are simply formed by a number of long slender poles, bent and inverted towards each other, over which are placed slips of the coarse fabric of camel-hair, generally black in colour; they are, in fact, mat-sheds, and are known as *kirri* and also *ghedans.* Where a number of these are found belonging to one family, they are collectively called *bunghi,* but when belonging to several families of one tribe, *tumān.*

Diseases.—But little would appear to be known of the number and class of diseases prevailing among the people of Balochistan; but one of the most dreaded is the *poto,* or casual small-pox, which at times makes extensive ravages among them. Vaccination seems to be unknown to the people, but inoculation is occasionally resorted to, the operation being performed by *saiyads* and priests, who receive presents in kind for their trouble. It is generally done with a razor on the inner portion of the arm, an inch or two above the wrist, and over the divided skin is bound the dried matter of pustules. Fevers of a bad type prevail in Makrān, especially in the tract south of the mountains, and are accompanied by great hepatic derangement. Among animals there is, in the Las district, a disease known as the *poto-ghau*, or cow small-pox; and the camel is at times similarly afflicted with what is called the *poto-shutar*, or camel small-pox. No fatal results are said to follow from either of these *potos*.

Manners and Customs.—In the matter of marriages, births, and deaths, as the Balochis are of the Muhammadan persuasion, these ceremonies are mainly regulated by the Kurān, and are thus similar to like ceremonies among Musalmāns generally. With the Balochis marriage is always attended with great festivities. The first step is the *sang*, or betrothal, which is regarded as of a very sacred nature, the final rite being known as *nikkar*. A few days before this latter takes place there is much vocal and instrumental music. On the wedding-day the bridegroom, gorgeously arrayed and mounted on a horse, proceeds with his friends to some notable *ziārat*, or shrine, there to implore a blessing, after which the *urus*, or marriage form, is gone through by a Mālla. Much food is prepared and eaten on these occasions, the expense of this, as indeed of the entire marriage, falling upon the bridegroom. Very frequently a circle of stones laid flat on the ground, with a central one set upright and projecting above the surface, is to be seen in different parts of Balochistan. It commemorates, says Bellew, a wedding among the Brahui clans, and occupies the exact spot on which the reel, here called *chap*, accompanying the ceremony, was danced. On the birth of a child there is also much rejoicing and music, as well as a large distribution of food. On the fourth day after birth a name is given to the infant, and on the sixth an entertainment to friends.

On the following day the rite of circumcision (*kattam*) is performed, though not always, as this is sometimes postponed for a year or more. On this occasion large charitable distributions of food are made, and are known under the name of *kairats*.

When a death occurs, mourners are immediately sent for, and food is prepared at the deceased's house three successive days and nights for such friends as desire to be present at the reading of prayers for the dead. The *kairats*, or distributions of food, are again put into requisition for the benefit of the soul of the deceased person. The graves have not always headstones, but the mound is covered with white and black fragments of stone, neatly arranged. Pillars also, called *chedd*, are erected on the death of a tribesman who has died without issue; and it is, it appears, the custom for his surviving relatives to feast the clan to which he belonged on the first anniversary of his demise—if possible, in the vicinity of the monument. The wife, on the decease of her husband, neglects washing, and is supposed to sit lamenting by herself for not less than fifteen days. Her female friends, however, long before this, come and conjure her to desist from weeping, bringing with them the powder of a plant called *larra;* with this the widow washes her head, and then resumes her former enjoyments.

A very commendable trait in the character of the Baloch is his practice of hospitality (*zang*). The rites of friendship are never refused to the weary traveller who may visit the *tumān* of a Baloch tribe, and everything is done to entertain him, the person of a guest being looked upon as sacred. The reception of guests, says Pottinger, is simple, yet impressive. When a visitor arrives at a *tumān* a carpet is spread in front of the door of the *Mihmān Khāna*, or house for guests, of which there is one in every town or village in Balochistan; the *sardār*, or head of the *Khēl*, immediately appears, and he and the stranger having embraced and mutually kissed hands, the followers of the latter successively approach, and the *sardār* gives them his hand, which they press to their foreheads and lips. So far, the reception is conducted in profound silence, and the parties now sit down, prepared to enter upon a long list of complimentary questions. On this head it will be necessary to quote Masson, whose experience in these matters must evidently have been very considerable: "If the parties be acquainted, they alternately kiss hands; one commences a series of congratulatory inquiries, including the individual, his family, his cattle, etc., as '*Darakh! Darakh! Darakh jur! jur massan! massan Darakh!*' etc. etc., to which the other incessantly replies, '*Fazl! Fazl khuda! Shukr! alhamdlilla!*' etc., or if an inferior, he repeats, '*Mehrbāni! Mehrbāni!*' The first course of inquiries completed, he asks '*Kabar netti?*' (Is there any news?) Should a third person be present, he is first appealed to as to whether the inquiry for news shall be made, and answers, '*Ji ilam*' (Yes, brother). The party from whom intelligence is demanded then relates all he knows or has heard concerning the *khān*, the several *sardārs*, etc., and, public affairs dismissed, proceeds to private details, and relates circumstantially where he has come from, whither he is going, on what business he went or is engaged in, how it was or may be settled, and so forth, and having exhausted his subject, concludes by saying, '*Am in kadr awāl ast*' (This is the extent of my information). The parties then burst forth into a fresh repetition of gratulatory inquiries, which terminated, the individual who has communicated his intelligence asks of the third person if he in turn may inquire the news. Before being answered in the affirmative, he makes the demand, which is complied with in the same minute and important manner. The close is again marked by a renewal of '*Darakh! Darakh! Darakh jur,*' etc., etc."

Another strong but totally different custom prevailing among the Balochis is their system of blood-feuds, known with them under the name of "*Khun bāwar*," or satisfaction in blood. These blood-feuds are in many cases of long standing, and may have originated in some slight and trivial insult having been given and resented by the loss of a life. When once established, these feuds can hardly ever be extinguished, and a regular debtor and creditor account is kept on either side of lives taken and required, and this is carefully treasured up by the several parties interested. In their own intestine wars the loss of life among the Brahuis is not as a rule followed by much bloodshed, as when a few persons happen to be slain on either side the women and *saiyads* make it a point to interpose and stop all further hostility. The lives of women are greatly respected in these affrays, and if any be killed, or even wounded, it is accounted a great calamity; but, though this be the case, murders are very frequent in Balochistan, and Masson states that scarcely a chief existed in his time whose hands had not in some way or other been imbued with the blood of his kinsmen, and further, that the tribes of Kachh Gandāva murdered sometimes from motives of *mere wantonness.* All classes are very superstitious, and have a strong belief in *jins* (genii), *peris* (fairies), charms, and spells.

In matters of religion the Baloch is a Suni Musalmān, and entertains an inveterate hatred against the Shia class. Masson remarks that the Brahuis have no *saiyads*, *pirs*, *mūllas*, or fakirs, among them, and that in their religious observances there is less bigotry with them than with the Afghāns, as few of their *tumāns* possess any *masjid*, or place of worship. The Makrān Balochis are, on the other hand, it is said, remarkably observant of the various forms prescribed by their religion, though among the population of that province are several religious sects, which are held in abhorrence by the orthodox Musalmān. Of these may be mentioned the Zikris, so called from their practice of repeating a short *Zikr*, or formula, in lieu of the regular prayers. Their prophet is Mehdi, who, they state, appeared at Attok, in the Panjāb, and afterwards disappeared somewhere in Makrān, but is to be looked for in the latter days. They regard Mehdi as a much greater prophet than Muhammad. This sect is numerous in Eastern Makrān, and they are met with in Kēj, Kolānch, and Kolwah. This is evidently the same sect referred to by Cook under the name of the Dāis, a few of whom he saw at the town of Gajer, in Makrān. He states that their principal masjid, or place of worship, is on the top of a small hill near Kēj, in Makrān, called Kuh Murād, and that, instead of repeating the usual formula—"God is God, and Muhammad is his prophet!"—they exclaim in derision—"God is God, but the mother of Muhammad is his prophet!" The state of morals among this sect he represents as being of the lowest and most debasing description. Another of these religious sects—the Rafāis—is also found in the same province among the Korwahs, Mēds, and Raises—that is, the seafaring tribes of the coast. They are in the habit of submitting to a variety of tortures as a proof of their faith, such observances being obnoxious to the orthodox Muhammadan. They are, in fact, more of a class of devotees than anything else, and are excessively bigoted and fanatical. Their principal places of worship are said to be at Gwādar. In Makrān, also, are found the Khwājah sect, the followers of Agha Khān. Their religion, according to Ross, may be considered as Muhammadanism tacked on to Hinduism by the notable device of regarding Muhammad as a tenth *avatar* of Vishnu.

"The amusements of the Balochis are such," says Pottinger, "as may be expected among a wild and uncivilized people.

They are enthusiastically fond of every species of field sports, and much of their time is passed in shooting, hunting, and coursing, for which purpose they bestow a great deal of attention on the training of their greyhounds. Firing at marks, cudgelling, wrestling, practising with swords, and throwing the spear, are likewise all favourite diversions with them. The four latter they understand scientifically, and at the first some of them are so incredibly expert as to invariably hit a target not more than six inches square off a horse at full gallop. The guides killed at a distance of 50 or 60 yards every small bird, such as larks or sparrows, at which they fired with a single ball, nor was this considered as any signal proof of their dexterity as marksmen."

The institution of slavery would appear to be very general throughout Balochistan, and there is no family of any consideration that does not possess a number of male and female slaves. The greater number are Sidis, or negroes from Maskat, but they also comprise the issue of captives taken in war. At Kalāt there are slaves of Baloch and Afghān origin. Masson observes that *Khānazādas*, or slaves born in the families of their owners, are well treated and comfortable, and are frequently employed by their masters in confidential and important matters. One of the Kalāt rulers, Mahrāb Khān, possessed a large number of these *Khānazādas*. Pottinger states that the slaves are the fruit of their *chupaos*, or plundering excursions, and that when first taken they are treated in a very harsh and cruel manner. They are blindfolded and tied on camels, and in this manner transported, to prevent the possibility of their knowing how to return. The women's hair and men's beards are also shaved off, and the roots entirely destroyed by a preparation of quicklime, to deter them from any wish to revisit their native soil; but they soon get reconciled to their fate and become very faithful servants.

The master has, it must also be mentioned, full power, even of life and death, over the slave, without any right of appeal by the latter.

The savage and predatory character of the Balochi is well exemplified in those lawless incursions called *chupaos*, when they plunder and devastate a large tract of country, committing at the same time the most unheard of outrages and cruelties on the wretched inhabitants, who are generally attacked during the darkness of night. Pottinger gives the following description of one of these plundering expeditions, which he says was mentioned to him by Balochis who had themselves taken part in them:—"The depredators are usually mounted on camels, and furnished, according to the distance they have to go, with food, consisting of dates, some cheese, and bread; they also carry water in a small leathern bag, if requisite, which is often the case in the midst of their deserts. When all is prepared they set off, and march incessantly till within a few miles of the point where the *chupao* is to commence, and then halt in a *jangal*, or some unfrequented spot, in order to give their camels rest. On the approach of night they mount again, and as soon as the inhabitants have retired to repose, they begin their attack by burning, destroying, and carrying off whatever comes in their way. They never think of resting for one moment during the *chupao*, but ride on over the territory on which it is made at the rate of eighty or ninety miles a day, until they have loaded their camels with as much pillage as they can possibly remove; and as they are very expert in the management of those animals, each man, on an average, will have charge of ten or twelve. If practicable they make a circuit, which enables them to return by a different route from the one they came. This is attended with the advantage of affording a double prospect of plunder, and also misleads those who pursue the robbers, a step generally taken, though with little effect, when a sufficient body of men can be collected for that purpose. In these desperate undertakings the predatory robbers are not always successful, and when any of them chance to fall into the hands of the exasperated villagers, they are mutilated and put mercilessly to death. It may also happen that the threatened district receives timely intimation of the intended *chupao*, in which case means are taken to repel the marauders. The fact, however, of such plundering expeditions being an institution in Balochistan, must serve to show how slight is the power wielded by the paramount rulers, and what risks to the safety of both person and property must be run by those engaged in the business of trade in such a country."

Government and Revenue.—In treating of the administration of government in force in Balochistan, it will be necessary to remember that, as previously mentioned, the country may be considered as divided into two portions—the one, Kalāti Balochistan, or that either really or nominally under the rule of the Khān of Kalāt; and the other as Persian Balochistan, or that part which is more or less directly under the domination of the Shāh of Persia. Of the government of this latter territory, it will suffice to say that it is at present administered by the Governor of Bam-Narmashir, a deputy of the Kermān Governor; but the only district that is directly under Persian rule is that of Banpur—the rest of the country, says St. John, is left in charge of the native chiefs, who, in their turn, interfere but little with the heads of villages and tribes. The annual revenue paid into the Persian treasury by this portion of its Baloch possessions is not supposed to exceed £1500, but this is exclusive of Banpur and the neighbouring villages, which are cultivated, it is said, by the Persians on their own account. It would thus appear that the supremacy of the Shāh over a very large portion of the immense area (60,000 square miles) known as Persian Balochistan is more nominal than real, and that the greater number of the chiefs only pay revenue to their suzerain when compelled to do so.

As regards Kalāti Balochistan, the government is, so to speak, vested hereditarily in the Brahui Khān of Kalāt, but his sovereignty in the remote portions of his extensive territory (80,000 square miles), though even in former times more nominal than real, is at the present moment still more so, owing to the almost constant altercations and quarrels which take place between the reigning Khān and his Sardārs, or chiefs. The government of the country, though vested, as has been mentioned, in the Khān, was not, as a rule, administered by him absolutely. There were two hereditary counsellors associated with him, without whose consent nothing of importance could be done by the ruler. These were the Sardārs of Sarawān and Jhalawān, the privilege of the first being to sit on the right of the Khān in *darbār*, and that of the second on his left; the priority of consideration and statement of opinion on any public matter being with the Sardār of Sarawān, and after him with the chief of Jhalawān. This system of government naturally placed the Khān, at times, in a very dependent position. There was also another special adviser of the sovereign, whose office, too, was hereditary. This was the Vazir, chosen from among the Dehwar or Tajik community, the class from which the revenue of the country was principally derived. This selection was no doubt made with the object of conciliating that important portion of the Khān's subjects. It was only, in fact, when the reigning prince was a man of strong will and energy, like the great Nasir Khān, for instance, that he was able to exercise any absolute supremacy in public affairs. Owing to the state of anarchy at present prevailing throughout Kalāti Balochistan, due to the constantly recurring revolutions and rebellions of the chiefs against their Khān, it is difficult to define the various rights of the ruler and those of his subjects. Pottinger states that the power of declaring war and making treaties lay entirely with the Khān; that he was empowered to fix the limits of all landed property, and where boundary disputes arose and reference was made to him as *lord of the soil*, he gave his decision, which was always regarded as final. It was the Khān who, as supreme ruler, could order, when necessary, the chief of each tribe to attend in person with his quota of troops. This collective army was divided into three parts, each of which was distinguished by a particular banner. Thus the division of armed men from Kachh Gandāva and the Kalāt and Nushki districts was known by their red flag. That of Sarawān by a green, forked pennant, and the troops of Jhalawān and Las by one of a yellow colour. This claim on the chiefs of military service would seem to be universally acknowledged, it being *the condition* on which the several tribes held their lands. The numbers of the armies assembled by the different Khāns of Kalāt seem to have varied according to the popularity or otherwise of the ruler and his cause. Thus, Nasir Khān (I.) was enabled to collect without difficulty a force of 30,000 men; but his successor, Māhmud Khān, could only get together half that number, while Mehrāb Khān, the successor of Māhmud, could barely raise 12,000 men, and this with considerable difficulty. Nasir Khān is said to have had a small standing army, and so had his son, Māhmud Khān; among the troops of the latter were men in red jackets, similar to the sepoys in the British Indian army. Pottinger, in 1810, saw at Kalāt a register of the Baloch army which showed a strength of 250,000 men—an absurd estimate, and grossly exaggerated, since it is calculated that the entire number of males throughout the country did not much exceed *half* that amount. The present reigning prince, Khudadād Khān, has a small standing army, of artillery, cavalry, and infantry, in his pay, and this has been made a subject of complaint on the part of his chiefs. The *yearly* cost of this military force is believed to be a little over one lakh of rupees, or, say, about £10,000; but his troops are never paid, it seems, with any regularity, and are but too frequently kept in long arrears.

It is believed by some writers that no code of laws and regulations ever existed in Balochistan, but this is not borne out if what Pottinger has written be correct. He clearly states that laws for the administration of justice were drawn up by one of the earliest princes of the Kamburāni tribe, and that these were revised during the reign of the great Nasir Khān. From these it is found that in cases of murder the usual punishment, provided the deceased's relatives were agreed on this point, was imprisonment and heavy fine; otherwise blood for blood was demanded. Generally speaking, the offender was given up to the murdered person's friends to do with him as they liked, but if the victim happened to be a *foreigner*, the murderer was at once executed; nothing could save him. The previous permission of the Khān, in such cases, was not even necessary, though an immediate report of the circumstance had to be sent to him. The crimes of burglary and robbery by night were, when sufficient evidence for conviction was forthcoming, punished with death. For thefts and other ordinary crimes, flogging and imprisonment were usually awarded. Adultery was, as is common in oriental countries, visited with severe punishment, on due attestation of the fact by credible witnesses. Petty quarrels, thefts, etc., occurring among a *khēl* or society, were usually adjusted by the chief, an appeal against his decision lying to the chief of the tribe to which the *khēl* belonged. There was certainly a further right of appeal to the Khān himself against the sentence of the chief, but this was seldom if ever resorted to. For the government of that part of Makrān falling within Kalāti Balochistan, the Khān usually sent *Naibs*, or deputies, to Kēj and Panjgur, the two most important districts in that part of his dominions, to watch his interests and get such revenue from them as they could. These authorities, however, seldom interfered with the administration, which was almost entirely left to the local chiefs, and these exercised *unlimited* powers within their respective districts.

The revenues of Kalāti Balochistan seem to vary in amount with the ability or otherwise of the reigning Khān to enforce the payment of the State dues. In the time of the great Nasir Khān—the Augustan age, evidently, of Balochistan—the revenues are said by Pottinger to have exceeded 30 lakhs of rupees (£300,000), but in the time of his successor, these had dwindled away to 3½ lakhs, and the present Khān's revenue is believed not to exceed 2½ or 3 lakhs at the most. It must, however, be remembered that in Nasir Khān's time, Makrān, Las, Kharān, and other districts, paid tribute to this energetic ruler, which does not appear to be the case at present; and, again, his treasury was augmented by the customs dues derived from the port of Karāchi, then belonging to the Kalāt State. One great reason for the ridiculously small amount of revenue obtained by the Khān of Kalāt is the fact of the lands of the Brahui tribes in the Sarawān and Jhalawān Provinces being altogether free from taxation; while in Makrān it is the poorer class only of agriculturists who pay any dues, the rich and powerful being usually exempted. In that province one-tenth of the produce of the fields and groves, says Ross, is the property of the State, added to which is a tax on inheritances. In the other districts of this Khānate, revenue is paid by the Afghān agriculturists of Shāl, the Dehwar cultivators of Mastung, Kalāt, Nichāra, etc., at the rate of *one-third* of the produce (*sehkot*). The Jat cultivators in

Kachh Gandāva paid, it seems, according to Masson, *one-half* of the produce (*nimāghi*); from other parts of the country, one-fourth, one-fifth, or one-sixth was levied, according to their nearness to the capital, or, as Masson no doubt correctly terms it, *the chance* of getting it. When Pottinger wrote (1810), neither horses nor cattle paid anything throughout Balochistan in the way of taxation to the State, and it is believed that no change in this respect has taken place up to the present time. Commerce and manufactures in Makrān seem to be altogether exempt from taxation, but this is not the case as regards trade in Kalāt proper, and Las, where duties are levied at various places both on the sea-coast and in the interior.

Trade.—The trade of Balochistan is very small indeed in comparison with the great extent of the country, but this is not to be wondered at when the semi-barbarous condition of the people, and the consequent risks to both person and property, are taken into account. The export trade of the interior is very trifling in quantity and value, though capable, under a wise and beneficent rule, of great expansion. The wool of the hill country is excellent in both quality and staple, and would no doubt, under a good system of government, be a highly remunerative article of export. Madder from Shāl, Kalāt, and Mastung, almonds and dried fruits generally from the latter district, a little grain from Khozdār and its neighbourhood, small quantities of asafœtida from Nushki, and sulphur from Kachh Gandāva, comprise all the exports. Sometimes Kalāti-reared horses form an item of export. From the Makrān and Las Provinces the export trade is in *roghan*, hides, tobacco, bdellium (a gum), salted fish, isinglass, *ghi*, a little cotton, oil-seeds, dates, and a few other miscellaneous articles.

The imports are rice, pepper, sugar, spices, indigo, wood, metals, piece-goods, received mostly at the port of Sonmiāni, in Las. No *accurate* or reliable statements of the entire value of the export and import trade of Balochistan can here be given, but the traffic as at present existing between Makrān, Sindh, and Bombay, can be so shown, and will be found entered in the description of the Coast Provinces.

The different trade routes in the Sarawān and Jhalawān districts of Kalāti Balochistan are those leading from Shikārpur, in Sindh, to Kandahār, *viâ* Quetta; from it other routes branch off to Kalāt, Mushki, Ghazni, and Kābal. Formerly a much-frequented camel-caravan road was that running from the port of Sonmiāni, in Las, to Kalāt, but this, owing to the superior and safer trade routes through British Sindh, is supposed not to be so much used as formerly. A *kāfila* from Shikārpur to Kandahār occupied generally one month in transit, and from Sonmiāni to Kalāt about 40 days. In the Makrān Province the chief trade routes are between Panjgur and Kēj and Gwādar; Kolwah and Ormāra, Panjgur and Karāchi, *viâ* Las Bēla; Bahu and Gwādar; Dizāk and Gwādar; Kolānch and Gwādar, and between Geh, Kasrkand, and Chāhbār. Of the trade of Persian Balochistan little or nothing appears to be known, but it is most likely as trifling in extent as is that of the Kalāti Provinces.

Ruins and Antiquities.—Masson has well observed that no splendid vestiges of the olden times are, as in Afghānistan and Persia, to be found in Balochistan, though no doubt in by-gone ages, when the country was probably at one time a dependency of the great Persian Empire, subsequently included in one of the provinces of the Syro-Macedonian kings, and after that, as Arachosia, under the sway of Demetrius of Bactria, it was far more populous and civilized than at present. Ancient cities are still traceable in various parts of Balochistan; the sites of three are to be found near the present town of Kalāt, the names of two of them being Sorra and Bek-Kuki, but that of the third is unknown; another, known as Shahr Roghan, is to be seen not far from Bēla, in Las, and near the town of Gwajak, on the north-east border of Makrān, are the remains of an ancient city covering a very large area. Ancient writings on rocks are not uncommon; one daubed in red and black colours exists on the face of some hills lying between the Habb river and the Pabb mountains, in the Las district. Another was found on the scarped surface of a rock near the town of Panderan, in the Jhalawān Province. *Gaur-bastas* (or *Gaur-bands*), which are great walls and parapets of stone, said by the natives of the country to be the work of Kafirs (or infidels) in a former age, are frequently met with in various parts of the Sarawān and Jhalawān Provinces. Some writers have argued that they were constructed as defensive works, but Cook, who had an opportunity of seeing a large number of these structures in the course of his tours in that part of Balochistan, and who noticed that they were invariably placed on declivities, or across the mouths of ravines, has arrived at the conclusion that they were undoubtedly connected with the irrigation of the country; but by what race they were erected, and when, are questions still requiring to be satisfactorily answered. Caves have also been discovered in some parts of the Jhalawān Province, in the recesses of which the bodies of infants only have evidently been regularly placed, and these were so found by Cook in the course of one of his tours in that district. It has not unnaturally given rise to the idea that infanticide was formerly practised, and that the bodies were deposited there by some Rājput tribe that had settled in Jhalawān and had become incorporated with the Brahuis. Among the hills eastward of Kalāt are other caves and cave-temples, which are supposed to be religious and sepulchral localities, and in the Gurghina district is a subterranean chamber, presumed to be artificial, which may have also served the purposes of either a cemetery or temple in a by-gone age. In the immediate vicinity of the Hinglāj temple, in the Las district, the great place of pilgrimage for Hindus, are said to be figures of the sun and moon hewn out of the rock; and while mentioning Hinglāj, another spot sacred to the same race must not be omitted—this is the small island of Satadip, situate a short distance off the Makrān coast, between Ormāra and Pasni, whither many pilgrims proceed after visiting Hinglāj. This island is the Asthilāl of the Arabs and Balochis, and anciently known by Ptolemy as Asthæ, and as Kamina by Nearchus. Masson states that many of the names of places on the Las and Makrān shores, as given by the Greeks, are retained to this day, and he instances the stations of Malāna, Araba, Kalama, Derembosa, and Kophas, as mentioned by Arrian, to be readily recognizable in the present Malān, Araba, Kalamat, Darambāb, and Kaphān, as named by the natives.

CHAPTER III.

A GENERAL DESCRIPTION OF PERSIAN BALOCHISTAN, AND THE SARAWĀN AND JHALAWĀN PROVINCES OF KALĀTI BALOCHISTAN.

In the foregoing chapters a general description has been given of the country of Balochistan taken as a whole, but it will now be necessary to enter somewhat more minutely into an account of the different divisions, political and otherwise, of which it is composed. It has also been mentioned that the country is divided politically into two great portions—one part, about 80,000 square miles in extent, forming the territory of H.H. the Brahui Khān of Kalāt; the other, known as Persian Balochistan (some 60,000 square miles in area), of which a large slice out of the western portion of the Makrān Province forms a part, being subject to Persia. Some account of this latter extensive tract of country it is now proposed in the first place to give, so far as is possible; but it must be borne in mind that it is only within the last ten or eleven years that any correct or reliable information in connection with it has been obtained. In the years 1809 and 1810 two British officers, Captain Christie and Lieut. (afterwards Sir Henry) Pottinger, both belonging to the East India Company's native army, certainly travelled, in the interests of the English Government, through portions of Balochistan, and gained a considerable amount of valuable information, which was published in one volume by the latter officer in the year 1816. But from that date up to 1865, when Sir Frederick Goldsmid made his first journey through the interior of western Balochistan, to ascertain whether or not a line of telegraph could be laid down between Gwādar and Ispahān, no other European had penetrated into the inner part of the country. Since the great Indian Mutiny of 1857 it had become a matter of the first importance to connect India and England by a direct chain of telegraphic communication, and this, which was completed in 1864, had led to a careful exploration of the sea-coast of the Las and Makrān Provinces, and to the acquisition of much useful information in connection with those parts of Balochistan. Another cause was also at work which was destined, at a later period, to afford a still better opportunity of viewing the interior of this, so to speak, modern *terra incognita.* This was the fact of Persia having, during the past fifty years, been slowly but surely extending her rule over districts in western Balochistan which she had no doubt, at a previous period, held in subjection, but which her own weakness, arising from foreign wars and intestine strife, had long made independent of her. As these Persian conquests, however, seemed to threaten districts belonging to the Khān of Kalāt, then in alliance with the British Government, it was deemed advisable, in 1870, to appoint a mixed commission to settle a frontier beyond which Persia should not be permitted to push her conquests to the eastward. Sir Frederick Goldsmid, with a suitable party, was deputed to undertake this settlement on the part of the British Government, and it resulted in the acquisition of much important information in both a geographical and geological point of view. The settlement effected by this mission in 1872 shows the boundary of the western frontier of the Kalāt Khānate to be as follows:—From the coast at Gwattar Bay, in the Makrān Province, and between the mouths of the rivers Dasht and Dashtiyāri, are two creeks, and it is from the centre of the more western of these that the boundary runs northward, in the direction of the western slope of the Darabal hills. From the Darabal hills, to quote the words of St. John, the boundary follows an imaginary straight line across the alluvial plain (inundated after rain), in a direction slightly east of north, as far as the southern ridge of the Jambki hills. Here a prominent white cliff (name not known) marks the frontier, which thence follows the water-parting between the torrents called the Kalaki (on the Persian side) and the Samān (on the Kalāt side) as far as the east cliff of the Puru hill. It then turns east along the summit of the ridge connecting the Puru with the southern of the two Jambki peaks and of that between them. From the north Jambki peak it is carried along an imaginary line, in a north-north-east direction, to the junction of the Kastag and Ghistan torrents. From Kastag the boundary follows the water-parting of the Dasht and Dashtiyāri rivers to the westernmost peak of the range called Nākuh, a short distance south-east of the Persian village of Pishin. Five or six miles north-east of Pishin are two small patches of cultivation called Bok and Mazamband, near two small torrents of the same names. The latter, though on the watershed of the Bahu river, belongs to Mand, and is therefore on the Kalāt side of the frontier. North of this the Talār hills are entirely on Persian ground, as are the northern slopes of the Shairas hills, their southern belonging to Mand. From the Shairas hills the boundary line follows the centre of the Hamzai torrent to the point where it joins the Nihing river, along the centre of the bed of which it is carried to its source on the Sar-i-Sham plain, south-east of the Persian village of Gishtigan. A prolongation of the line due east defines the frontier as far as the meridian of the westernmost peak of the Sagarkand hill, along the ridge of which the boundary line runs sufficiently far east to enclose both banks of the torrent on which the Persian villages of Pātkuk and Kolān are situate, until the torrent joins the Māshkid river. Here the Persian and Kalāt frontiers cease to be conterminous, being divided by the land of the independent villages of Kuhak (including Konarbasteh) and Isfandak. These cover a space of about 40 miles from east to west, with an average breadth of 12, and are bounded by the Māshkid river on the south and east, the Siāneh mountains on the north, and on the west by an imaginary north and south line across the desert, half-way between the village of Isfandak and the Persian village of Dehak. North of the point where the Māshkid river issues from the hills between the Siāneh and Kuh-i-Sabz ranges, the frontier of Kalāt is undefined, but the Washati mountains, which run up to the extreme southern part of the Kharān district of Kalāt, may be taken as the probable boundary between it and Afghānistan.

Persian Balochistan consists of two mountain plateaus, known as the Baloch and Sarhad, though a portion only of the former—that is to say, the western half—is in this district. A description of both these plateaus was given in the first chapter of this work, so it will be unnecessary to repeat it here.

The rivers are the Banpur, Māshkid, the Dasht, or Nihing (or Nihang), the Sarbāz, and the Kāju (or Dashtiyāri). The first-mentioned stream flows in a direction north by west as far as the 59th meridian of longitude; here it joins another stream from an exactly opposite direction, the waters of both combined being, it is supposed, afterwards lost in a sandy desert. The Māshkid drains the Baloch plateau to the north, and, like the first, is said to be also lost in the desert about the 29th parallel of latitude; but it is surmised that it again appears, to assist in forming the great Zirreh swamp lying in Afghān territory. A portion only of the Nihing flows for about 50 miles through Persian Balochistan, the remainder being within the Kalāt border, where it is known as the Dasht. The Sarbāz river lies wholly within Persian Balochistan, rising about 20 miles north of the village of the same name, and after a very tortuous course is joined by the Kāju (or Dashtiyāri), in Makrān, their united streams falling into the sea at Gwattar Bay. The Kāju rises, it is said, from the same ridge of hills as the Sarbāz; in the lower part of its course it is known as the Dashtiyāri, and meets the Sarbāz river a few miles from the sea. These are the principal streams in Persian Balochistan, and all, excepting perhaps the Banpur, which has a continuous flow above ground, are merely disconnected pools of water during the greater part of the year.

The chief districts making up Persian Balochistan are four in number, namely:—Sarhad, Dizak, Sarbāz, and Geh, but a large portion is as yet unexplored. The sub-divisions of these districts, with other information concerning them, are contained in the accompanying table:—

Districts.	Estimated population.	Sub-divisions.	Remarks.
1. Sarhad...	Unknown	Unknown	Is an unexplored district; the inhabitants, who are Balochis, are nomadic—there is only one village, that of Washt.
2. Dizak ...	30,000	Dizak (proper), Jalk, Kalagan, Sib, Magas, Bampusht, and Irafshān.	Inhabitants are mostly Balochis, but the cultivators in some of the districts are Arbābis.
3. Sarbāz...	35,800	Sarbāz (proper), Kasrkand, Kughi, Dashtiyāri, and Pishin; also port of Gwattar.	In this district is Banpur, the capital of Persian Balochistan.
4. Geh ...	35,000	... ...	Very little is as yet known concerning this district.
Total ...	100,800		

The population of the three divisions here entered is altogether *approximative*, and is shown on the authority of Ross, who wrote upon the Makrān district in 1868. It is also to be observed that the inhabitants of Kasrkand have been included in the Geh district, and not in that of Sarbāz, of which it is a sub-division. If to this number (100,800) be added a little over 9000 souls, as the *probable* population of the hill district of Sarhad, the inhabitants of which may be considered as altogether nomads, this would give a total of about 110,000 souls, or, say, not quite *two* to the square mile. Nothing reliable seems to be known as to the particular tribes inhabiting these districts. It would seem to be a doubtful point to what district, whether Geh or Sarbāz, the port of Chāhbār, containing about 800 inhabitants, properly belongs, but it is conjectured to the latter. It was recovered by the Persians, so late as 1872, from the Arab state of Maskāt, of which it had been a dependency for nearly eighty years, having been captured during the reign of Sultan Bin Ahmad of Maskāt.

Persian Balochistan is ruled by the Governor of Bam-Narmashir, a deputy of the Governor of Kermān. He resides at Banpur, in the Sarbāz district, a town 1700 feet above the sea, with 200 houses, or, say, about 800 inhabitants, and a small fort. The town of Banpur, with a few villages, is alone under the direct rule of the Persians, the rest of the country being left in charge of the native chiefs, who, in their turn, interfere but little with the heads of villages and tribes. The revenue received by Persia from the whole of their territory in Balochistan is believed to be very small and trifling, not exceeding the sum of £1500 (or Rs.15,000), but this is exclusive of Banpur and the neighbouring villages, which are cultivated by the Persians themselves. Of this sum the Dizak district is supposed to contribute no more than £500 (Rs.5000). Unequal taxation, as in the Kalāt

State, would seem to be the rule here; and when the cultivators refuse, or are unable, to pay the State dues, which are generally *one-tenth* of the produce, an armed force is sent into the refractory district to collect them.

The ports of Gwattar and Chāhbār are considered to be the most important places in Persian Balochistan, the population of each being, however, not more than 250 and 600 respectively; after them come the towns of Banpur, Pishin, Hichān, Kasrkand, and Bahu-Kalāt, in the interior; other places on the coast are mere hamlets.

KALĀTI BALOCHISTAN.

The remaining portion of Balochistan, which it is now necessary to describe, is that part of it belonging to his Highness the Khān of Kalāt, the boundaries of which, so far as the eastern, northern, and southern borders are concerned, were described in Chapter I.; while the comparatively speaking newly settled line of frontier on the western side will be found fully entered into in this present chapter. This extensive territory, covering about 80,000 square miles, and inhabited by a population very roughly estimated at not more than 350,000 souls, or, say, but *four* to the square mile, comprises five large districts, the area and population of which, given *approximately* it must be remembered, together with such other information as is available, are contained in the following tabular statement:—

Name of Province.	Estimated area in sq. miles.	Estimated population.	Sub-districts.	Towns and Villages.
I. Sarawān...	15,000	70,000	1. Nushki ...	Only Nushki, the population being mostly nomads.
			2. Kharān ...	Kharān and Wāshak (both small).

Name of Province.	Estimated area in sq. miles.	Estimated population.	Sub-districts.	Towns and Villages.
I. Sarawān ... (*continued*)	15,000	70,000	3. Shāl (or Quetta) ...	Shāl (or Quetta), Barg, Kuchlak, and Ispangli.
			4. Mastung...	Mastung, Khānak, Pergawad, Tiri, and Feringabad.
			5. Mangachar	Mangachar.
			6. Kalāt ...	Kalāt, Nichāra, and Siālkoh.
			7. Kirta ...	Johan and Rodbar.
			8. Gurghina	None.
II. Jhalawān	16,000	40,000	1. Sohrāb ...	Sohrāb, Nogrāma.
			2. Zehri ...	Gwatt.
			3. Baghwāna	Kamāl-Khān villages.
			4. Khozdār...	Khozdār.
			5. Zedi... ...	Zedi.
			6. Kappar ...	...
			7. Wadd ...	Wadd.
			8. Nāl	Nāl.
			9. Greshar ...	...
			10. Gidar ...	Gidar.
			11. Bessemer	...
			12. Matt ...	Matt.
III. Kachhi. or Kachh Gandāva	9,000	100,000	No sub-divisions.	Gandāva, Bāgh, Dādar, Kotri, and Nasirabād.
IV. Las	8,000	30,000	,,	Bēla, Sonmiāni, Utal, Liyāri.
V. Makrān ...	32,000	110,000	1. Ormāra ...	Ormāra.
			2. Pasni ...	Pasni.
			3. Gwādar ...	Gwādar.
			4. Kolwąh ...	Balor, Chambar, Gushanak, and Rudkhān.
			5. Panjgur ...	Panjgur.
			6. Kēj	Kēj, Turbat, Kappar, Nogbarr, and Jiuni.
			7. Tump ...	Tump.
			8. Mand ...	Mand.
			9. Mushki ...	Shahr-Kalāt, Mushki, and Gajar.
Total ...	80,000	350,000		

THE PROVINCE OF SARAWĀN.

The Province of Sarawān, the most northern in Kalāti Balochistan, is somewhat peculiar as regards its configuration, and is bounded on the north and west by the Shorāwak, Pishin, Toba, Sherrud, and other districts of Afghānistan; on the east by Kachh Gandāva, from which it is separated by a range of hills of the Brahuik plateau known as the

Takāri, and on the south by the Jhalawān and a portion of the Makrān Provinces. Its area may be roughly estimated at 15,000 square miles, and it comprises the districts of Shāl, Mastung, Mangachar, Kalāt, Nushki, and Kharān, as also the hilly tracts of Gurghina and Kirta. This province, in its physical aspect, is very mountainous, the Brahuik plateau, which covers it, containing the most elevated land as yet known throughout Balochistan. The parallelism of the hill ranges in Sarawān, says Cook, is extremely marked, and hardly ever varied to any appreciable extent. Lines of disruption appear to run from east to west in several places. Gorges cut through five ranges in succession, and the water-drainage is almost for that distance due east. It is these gorges which form the only means by which horsemen can manage to travel from one village to the other, the hills being otherwise impassable. The mountains of Sarawān are, according to the same authority, almost entirely composed of nummulitic limestone, and the Harbui range, eastward of Kalāt, is probably the most extensive, as well as the loftiest, in the province. It is many miles in length, and is composed of some five or six ranges, rising one behind the other until a height of more than 9000 feet above the level of the sea is attained. Eastward this mass of mountains stretches away, range after range, until the plains of Kachhi, 40 miles distant, are reached.

In the northern part of the Shāl district is the Tokātu chain of hills, running nearly east and west; one of its summits—a two-forked peak—being, it is said, about 12,000 feet above sea-level. On the western side of the same district is the Chehel-Tan range, having at its southern extremity the towering mass of Chehel-Tan, the most elevated mountain yet known in Balochistan, and one which has more than any other attracted the attention of those European travellers who have visited the country. Two

Europeans only have ascended this mountain to its summit, on which is a *ziārat*, or shrine. These are Masson and the present Sir Henry R. Green, Bombay Army, and at one time Political Agent at the Court of Kalāt. The latter found the height to be 12,300 feet. Masson states the route to be difficult, and dangerous as well, on account of the Khāka tribe, who infest the neighbourhood and are at deadly enmity with the Brahuis. He mentions juniper-cedar trees as growing on the sides of the mountain, and that the wild white-rose tree was also seen. He observed, too, several marine shells of the same kind as those found on the sea-coast of Makrān. Other trees and plants noticed are the *mashmuk*, a large thorny bush, the *siah-chob* (blackwood), the *gwhen* (*pistacia kabulica*), the fig-tree, and a few others. Wild sheep and the *peshkoza* range about the hill. The view from the top is said to be vast and magnificent; the line of the Bolān pass is seen running through the great chain towards the plains, and even the lowlands of Kachhi can, it is affirmed, be readily distinguished on a clear day.

The word Chehel-Tan means "forty bodies," and Masson relates the following ridiculous legend, current among the Brahuis, from which the mountain is reported to have taken its name:—"A frugal pair, who had been many years united in wedlock, had to regret that their union was unblessed by offspring. The afflicted wife repaired to a neighbouring holy man, and besought him to confer his benediction that she might become fruitful. The sage rebuked her, affirming that he had not the power to grant what Heaven had denied. His son, afterwards the famed 'Hāsrat Ghous,' exclaimed that he felt convinced he could satisfy the wife, and casting forty pebbles into her lap, breathed a prayer over her and dismissed her. In process of time she was delivered of forty babes—rather more than she wished or knew how to provide for. In despair at the overflowing bounty of superior powers, the husband exposed all the infants but one on the heights of Chehel-Tan. Afterwards, touched by remorse, he sped his way to the hill, with the idea of collecting their bones and interring them. To his surprise he beheld them all living and gamboling among the trees and rocks. He returned and told his wife the wondrous tale, who, now anxious to reclaim them, suggested that in the morning he should carry the babe they had preserved with him, and, by showing him, induce the return of his brethren. He did so, and placed the child on the ground to allure them. They came, but carried it off to the inaccessible haunts of the hill. The Brahuis believe that the forty babes, yet in their infantile state, rove about the mysterious mountain." Pottinger, however, accounts for the forty bodies in a more reasonable manner by stating that the Brahuis "believed themselves to be peculiarly favoured by the prophet, who, they aver, paid them a visit one night mounted on a dove, and left several *pirs*, or saints, amongst them for their spiritual guidance. The remains of forty of these deified preceptors are believed to be buried under a mountain about 76 miles north of Kalāt, whence it is called the Kuh Chehel-Tan, or mountain of the forty bodies, and is flocked to as a place of *ziārat*, or pilgrimage, by both Musalmāns and Hindus."

It is in the valleys among these hills that towns, villages, and cultivation are found, and though there are no rivers in the province excepting the Lora, in the extreme north, the Bolān, and Mula (and these two latter are merely *mountain torrents* on a large scale), there are nevertheless numerous rivulets issuing from the hills, as also *karēzes*, or subterranean aqueducts, which lead from the bases of the hills towards the centre of the valley, and these, conjointly with occasional rain, supply all that is necessary for irrigational purposes. The names of the various valleys lying on the Brahuik plateau in this province, with their areas and such other information connected with them as is obtainable, are given in the following statement :—

Name of Valley.	Estimated area in sq. miles.	Elevation above sea-level.	Remarks.
		Feet.	
1. Quetta, (or Shāl)	90	5600	Soil rich and good; cultivation comprises wheat, rice, madder, tobacco, lucerne, melons, apricots, peaches, plums, apples, quinces, mulberries, grapes, figs, pomegranates, and walnuts; the grasses are numerous.
2. Kanhi ...	150	5500 (?)	Is south of the Quetta valley; soil light and sandy, but more stony than that of Quetta; productions: wheat, and garden produce generally.
3. Mastung ...	280	6000	Situate south of the Quetta and Kanhi valleys; soil light and rather sandy, but very fertile when irrigated. Productions the same as those of Quetta, but better in quality; the melons, as also the grapes, are celebrated.
4 Mangachar	...	5900	Is south of Mastung and smaller in area; productions are wheat, lucerne, tobacco, etc. In this valley there is a great want of trees.
5. Girāni ...	...	6600	Is south of the Mangachar valley; the soil and productions are not known.
6. Ziārat ...	...	Lower than Girāni	Is west of the Girāni valley; soil and productions unknown.
7. Chappar ...	...	...	Is west of the Ziārat valley, and is largely cultivated; its melons are later in season than those of the Kalāt valley.
8. Kalāt... ...	16	6800	Soil is good; productions are wheat, barley, millet, *juār*, lucerne, tobacco, turnips, carrots, lettuces, radishes, onions, beetroot, cucumbers, melons, and many kinds of fruits, as at Mastung.
9. Katringal...	16	6900 (?)	Soil of this valley is good, and it is well cultivated at its northern end.
10. Rodinjo ...	...	6580	Soil in some parts good, more especially to the south, where there is a fair amount of cultivation; but in others there is merely an out-crop of common salt in an efflorescent state; productions not known.

"The fruits of Mastung," says Cook, "are deservedly famous. Of the grape there are no less than *five* varieties: —(1) a fine, long white grape, measuring 1¼ inches, and weighing about 80 grains—it is fleshy, and resembles an English hot-house grape; (2) a smaller one of peculiar shape, resembling a pear; (3) an oval one of ordinary size; (4) a small oval one having no seeds, the flavour resembling the muscatel; and (5) a large purple-coloured grape."

In the Sarawān Province, as, indeed, throughout Balochistan generally, there are no made roads, with the single exception of one over a portion of the Nishpa *lak*, or pass, between Mastung and Sir-i-Ab, which was constructed, it is said, by the British army in 1839–40, when temporarily occupying that part of the country. All other means of communication are simply paths, and transit through the country is effected either on foot, or mounted on horse or camel-back. It is, according to Cook, when travelling *east* or *west* that difficulties are found to occur, the camel-tracks and footpaths crossing many hills and leading through deep and sombre ravines; but in proceeding either *north* or *south* these tracks are comparatively easy, and hardly an obstruction is met with that would prevent the passage of artillery.

The hilly tract of Gurghina, situate west of the Mastung and Mangachar districts, comprises the sub-divisions of Kurdigap, Ashikhān, and Pudēn. It is poorly supplied with water, and cultivation is carried on by means of *bandhs*, or mounds of earth thrown up to preserve the rain-water. In the hills of the Kirta district, on the extreme eastern border of Sarawān, are a few small valleys known as those of Rodbar, Kajuri, Ghazg, Merv, Isprinji, Kuhak, Narmak, Lup, and Kishān. North-east of Mastung lies the "Dasht-i-Bidaulat," or the unpropitious valley, a plain at the head of the Bolān pass; but this depreciatory name only applies to it after the harvests have been gathered in, for in spring it is covered with flowers, especially with the fragrant *tark* plant. There are but two wells upon it, cultivation there being mostly dependent upon rainfall and heavy dews. The proprietors of this plain are nomad Kurds, whose *tumāns* cover it during the spring and summer.

The only other districts of Sarawān requiring notice are those of Nushki and Kharān, both lying westward of those already described. The Nushki district, which is very extensive, borders directly on the Afghān desert, having the Kharān district to the south, while hill ranges to the eastward separate it from the hilly tract of Gurghina. There are several *laks*, or passes, léading from the upper or hill country into Nushki; one of these is mentioned by Pottinger (who travelled through this part of the country), as being eleven miles in length and extremely steep. The people of Nushki are nearly all nomads. The vegetable productions are wheat and *rawash* (native rhubarb), but failure in the crops is of very frequent occurrence. Asafœtida (*hing*), is found on the hills. The wild ass (*gurkhar*) is still to be seen, it is said, on the level wastes of Nushki.

The Kharān district comprises the extreme western part of Sarawān, but though entered here as a part of that Province, it is believed to be to all intents and purposes independent of the Brahui Khāns of Kalāt. If it owns allegiance to any one, it must be to the Afghān governor of Kandahār alone, and even this is understood to be but nominal. It has the Sohrāb valley in the Jhalawān Province to the west, Nushki to the north, Mushki, in Makrān, to the south, and the Afghān desert to the west. Some of the sub-districts in Kharān are Jalalan, Khargoshki, and Bhagat. Parts of this district are very mountainous, but the sandy deserts greatly preponderate, and Pottinger, who passed through this portion of Balochistan in the month of April, has stated that water is very scarce at times, and only to be got at certain places from very deep wells. Owing to this difficulty, and also to the destructive and scorching nature of the winds in these deserts during the hot season, that is to say, from June to September, travelling becomes simply impossible. As regards the effect of this hot wind, which is known here under the name of *juloh*, or the flame, and *badē simum*, or the pestilential blast, Pottinger remarks that so powerfully searching is its nature, that it has been known to kill camels and other hardy animals, and its effects on the human frame are said, by those who have been eye-witnesses of them, to be the most dreadful that can be imagined. The muscles of the unhappy sufferer become rigid and contracted, the skin shrivels, an agonizing sensation, as if the flesh were on fire, pervades the whole frame, and in the last stage it cracks into deep gashes, producing hemorrhage, which quickly ends his misery.

The productions of the Kharān district are wheat, but in small quantities only, so that it has to be imported, at times, from Mushki, and barley, which is grown on *khushkāwah*, or rain lands. *Shakar-gaz*, a sweet gum, is obtained from a species of tamarisk, and asafœtida is grown on the hills; the date and melon are the only fruits, the first being cultivated in the level country. The camels bred in the Kharān district are deservedly noted for their great strength and powers of endurance, and in this respect are found very useful in predatory expeditions. But very little is known of the Kharān district; Pottinger and Christie are, up to the present, the only travellers who have ever passed through it. The only two villages in this large tract of country are Kharān and Wāshak, and these are both very small and unimportant.

Climate.—The climate of the hill country of Sarawān may be said to be truly delightful when compared with that of the plains. The summer season includes the months of May, June, July, and nearly the whole of August, but it is, of course, cooler and more agreeable at Kalāt, the highest occupied table-land in the province, than at either Quetta or Mastung, which are both lower in altitude. During the months of June, July, and August, Cook found the extreme maximum of heat at Kalāt to be but 103°, and the extreme minimum 48°, the *mean* between sunrise and sunset being 76°. It has been noticed that the heat at Mastung is much more *oppressive* than that at Kalāt, and the air at the former place is by no means so buoyant or elastic, nor has it the same bracing effect. The winter commences about the end of October, and lasts till the middle or end of February. The cold is at times exceedingly severe, and heavy falls of snow also occur. In the Shāl district snow falls and remains on the ground for about *two months*. All the inhabitants that can do so migrate in the latter part of the autumn to the warmer climate of Kachh Gandāva. In the Nushki district snow rarely falls, but the heat of summer in the desert portion is said to be very great.

Towns and villages.—The principal towns and villages in the Sarawān Province, in the order of their importance, are the following:—(1) Kalāt (the capital), (2) Mastung, (3) Shāl (or Quetta), (4) Rodinjo, (5) Tiri, (6) Pergawad, (7) Khānak, and (8) Siālkot.

KALĀT, the capital town of the Khān, is situate in lat. 29° N. and long. 66° 40′ E., and stands on the northern spur of a limestone hill called the Shah Mirdan. It is about 6800 feet above sea level, and has, in consequence, a climate more nearly approximating to places situate in much higher latitudes, but the temperature of this part of Sarawān has already been referred to, both in the first and present chapters of this work. Kalāt is a fortified town built in terraces, and has three gates, known as the Khāni, Mastung, and Bēlāi, the two latter named, no doubt, from the roads leading to Mastung and Bēla which pass through them. The streets are extremely narrow, tortuous, and dirty, and this Bellew, on his passing through the place in 1872, confirmed by saying that the approaches were filthy, and full of all sorts of refuse. The walls of this town are built of mud and have bastions at intervals, and both walls and bastions are said to be pierced with numerous loopholes for musketry. Only a few guns are mounted on them. The bazar of Kalāt is reported to be large and well supplied with all kinds of necessaries, and the town itself is furnished with very clear and pure water from a stream which rises from the base of a limestone hill on the eastern side of the valley. The *miri*, or fort, the palace of the Khān, overhangs the town, and is made up of a confused mass of buildings crowded together and adjoining one another. Cook says it is an imposing and antique structure, and probably the most ancient edifice in Balochistan, owing its foundation to the Hindu kings who preceded the Muhammadan dynasty. From the *darbār* room in this building, which has an open balcony, a most extensive view is obtained, embracing the whole valley and surrounding hills.

The suburbs of Kalāt are two in number, one on the west and the other on the east side. They would appear to be extensive, and it is here that the Bābi portion of the community reside. The number of houses, according to the latest authority—Bellew—is said to be 3500, which would give a population of about 14,000 people; but this no doubt includes the suburbs. Masson states the number of houses in all to have been, *in his time*, only 1100, which would give probably not more than between 4000 and 5000 inhabitants in all; but he has nevertheless estimated the population of Kalāt and its environs at 14,000 souls, which would thus show Bellew's calculation to be correct. The town of Kalāt is inhabited by Brahuis, Hindus, Dehwars, and Bābis, or Afghāns, the latter residing mostly, as has previously been stated, in the suburbs. The Brahuis form the great bulk of the inhabitants; but the cultivation is chiefly carried on by the Dehwar community. There are several villages and walled gardens clustered together in the valley east of the town; of these Siālkoh is one of the largest, having about 100 houses, or, say, 450 people. The trade and manufactures of Kalāt are in every way slight and unimportant.

The next largest town in Sarawān, after Kalāt, would appear to be MASTUNG, in lat. 29° 48′ N., and long. 66° 47′ E., 61 miles north of Kalāt, and 42 miles south from Quetta. It is nearly 6000 feet above sea-level, and is situate about 12 or 14 miles from the extreme northern end of the valley of the same name. It is a fortified place, and the old fort, which is slightly raised above the rest of the town, is built of sun-burnt bricks, and has a few guns mounted upon it; the garrison consists of a small force of infantry, and a few artillerymen. Bellew says that Mastung possesses a thriving bazar, and the people, among whom are many Afghāns, appeared well-clothed, and looked a prosperous community. The same authority considers the number of houses to be about 1200, though Cook reckons them at only 400; the population may, however, most probably be estimated at, in round numbers, 4000 souls. The town of Mastung is entirely surrounded by gardens and orchards, in which the finest fruit in Balochistan is produced. The climate of this place is considered to be mild and salubrious, and Cook states that it is very much warmer throughout the year than either Kalāt or Quetta (Shāl). Those of the inhabitants who can do so migrate during the winter to the lowlands of Kachh Gandāva. The principal tribes inhabiting the town are the Raisāni, Sherwāni, Mahmudshāhi, Banghlzai, and a few Dehwars.

The town of SHĀL, so-called by the Brahuis, or Quetta (Kwatta), as designated by the Afghāns—meaning *the fort*, or *kot*—is situate at the northern end of the valley of the same name, and is on the direct route from Kandahār to Jacobabad and Shikārpur, *viâ* the Bolān pass, being at the same time very conveniently placed as regards Kalāt (from which it is distant 103 miles north) and other Baloch towns. It is in lat. 30° 8′ N., and long. 66° 56′ E., and is 5600 feet above the level of the sea. The town is surrounded by a mud-wall, and has two gates, the eastern and southern, the latter being known as the Shikārpuri gate. In the centre of the town, on an artificial mound, is the *miri*, or fort, in which the governor of the place resides, and from it there is a very fine and extensive view of the neighbouring valley. This fort, it would seem, possesses but a single gun. Shāl is said to be about the same size as Mastung, and has probably about 4000 inhabitants, of whom a large number are Afghāns. Bellew remarks that in 1872 the garrison of the fort consisted of 100 infantry, mostly Afghāns, 40 horsemen, and a few artillerymen. The same authority also mentions that when there, on the 30th January, 1872, the thermometer stood at 7 a.m. at 18° Fahr., and that four or five inches of snow had fallen during the previous night. In summer the climate is considered to be very pleasant, the heat being tempered by cool breezes from the lofty hills which on all sides surround the valley. Numerous gardens and orchards abound in the suburbs, and the water supply is good.

The village of Rodinjo, on the southern border of the province, 14 miles south from Kalāt, and 29 miles north of Sohrāb in Jhalawān, is, perhaps, as regards number of inhabitants, the next most populous place after Shāl (or Quetta). Bellew speaks of it as a flourishing village of about 200 houses or so, representing a population of about 800 or 900 souls. It is freely irrigated by numerous hill-streams, and is seated on high ground, being, according to Cook, 6580 feet above sea-level. The towns of Tiri, Pergawad, Khānak, and Siālkot are small and insignificant, and do not require any particular description.

Though mention was made at page 33 of the several sub-tribes of the Brahuis inhabiting the Sarawān Province,

BRAHUI SARDĀR AND FOLLOWERS. (GHULAM JĀN, NEPHEW OF THE SHĀHGASSI, WALI MUHAMMAD.)

To face page 74.

it will not be superfluous to refer again to this subject, and to detail as succinctly as possible the names of those tribes dwelling in the various valleys, hill-districts, and plains of the Sarawān Province which have already been described. Thus the Raisāni tribe of Brahuis, as also a numerous body of Afghāns, dwell in the Shāl (or Quetta) valley; the Raisāni, Samalāri, Shirwāni, Mahmudshāhi, Bangulzai, Shēkh Husaini, and Lari tribes of Brahuis, together with some Dehwars, inhabit the Mastung district; Brahuis, Afghāns, Dehwars, and a few Hindus the valley of Kalāt; the Langhau tribe of Brahuis the valley of Mangachar; Kurds the Dasht-i-Bidaulat and Merv; the Sirperra and Rodāni tribes the Gurghina hill-district; the Ghazghi, Kalhui, Kuchik, Puzh, Mandarāri, and Pugh tribes the hill-district of Kirta; the Zigar Minghals and Rakshānis the Nushki district, and the Nurshirvāni tribe that of Kharān.

In the Sarawān Province, near Kalāt, are to be seen the sites of three ancient towns, and not far from Nichāra the remains of an infidel city. Masson states that several Greek coins have been found in the vicinity of Mastung, and also that *gaur-bastas*, or great walls and parapets of stone, constructed, it is supposed, in some past age, but by whom is not known, exist at Rodbar, in the hills between Kalāt and Kirta.

THE PROVINCE OF JHALAWĀN.

The Kalāti province of Jhalawān, next to Makrān the largest in area of the districts making up the country of Balochistan, occupies an easterly position on the map, and has Sarawān on its north, portions of Kachh Gandāva and of the British province of Sindh to the east, while

Makrān and Las respectively bound it on the west and south. In area the Jhalawān Province is about 16,000 square miles, being on an average 160 miles in length from north to south, by 100 in breadth from east to west. It comprises, so far as is at present known, eight districts, that is to say:—(1) Sọhrāb, (2) Zehri, (3) Baghwāna, (4) Khozdār, (5) Zedi, (6) Kappar, (7) Wadd, and (8) Nāl; but there are doubtless others on the extreme south-western and south-eastern borders, which have as yet scarcely been visited by any European traveller. In its physical aspect, this province, like that of Sarawān, is exceedingly rugged and mountainous, being, in fact, a continuation of the Brahuik mass of mountains, which covers almost every part of it, and leaves but few level spots of any extent. Range rises up after range in an apparently interminable succession, many of these being distinguished by local names, such as the Hāla, Harbui, Dauwaru, and other chains. The parallelism of these mountain ranges is as marked as in the Sarawān Province. The most elevated portion of the Jhalawān district is in the north, at Sohrāb and Panderan, and again in the south-west at Vaju, near the Kalgalli pass; thence it decreases in a southerly direction, being but 3800 feet above sea-level at Khozdār, and very much less than this on the southern border. Hardly any of the passes leading from the western part of the Jhalawān mountains into the Kharān district on the north-west, and again into the low land of the Mushki district of Makārn on the south-west, are at present known to Europeans. Several of the valleys, which, as in Sarawān, are found lying at a considerable elevation among these mountains, are extensive in area, and tolerably fertile as regards soil. The prevailing rock of which these hill-chains are composed, at least in the northern and middle portions of the province, would seem to be the usual limestone, of different kinds, but mostly nummulitic. Towards the south and west ranges of clay-slate are met with, while at Nāl, and at other places still further south, trap forms, in conjunction with other igneous rocks, an important element in the constitution of entire chains of hills. What it may be in the extreme south-west and south-east directions does not appear to be known, since no geological researches have as yet been carried on in those parts of the province. Of the rivers of the Jhalawān district there are hardly any that deserve the name. The Mula, which rises at or near Angira, is merely a mountain torrent on a large scale, and the same may be said of the Nāl, the Urnach and Purāli streams, which, when in water from heavy rain, flow partly through this province, and are lost in the plains. Of these, the Purāli may be considered, perhaps, as the most important. It rises in about the middle of the Jhalawān Province, but is only in water after a heavy rainfall, when it becomes a furious torrent, sweeping along with it trees and stones. It leaves the southern boundary of Jhalawān at a spot in the hills near Kunarcharri, about 18 or 20 miles north of the town of Bēla, and, entering the Las territory, still bears out its character of a mountain torrent on a gigantic scale. There are, besides, numerous rivulets in some parts, which afford water sufficient for good and careful cultivation; but, compared with the Sarawān Province, Jhalawān may on the whole be considered as deficient in water supply, and the natural consequence is much barrenness and a scanty population.

Of the principal valleys in Jhalawān, that of Sohrāb, situate in the north-west, has a good deal of cultivation, and is fairly watered. From its great altitude (being between 5000 and 6000 feet above sea-level) it is cold and dreary in winter, but in the summer displays much luxuriant verdure. Zehri, another of these valleys, lying to the eastward of Sohrāb, and containing several villages, has a comparatively fertile soil, and is watered by numerous rivulets. It produces grain, pulse, and vegetables. The Baghwāna valley lies a considerable distance south of that of Zehri, and is surrounded by high ranges of limestone hills; it is fertile, and possesses several villages, but, as its elevation (4400 feet) is considerable, the cold in the winter season is severe. In the valley are numerous gardens and orchards, and, besides an abundance of grain and grass, it produces figs, apricots, pomegranates, apples, plums, grapes, and melons. The valley of Khozdār, south of that last mentioned, is extensive, but in parts fertile, well-watered, and highly cultivated; in others it is sterile, stony, and much cut up by ravines. The valley of Nāl, westward of that of Khozdār, is broad and very extensive, and in places fertile and well-watered; there is a fair amount of cultivation carried on in it. South of this, again, is the great plain of Wadd, the eastern portion of which is considered the most fertile, producing large quantities of wheat and millet. There is also the large and open plain of Greshar, west of Nāl, which is in parts perfectly flat and sandy; but the height here is still considerable, being, according to Cook, 4100 feet above sea-level. Water is, however, scarce, and this portion of the province is in consequence very thinly inhabited. There are numerous other valleys scattered over this large tract of country, but little is at present known concerning them.

Climate.—The climate of Jhalawān, from its northern border to as far south as Baghwāna, in lat. 27° 55′ N., is not unlike that of Sarawān, but from this parallel of latitude down to its extreme southern border it is very much warmer. Snow rarely falls south of the Khozdār and Baghwāna valleys. So early as the beginning of November, Cook found the cold at Kapote, a march or so south from Kalāt, very great, the thermometer showing a minimum of 24° during the night. Again, when at Khozdār (3800 feet

VALLEY OF KHOZDĀR.

To face page 73.

above sea-level), towards the latter end of February, he states that the thermometer fell many degrees below freezing point; severe frosts took place nightly, succeeded by intensely cold winds and heavy rain, the mountains being covered with snow. When at Matt (5330 feet), in the north-western portion of the province, and about 25 miles south-west from Sohrāb, the thermometer, which on the 16th of April had risen to 90° during the day, fell in the night to 32°, showing the great variation of 58° during the four-and-twenty hours.

Inhabitants.—The Jhalawān Province is, for its immense size, but very sparsely populated, the number of inhabitants being estimated at not more than 40,000 in all, or but *two* persons to the square mile; but so much of the province is covered with hills, and the quantity of arable land is so restricted, owing to a scarcity of water over a great part of its surface, that this low rate is scarcely to be wondered at. The names of several of the tribes comprising this scanty population have already been given (at page 32), and it will therefore be only necessary here to remark that the Minghal and Bizanju tribes are the most numerous in the province, the former inhabiting its southern portion, with their capital town at Wadd, where their chiefs reside. They are broken up into two great divisions, the Shahizai, and the Pahlawanzai, and in character are rude in manner and predatory in habit. The Bizanju tribe are also divided into two great branches, the Amalāri and Tambarāri. Their chief resides at Nāl. The people of this tribe are violent and much addicted to rapine, and have long been the terror of *kāfilas*, or caravans, proceeding from Kalāt to Sonmiāni. The Zehri tribe, inhabiting the Zehri valley, are numerous, and are generally respected for their orderly habits. The Jataks, who occupy the hills east of the Zehri tribe, are essentially nomads, and have no permanent villages; but this may also be said to apply to the majority of the tribes inhabiting the Jhalawān Province.

Towns and Villages.—There are no towns, in the proper acceptation of the word, in Jhalawān, and but few villages, and this is mainly owing to the nomadic character of the people. Khozdār, Wadd, Nāl, and Gwatt are the only villages of any importance throughout the province, and these are very small, and have but few inhabitants in them. The first of these, Khozdār, the ancient capital of Jhalawān (3800 feet in elevation), is attractive by position, and is situated in lat. 27° 45′ N., and long. 66° 23′ E., being 16 miles south from the Baghwāna villages known as Kamāl-Khān. Several roads converge to this place from Kalāt, Sonmiāni, the Makrān Province, and from Gandāva, in Kachhi; yet it is small in size, Cook stating that in 1860 there were not more than perhaps 200 houses, representing a population of between 800 and 900 souls. Pottinger, who visited it about 64 years ago, considered it to possess 500 houses, mostly occupied by Hindus. Thirty years afterwards, Masson found but 60 or 70 mud-houses in the place, so much had it decayed since Pottinger's time. In 1872, when Bellew passed through it, he saw but a small collection of inhabited huts, but a good many *uninhabited* ones. There is, however, a fort at some short distance from the town, which, says Bellew, is an oblong with bastions at the angles, and a fortified gateway in the west face. The curtains are loopholed and crenulated, and there is no ditch. It was built in 1871 to protect the caravan routes converging at this spot. The garrison consists of 50 regular infantry, and 60 Brahui levies, with a few artillerymen and two guns. There is a good deal of cultivation around Khozdār, irrigated by small streams brought from a spring in the hills to the north. Wild duck and geese are said to frequent the river, and partridges the cultivated ground, while deer roam over the stony tracts, and wild sheep (*gad*) and ibex on the neighbouring mountains. The Saholi and Kaidrāni tribes inhabit the neighbourhood.

Wadd, the principal village of the Minghal tribe (lat. 27° 19 N., long. 66° 31′ E.), situate in a plain of the same name, is small and ill-built, and in Masson's time had not more than 70 houses in all, representing a population of only 200 or 300 people. It is on the caravan route, leading from Sonmiāni to Kalāt, and derives a little importance from this circumstance, as well as from the fact of the chief of the Minghal tribe residing there.

The village of Nāl is situate on the western side of the extensive valley of the same name, near a range of hills which bounds it in that direction. The town is small, about the same size as Wadd, and has a square fort. It is the headquarters of the Bizanju tribe, and it is believed that the *kāfila* route from Kalāt to Sonmiāni formerly led by it, but the bad reputation of this tribe for violence and plunder no doubt caused it to be deserted. Nāl is, according to Cook, 3390 feet above sea-level.

Gwatt, a village in the Zehri valley, is situate close under the western range of hills, is surrounded by gardens, and merely derives some little importance from the fact of its being the residence of the Jhalawān Sardār. The number of its houses or inhabitants is not known. In the Baghwāna valley is a cluster of villages known as Kamāl-Khān, about which is a good deal of cultivated land, the water for irrigation purposes being brought from a spring two or three miles distant. Corn, fuel, fodder, water, and other supplies are obtainable here in abundance, as the valley of Baghwāna is considered one of the chief corn-growing districts in Balochistan, and is noted also for its fruit.

Lead Mines.—About twelve miles west from Khozdār are the lead and antimony mines of Sekrān, which were in 1860 twice visited by Cook, who thus describes what he saw of them :—"As soon as our horses came up we mounted, and rode to the mines for which Sekrân is celebrated. We first passed northward up the valley, and then, turning westward through a gorge in the hills, ascended a rugged *nāla*, and in half an hour found ourselves in a narrow semi-circular valley surrounded by high hills. The strata dipped east ; the hill on the westward was composed of the dark blue limestone, that on the east, in which the mines were situated, wearing a blackened and cinder-like aspect. Vast quantities of black, metallic-looking *débris* covered the base of the hill, in the sides of which, here and there, at various elevations, were observed the low, cavern-like mouths of the many mines which riddled it. Taking with us candles, rope, and a lamp, we ascended this vast mass of slag-like looking stones, and climbing the sides of the hill for about 150 feet, reached the mouth of a mine. The rock resembled an altered claystone, variously mottled, black, purple, and metallic grey, veined and dotted red and white, and containing small cavities filled with bright red and yellow ochres, and the fracture of some specimens showed a metallic appearance of steel-grey. The stone was heavy and massive, and some parts of it effervesced with acid. It was stratified, the strata dipping east, and the upper strata was composed of the dark blue limestone. Near the mouths of the excavations were small masses of granite, which had apparently been brought up from the bowels of the mine. The gallery ran downwards at a steep inclination, following the dip of the strata. We passed down some distance on our hands and knees, but finding it almost blocked up with earth, rock, etc., and the air unpleasantly close, we did not carry on its exploration, but going along the side of the hill some two hundred yards, came to the opening of a mine which had, on a former occasion, been entered by Major Green. Here we lit our candles, and crawled downwards on hands and knees along the narrow passage. Fragments of bones lay about, evidencing the occupation of the excavations by wild animals. After proceeding for some time in this constrained position, we came to a spot where there was a sudden drop of some six or eight feet, like a well. Descending this, we found a hole at the bottom leading horizontally inwards. Through this we struggled, and along a narrow gallery, the roof of which was so low that it obliged us in some places to lie flat. We then emerged into a wider space, and sufficiently high to allow of one sitting up. From this branched several low galleries; selecting one of these, we crawled along some yards, and found another well-like gallery penetrating at a considerable angle downwards. It was so choked up that we could not force a passage, but proceeding along the horizontal gallery, we reached its extremity. Here were many bones of oxen, camels, etc., and the excrement of the hyena, not a pleasant fellow to meet in these narrow passages, coward as he is. The surface of the walls and roof was spangled with glittering crystals of sulphuret of *lead*, and coloured with ochres; bright white, needle-shaped crystals also sparkled on every side. The rock is rather easily worked, and I hammered away a good portion of it. Retreating now, as the atmosphere was becoming very oppressive, we reached the central excavation, and taking another gallery, soon discovered daylight at its further end. There were many other excavations in all directions in the side of the hill, some large enough to admit a man in an erect posture; but these only extended a short distance: others were so narrow and choked with *débris* that we could find no means of entrance. The mines have evidently been most extensively worked at some remote period, but the Brahuis have too great a dread of the supernatural beings who, they believe, inhabit them, to enter them themselves, and are contented to break off portions of the rock from the hill sides, and extract the lead and antimony as required. There is a peculiar tribe called the 'Mardui,' residing some few miles distant, who more especially work at this. . ." On a second visit paid by Cook to these mines, he says:—"I succeeded in reaching the bottom of the one near the mouth of which I had seen the granite lying on our last visit to this place, but I was disappointed in not finding the spot whence the granite had been taken. I searched minutely every portion of the interior, but the walls were entirely composed of what I have termed metamorphosed claystone. I then climbed the hill and found a large entrance leading into a kind of chamber where cattle had recently been kept; the back part of it was blocked up with brushwood. On removing this, I found two passages, one leading vertically upwards to another excavation, and the other downwards. Lighting the candles, I descended some yards on hands and knees, and found myself in a large chamber with a vaulted roof, capable of holding a dozen men. Leading out of it were two passages—one passed about fifteen yards into the rock and then ceased abruptly; the other being nearly closed with *dèbris*, and descending at a considerable angle, I was obliged to lie perfectly flat and creep along it. After passing some distance in a tortuous manner it turned to the right, apparently crossing behind the other passage, but I thought it hardly advisable to proceed further, as the passage was so narrow that I could not turn, and I was obliged to back out, my feet being considerably higher than my head, and the atmosphere, from the burning candles and my own hurried breathing, was becoming very oppressive. These passages must have been much deeper at one time, and were probably ventilated by shafts which are now stopped up, as no human being could work in them in their present condition. They possibly led into larger vaults, where several men could work at a time, and through these the ore was carried out." This lead ore is obtained by the Mardui tribe of Brahuis, before alluded to as the people who make it their business to search for and reduce it, and their method of smelting it is thus described by Cook, who witnessed the operation:—"Some of this tribe smelted a quantity of ore for us at Khozdār; their implements were very rude, and their mode of smelting very simple. They first built a rough furnace with four upright square stones, leaving a hole below in which to insert the nozzle of a pair of bellows. The bellows is a leather bag, formed of the skin of some small animal, having an opening posteriorly, to which are attached two sticks that serve to open and shut the aperture. The floor of this furnace is formed of clay. On this a fire is lighted, and a heap of charcoal kindled; when at a white heat, three or four handfuls of ore are thrown on and then covered up with a thick layer of charcoal. The whole is kept to a white heat for some time. A stone of the furnace is then pulled away, and the dross, ashes, etc., raked off from the melted metal. Fresh charcoal is then thrown in, with more ore, and again charcoal till the furnace is full, when the fire is kept up until the fresh supply of ore is reduced, and the operation continued till sufficient metal has been obtained. This mode of extracting the metal has been carried on for ages. The peculiar slag produced is met with all over this part of the country, and oftentimes in the most unlikely places. Vast quantities of it lie near the bank of the river, south of camp; many cartloads, I should think, of large angular pieces, some of them weighing several pounds." Masson also refers to the lead mines of Kappar (or Sekrān), and states that two hundred men were constantly employed there in extracting the ore.

Ruins and Antiquities.—Among the relics of a bygone age, existing in the Jhalawān Province, as well as in other parts of Balochistan, is some ancient writing (a Greek inscription, as some think) on a scarped surface of rock, a few miles from the village of Panderan, in the northern part of the district. Cook, who saw it, describes the letters as being from four to five inches in length, not cut into the rock, but raised above its surface about one-eighth of an inch. They appeared as if written in the first instance in *bitumen*, or some similar substance, which had had the effect of preserving the writing from the eroding effect of ages, as the surfaces of the letters were perfectly smooth, while the rock itself had become worn and eaten into a honey-combed condition. The following is a fac-simile of this ancient writing, taken from Cook's memoir on the subject :—

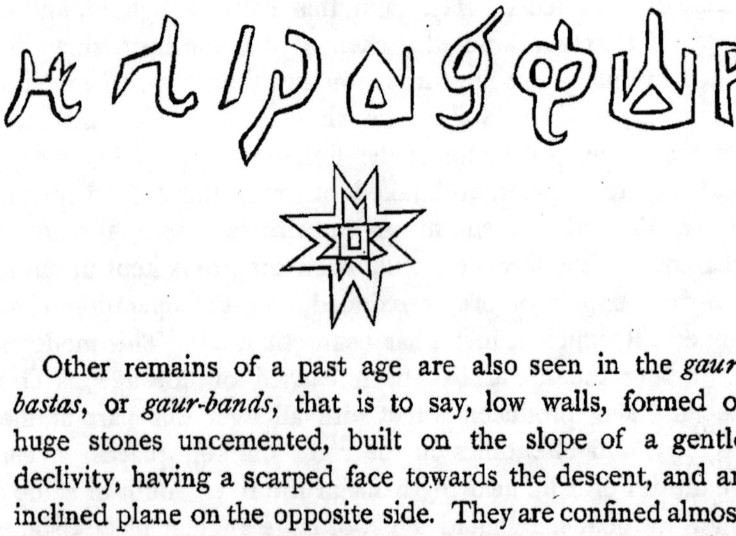

Other remains of a past age are also seen in the *gaur-bastas*, or *gaur-bands*, that is to say, low walls, formed of huge stones uncemented, built on the slope of a gentle declivity, having a scarped face towards the descent, and an inclined plane on the opposite side. They are confined almost entirely to the Jhalawān Province, the largest and most important being found in the southern and south-eastern portions of it. Bellew saw the remains of several of these structures in the Angira gap, near the top of the Mula pass, and again on the open ground a little in advance of the ridge towards Lakoriyan, in the same locality. He noticed that these *gaur-bands* were very solidly constructed, and that the greater number were built across gaps. From their appearance and position he concluded that they must have been erected as works of *defence*, and this, too, is Masson's opinion concerning them. But in this supposition Cook, who also had opportunities of seeing some hundreds of them, does not agree. He believes them to bear some resemblance to the Cyclopean remains in Europe, and to show evidently the traces of a people who occupied or passed through the country long anterior to the advent of the present inhabitants, who know nothing whatever of the builders, or of the uses, of these structures, and, with their usual bigoted ignorance, consider them as the works of *Kāfirs*, or infidels. Those built across ravines, Cook conceives to have been intended to form tanks for the preservation of the water that came down at irregular intervals in floods, while such as were on slopes were designed—he considers—to economize the distribution of the water, the surplus water of one terrace running over and flooding the lower one, depositing, as it went, a layer of surface soil. The following are the reasons put forward by him to show that these *gaur-bands* were *not* erected for purposes of defence, but solely with reference to the irrigation of the country :—"They are placed always on declivities, or across the mouths of ravines. Their solidity and size are proportioned to the steepness of the declivity; thus, where there is only a gentle slope, the walls are narrow and low, and slightly built, but where the descent is great, and the flow of water after floods and rains would be violent, they are of great thickness and height, and, as seen in the valley beyond Baghwāna, supported or strengthened by buttresses or walls built at right angles. They always present a scarped face to the descent, and the opposite side, when well preserved, is levelled off with the surrounding and superior ground.

Those built across the mouths of ravines are very solid and high, and usually the builders have taken advantage of some mass of rock jutting out as a sort of foundation. Those on slopes are never seen singly, but always in numbers, varying with the extent of the ground to be covered, and placed in succession one behind the other. The intervening ground, being levelled, is thus formed into a succession of terraces. These facts can lead, I think, to but one conclusion, namely, that they were connected with the irrigation of the country." It is supposed that from the great number of these *gaur-bastas*, or *gaur-bands*, this part of Balochistan must, at one time, have been very populous, and that the builders of these structures were, as regards energy and ingenuity, vastly superior to the present race of inhabitants; but whence these builders came, how long they remained here, and whither they subsequently went, are questions altogether unanswerable, and the subject is one that is consequently involved in much doubt and obscurity.

CHAPTER IV.

A GENERAL DESCRIPTION OF THE KACHHI PROVINCE, INCLUDING THE BOLĀN AND MULA PASSES, WITH MENTION ALSO OF THE MAZĀRI, GORCHĀNI, BUGHTI, AND MARRI BORDER TRIBES.

THE large province of Kachh Gandāva, or Kachhi, the easternmost territory of Kalāti Balochistan, has the still larger districts of Sarawān and Jhalawān on its western side; on the north and east it is surrounded by Afghān territory, the hilly country of the Marri, Bughti, and other tribes, and on the south by the British Province of Sindh. Its area is calculated at about 9000 square miles, but, unlike Sarawān, it is not broken up into any lesser divisions. In its physical aspect, the Kachhi district is peculiar, and differs very much from the temperate hill regions of Sarawān and Jhalawān. Its chief characteristics are its level surface, excessive heat in the summer season, and at times its great scarcity of water, which latter drawback makes agricultural operations in this province of a very hazardous and fluctuating nature. The land generally is extremely low as regards elevation, no part of it being much higher than 500 feet above sea-level. On the west and north-east it is surrounded by hills, those on the west being the lofty barrier of the Brahuik mountains, through which, by means of the Bolān and Mula passes, it has communication with the upper or hill country of Sarawān.

The rivers, or perhaps it would be safer to call them the mountain-torrents, are the Bolān and Mula, running down the great clefts or passes of the same name in the Takāri range, and entering the plains of Kachhi, the former near the town of Dādar, and the latter between the villages of Kotri and Jhal. Here are also the Nāri and Lhāri streams: of the two, the Nāri is the larger and more important. It rises, it is believed, to the north of the Sibi (or Siwi) district, belonging to Afghānistan, and enters the plain of Kachhi about 12 miles east of Dādar. When in flood after heavy rains, it is a strong and turbulent stream, running through the whole length of the province, and joining even the waters of the Indus, in the canals at Khairo-Garhi, in the frontier district of Sindh; but at other times it is for months together almost dry, and as its stream is said at such a time to be dammed up for irrigational purposes in the Afghān district of Sibi, little or none is left for the more thirsty soil of the plain country of Kachh Gandāva till the rainy season sets in, when its bed again fills, to the delight of the Jat cultivators. There are numerous other springs and rivulets flowing from the Brahuik range, its mountain-barrier on the west; but these, after a very short course, lose themselves in the *pat*, or desert, lying between them and Sindh. This desert tract, known as the "Dasht-Bedār," or treeless waste, is between 30 and 40 miles in width, perfectly flat, and has a firm, dry clay surface. Water is obtained with some difficulty during the cool season from wells of great depth; in the sultry summer months this tract is almost impassable from the absence of water and the prevalence at that season of deadly hot winds.

As has previously been mentioned, ingress into Kachh Gandāva from the upper or hill country of Sarawān is usually made by one or other of two passes, the Bolān and Mula (or Muloh), the entrance by the first being near the town of Dādar in the north, and by the other at a spot called Pir Chatta, nine miles or so west of the town of Kotri, and 60 miles south of the Bolān pass. But these are not the only *laks*, or passes, leading over that portion of the Brahuik range of mountains; there are others, very steep and difficult, it is true, but which Bellew states are usually traversed by the natives in seven days.

In an extent, indeed, of 60 miles or thereabouts, there are, including the Bolān and Mula, not less than *eleven* passes leading from the plains of Kachhi to the highlands of Sarawān and Jhalawān. To some of these—such, for instance, as the Mula and Gazak passes—there are several different entrances. The following tabulated list will give the names of these passes, with other information connected with them:—

Pass.	Where situate.	Remarks.
1. Bolān ...	Plain entrance near Dādar	Will be described in detail below.
2. Kahun-ka-rastah	Is 12 miles north of Shuran, and near the sulphur mines	Roads from Bāgh, in Kachhi, lead to this pass; it abounds in numerous strongholds, well calculated for sheltering marauding parties. The country beyond the plain entrance is very broken and intricate.
3. Gazak ...	Has three entrances: 1st, at Shuran; 2nd, at Mukhali, 13 miles S.W. from Shuran; and 3rd, Tang-i-Gazak, which follows the course of the Gazak river	Roads from Gandāva lead into this pass. The path through a portion of the third entrance is so difficult as to need the assistance of ropes to get through it. After heavy rain, water suddenly rises to from 60 to 100 feet, carrying everything before it. Half-laden camels perform the journey to Kalāt from Gajen (near the second entrance) in 14 days; from Shuran in 15 days.
4. Mekh-ka-rastah	Entrance from plains 12 miles north-west from Kotri (or Kotra)	A very difficult pass, and so named on account of some wooden pegs fastened in the face of a precipitous ridge of rock, 30 feet high, to assist the traveller in ascending and descending; is impracticable after rainfall.
5. Ladau (or Muāj)	Entrance from plains six miles west from Kotri	Ascent very difficult in parts, and goes by Zehri, in Jhalawān. Half-laden camels perform the journey by this pass from Kotri to Kalāt in 15 days; *kāsids* (foot travellers) in two and a half days.

Pass.	Where situate.	Remarks.
6. Takari ...	North of the Ladau pass, and is entered from Kotri	Is rarely travelled over, owing to the many difficulties presented. Half-laden camels perform the journey to Kalāt in 12 days, *kāsids* in three days.
7. Mula ...	Has three entrances: 1st, at Perchatta, near Kotri; 2nd, the Taphoi, leading from Jhal, nine miles south of Kotri; and 3rd, the Gatti, a very difficult road	This pass will be found fully described further on.
8. Naghau	Is the direct road from the village of Sunni, in Kachhi, to Kalāt	
9. Bhore ...	Direct road leads by this pass from Naushahra, in Kachhi, to Kalāt	Meets the road from Sunni by the Naghau pass near Geytāni, about 30 miles from Kalāt.
10. Shadihar	Is about 25 miles south of Jhal, in the Maghzi country	Very little is known of this pass, but it is said to be a very difficult one to get through.
11. Nurmak	Is north of the sulphur mines near Sunni	Little or nothing is known of this pass.

Bolān Pass.—The Bolān pass, from the low country of Kachh Gandāva, commences at a spot said to be in lat. 29° 30′ N., and long. 67° 40′ E., about five miles north-west of the town of Dādar, the pass itself being a succession of narrow valleys between high ranges having a north-westerly course. Through it runs the Bolān river (or torrent), which rises at Sir-i-Bolān, one march from the western or upper mouth of the pass. From the entrance of the Bolān, about 250 yards wide, near Dādar, to the first halting-place, Khundilāni, seven miles distant, the road runs through a valley about a third of a mile in width and enclosed by low hills of clay-capped sandstone; these are succeeded by limestone hills covered with loose pebbles and boulders, and again by ranges of conglomerate of great height. The Bolān stream, up the course of which the road ascends, is frequently crossed during this first march to Khundilāni. After leaving this latter place for Kirta, the next stage, 14 miles in distance, the pass rapidly narrows, the conglomerate cliffs, some 800 feet in height, closing in upon each other and leaving but a narrow passage, through which the Bolān river finds its way, at times filled with water. It is this portion of the pass which Masson mentions as being the most dreaded by caravans. For three miles or so from this defile the road is very stony, but it afterwards opens out on a level valley, though the river has again to be frequently crossed and re-crossed. Five miles from the defile the hills of conglomerate cease, and their place is taken by a range of limestone of about 1000 feet in elevation. Here the route winds through a valley of about half a mile or more in width, in the middle of which runs the river, concealed by very high reeds and grass, after which the path emerges on a broad level valley, bounded by hills of nummulitic limestone. Here is situate the small village of Kirta, 1200 feet in elevation, which has a fort and is inhabited by Balochis, the river running under the base of the hills behind the town. Close by is Garm-Ab, or the warm spring, the source of one of the confluents of the Bolān stream. The next march from Kirta is the halting-place of Bibi-Nāni, 1695 feet in height, and nine miles from Kirta. It is a shrine of some repute, says Masson, and there are some curious legends extant regarding it. The road passes through two plains, and after entering a gorge, emerges into the valley of Bibi-Nāni. The rocks on either side are still found to be composed of nummulitic limestone, some being from 300 to 400 feet high, while the range bounding the valley to the westward cannot, Cook thinks, be less than from 1000 to 1500 feet in elevation. From here a mountain road leads by Rodbar to Kalāt, *vià* Baradi, Rodbar, Nurmak Takhi, and Kishan, distant 110 miles.

The next march from Bibi-Nāni is to Ab-i-Gum (or the lost water), 14 miles, so called because the small stream near which it is situate occasionally loses itself in the shingly soil and again appears elsewhere. The road to this place is over loose shingle and boulders, and is, as Cook remarks, extremely fatiguing. It is very gradual in ascent for the first four miles, but much steeper afterwards; the height of Ab-i-Gum above sea-level is about 2600 feet. It was in a low range bounding this valley on the right that Cook found in the clay a seam of *coal* much decomposed, and also some thick veins of gypsum.

The next stage from Ab-i-Gum is Sir-i-Bolān, 6 miles distant, and about 4400 feet in altitude. The road to this point is north-easterly in direction, but the ascent, though gradual, is very considerable; the inclination being, it is said, one foot in twenty-five. Here the Bolān river has its source, little streams of pure water issuing from many fissures at the base of a mountain of about 1000 feet in elevation. In the conglomerate hills near this place, Cook discovered some thin seams of coal strata dipping to the south. From the Sir-i-Bolān to the top of the pass at the Dasht-i-Bidaulat, the route takes a westerly course, and no water, for a distance of ten miles, is obtainable. It is in the last three miles of this march that the most dangerous portion of the pass is found. Here the road becomes narrow, until at last, by the approximation of the ranges on each side, it is only sufficiently wide to admit of three or four men riding abreast. The hills on either side, which are still of limestone, tower above to a great height, and can only be ascended at either end. After a time the pass becomes wider and the hills less precipitous, till at length it opens out into a narrow valley extending westward, at the end of which the path cross-cuts the crest of a hill about 80 or 90 feet high, and enters a broad plain called the "Dasht-i-Bidaulat," some 15 or 20 miles across from east to west, and about the same in length from north to south. The elevation of the crest of the Bolān pass is about 5,800 feet, the average ascent being ninety feet in the mile, and the total length from the entrance near Dādar, in the low country, is thus—to quote the words of Cook, from whose interesting report this description has been mainly taken—"about sixty miles in length, passing in a north-north-west direction through the great chain of the Brahuik mountains. It is formed by a succession of valleys of various widths, the broadest being the valley of Kirta, bounded by mountain ranges having a general north-north-west strike, and a height which greatly varies in different parts, but which, perhaps, attains to its greatest in the mountain near Bibi-Nāni. The pass is constricted at two principal points—namely, immediately after leaving Khundilāni, seven miles from the eastern entrance; and beyond Sir-i-Bolān, near its westerly termination, where a few determined men might hold it against vast odds. The ascent is inconsiderable till Ab-i-Gum be reached, when it becomes more marked, and in the last 20 miles 2800 feet have to be surmounted. The temperature in the pass during the month of May is very high, as the atmosphere is then excessively dry, and no amelioration of the heat is experienced until the point where the greatest ascent commences is attained. As regards supplies, water is abundant and good throughout the pass. Grass and *bhusa* are to be had only at Kirta, and a rank, coarse grass in the valley near Khundilāni; wood is scarcely to be procured at all. The mountains are excessively bare, and, with the exception of the last few miles beyond the Sir-i-Bolān, where a few straggling trees are found, produce nothing that can be used as firewood."

From a military point of view the Bolān pass is important, as artillery can be conveyed through it without any serious difficulty. In 1839 a Bengal column took six days to get up the pass, and its artillery, consisting of 8-inch mortars, 24-pounder howitzers, and 18-pounder guns, were safely carried through. There are, however, dangers to be apprehended at times from the Bolān torrent, which is subject to sudden floods, from one of which a Bengal detachment, in

1841, was lost with its baggage. The pass is unfortunately infested by the Marri and Khāka tribe of Balochis, who live mostly by plundering the caravans proceeding from Khorasān to Sindh, and this want of security to person and property prevents any of the peaceably disposed tribes from settling in the valleys, where, it is believed, a fair amount of good soil and an admirable command of water would allow of large quantities of rice and other crops being cultivated with success.

Mula Pass.—The Mula (or Muloh), or, as it is also called, the Gandāva pass, is the other route through the Brahuik range by which access is gained from Kachh Gandāva to the table-land of Jhalawān. In the low country the entrance of this pass may be said to commence at a place called Pir Chatta, where there is a *ziārat*, or shrine, nine miles distant from the town of Kotri. The route thence to the next halting place, Kuhau (1250 feet in height, and 12 miles distant), leads at first through a long, narrow, and stony hollow, with high hills on the right, and a low conglomerate ridge on the left, and afterwards into a wide basin in the hills, through which the Mula stream flows, when in water, over a broad boulder-strewn bed. It is here that the *noh lang*, or nine fords, are met with, and the stream has to be crossed that number of times in transit. A very narrow and tortuous passage, or defile, has then to be traversed, with perpendicular masses of rock on either side, the road being here completely filled by the Mula stream; this leads to another basin in the hills, with some cultivation, and ultimately to Kuhau, which is merely a halting-place in a glen, there being no village here, or any supplies obtainable, except cattle-forage, and this only in limited quantities.

From Kuhau to the village of Hatāchi, the next stage, is 16 miles, the ascent being easy along up the course of the Mula river, which has to be crossed several times; the pass afterwards widens considerably, and corn cultivation may be observed on either side of the stream, as well as some solitary scattered huts at the intermediate places, Paniwat and Jah. The route then leads into the Hatāchi valley, the village of that name consisting of about 30 detached huts. Supplies are abundant here. From Hatāchi to Narr (2850 feet), the next halting-place, the distance is 16 miles, the road at first leading, by a winding, stony path, through tamarisk jungle, and afterwards into a narrow defile, when the Pir Lakka basin is reached. The *ziārat* of this name was built in the time of Nasir Khān of Kalāt; it stands on an elevated site, and adjacent to it is a large burial place. A few *fakir* families have charge of this shrine, and possess some well-cultivated land in the neighbourhood. Another tortuous defile is met with after leaving Pir Lakka; it leads into the Hassnah basin, where there is a little cultivation, and afterwards, leaving the river on the right, emerges upon the great open tract of Narr, which is situate at the southern extremity of the Zehri valley. There is a good deal of cultivation at Narr, in scattered patches. Pasture is found on the neighbouring hills, and water from a little tributary of the Mula river; here a cross-road leads to the town of Khozdār, *viâ* Gaz, while the pass-route turns sharply in a north-westerly direction to Peshtar Khān, 3500 feet in elevation, and 12 miles distant from Narr.

Much of the description of the Mula pass, as far as Narr, has been taken from Bellew's mission record of 1872; but he left the route at Narr, and proceeded to Khozdār by the cross-road just mentioned. From Narr to Peshtar Khān the pass crosses the Mula frequently, and in the course of this stage, on the left, is to be seen a lofty hill with two remarkable peaks, known as the "Do Dandān," or two teeth. At Peshtar Khān there used to be some cultivation of wheat, rice and mung; flocks of sheep and goats are also numerous.

H

From Peshtar Khān to Patki (4250 feet), the next stage, distant 10½ miles, the road runs over, in the first instance, a considerable plain, and afterwards is difficult and fatiguing, being in the stony bed of the river. Pisi Bent (4600 feet) is the next halting-place, 12 miles distant. The route, which here runs through a wide valley, follows for some distance the course of the river, and again leaves it; but it has to be crossed several times during the march. A good deal of cultivation is carried on in this part of the pass.

Hence to the small village of Bapau (5000 feet) is another 12 miles in length, the bed of the river still forming the road for some distance. In this portion of the pass is a very constricted defile, where precipitous rocks, about 500 feet in height, close in on each other to such an extent as to leave only a narrow passage some 30 or 40 feet wide, which, as it cannot be turned, could be effectually closed against the advance of troops coming up the pass by simply rolling down heavy blocks of stone. Twelve miles further on to the source of the Mula stream, and near the village of Angira, the top of the pass is reached at an elevation of 5250 feet above sea-level.

The Mula pass is thus in all about 102 miles in length from its entrance in the low country to the source of the river, the *average* rise being about 45 feet in the mile. It is considered, on the whole, to be preferable, as a *military* pass, to the Bolān, the road being better, the ascent easier and more regular, and some supplies, at least, being obtainable in it. At the close of 1839, General Willshire's force, after storming Kalāt, returned to Sindh by this route; but the guns brought down with it were only light field-pieces. Masson, who traversed this pass, remarks that, in a military point of view, the route, presenting a succession of open spaces, connected by narrow passages or defiles, is very defensible, at the same time affording convenient spots for encampment, an abundance of excellent water, fuel, and more or less forage. It is level throughout—the road either tracing the bed of the stream or leading near to its left bank. It is not only easy and safe, but may be travelled at all seasons, and is the only camel route through the hills intermediate between Sarawān and Jhalawān and Kachhi from the latitude of Shāl (where the line of intercourse is by the route of the Bolān river) to Khozdār, from which a road leads into Middle Sindh. Danger from predatory bands is not even to be apprehended, and in this respect alone it has an immense advantage over the Bolān pass. Bellew, who, as previously mentioned, passed in 1872 over but a portion of it leading to Khozdār, says that in a distance of about 50 miles, extending from Pir Chatta to Gaz, it presents a succession of basins, connected by narrow *straits* that are very crooked. The basins are those of Pir Chatta, Kuhau, Pani-wat, Jah, Hatāchi, Fazzan, Pir Lakka, Hassnah, and Narr. Each of these is more or less cultivated, contains abundant water and fuel, but very little or no pasture, and limited camping surface. The rainy season is in July and August. During these months violent storms occur on the mountains, and the pass often becomes suddenly flooded by swift torrents that sweep all before them.

Climate.—The climate of Kachh Gandāva, owing to its low situation and to its being surrounded on the west and north-east by ranges of high and arid mountains, is, as a rule, excessively dry, and during the hottest part of the summer season, that is, from April to August, very oppressive. Cook, writing from actual experience, says that during a portion of May the nights at Bāgh were cool and pleasant; they might, indeed, be called cold, in comparison with the heat of the day. The wind was generally from the northward, during his stay there, and moderately cool; but occasionally accompanied with clouds of dust, when its temperature rose considerably. The great difference in temperature between the day and night has also been remarked upon by Bellew, who noticed that in the month of January, 1872, when near Barshora, the thermometer rose to 92° in the open air, though on the same morning, at eight o'clock, it had been as low as 38°. It is in parts of Kachh Gandāva that dust storms occur so frequently during the hot season, and, as these are at times attended with peculiar phenomena, it will be necessary to consider them somewhat in detail. Cook, who studied these dust phenomena with much care and attention, places them under three heads, that is to say, (1) atmospheric dust; (2) dust columns; and (3) dust storms. The first he attributes to a highly electrified condition of the individual particles of sand, which are then ready to repel each other, and are at such a time likely to be carried up into the air by the slightest current. At times the air is filled with dust to such an extent as even to obscure the sun at noonday, and so impalpably fine is this dust that it penetrates even watches, no matter how carefully protected against its action. Dust columns, again, are presumed to be caused by a similar condition of electrical disturbance or intensity, though under a different aspect. Their creation is thus described by Cook:—"On calm, quiet days, when hardly a breath of air is stirring and the sun pours down its heated rays with full force, little circular eddies are seen to rise in the atmosphere near the surface of the ground; these increase in force and diameter, catching up and whirling round bits of stick, grass, dust, and lastly sand, until a column is formed of great height and considerable diameter. This usually remains stationary for some time, and then sweeps away across country at great speed, and ultimately, losing by degrees the velocity of its circular movement, dissolves and disappears." By the Balochis these dust columns are called "Shaitans," or devils, and they have a superstitious feeling with regard to them, regarding them in the light of evil genii. Carless remarks upon this same feeling as prevailing among the Numri tribe, for, when travelling on a camel in the Las district, he says—"These dust columns moved over the plain with great rapidity, and whenever one came near us, I could hear the chief, who guided my camel, mutter to himself, 'Pass away from the road, good demon, and do me no harm: I am only going to Bēla with the English gentlemen, who have brought presents for the Jām!"

Cook also refers to a peculiar case where a body of water, forcing its way over a *perfectly dry surface*, excited a remarkable disturbance in atmospherical electricity, as will be clearly apparent from the following incident, which was mentioned to him on very excellent authority:—On the 13th of April, the river Indus having risen sufficiently, the water flowed up the Begāri canal and reached Jacobabad (in Upper Sindh and bordering upon Kachh Gandāva) about five o'clock p.m. Preceding it, about a quarter of an hour, a vast pillar of dust moved slowly along and crossed the cantonment. The sky was dark and cloudy, thunder muttered in the distance, and a slight shower of rain fell; distant lightning was observed all night. This was followed by an immediate and very considerable fall in the thermometer, and the weather, which before had been excessively sultry and oppressive, became pleasant and agreeable, and the nights as cool as they had been a month previously.

It is also a highly electrical and accumulative condition of the atmosphere which produces the dust storm, the third phase of dust phenomena mentioned by Cook, and one which he considers to be closely analogous to the tornadoes of the Indian seas. They frequently last many hours, obscuring the sun at mid-day to such a degree as to make artificial light necessary—producing, in fact, that darkness which is said in Holy Writ "to be felt," and the unfortunate traveller who happens to be caught in one of these in the desert not unfrequently loses his life. Cook thus describes a dust storm which he himself witnessed:—"The preceding weather had been hot and oppressive, with but little or no breeze, and an evident tendency for dust to accumulate in the atmosphere. This evening heavy clouds gathered and covered the sky; about nine p.m. the sky had cleared somewhat, and the moon shone brightly. A breeze from the west then sprang up, which increased in force, and bore along with it light clouds of sand. About half-past nine the storm commenced in all its fury—vast bodies of sand were drifted violently along; the stars, moon, and sky were totally obscured; it became pitchy dark; and it was impossible to see the hand, even when held close to the face. The wind blew furiously and in gusts, and heaped the sand on the windward side of obstacles in its course. Thunder and lightning accompanied it, and were succeeded by heavy rain. The storm lasted about an hour, when the amount of dust gradually decreased until it entirely subsided. The sky again became visible, and the moon shone brightly, although the wind continued to blow hard for some time longer." These dust storms seem to be felt in their greatest intensity in the centre of the desert tract of the Kachh Gandāva province, where neither irrigation nor cultivation are at hand to stay, or at least mitigate, their violence.

But far more deadly and fatal than these phenomena of dust is the *juloh*, or poisonous wind, that is found occasionally visiting the deserts of Kachh Gandāva, and which has already been briefly referred to in the description of the Kharān district of Sarawān as the *badē simum*, or *juloh*. It is this which makes travelling in parts of the Kachhi province at certain seasons of the year almost wholly impossible; and Cook, who has given this subject also great attention, has come to the conclusion that it is caused by the generation in the atmosphere of a highly concentrated form of ozone, by some intensely marked electrical condition. As evidence of its effect in destroying every green thing on its course, and in being frequently fatal to human life, he cites the following authenticated cases: 1.—In the year 1851, during one of the hot months, certain officers of the Sindh Horse were sleeping at night on the top of General Jacob's house, at Jacobabad. They were awakened by a sensation of suffocation, and an exceedingly hot and oppressive feeling in the air, while at the same time a very powerful smell of sulphur was remarked as pervading the atmosphere. On the following morning a number of trees in the garden were found to be withered in a very remarkable manner. It was described as if a current of fire about two yards in breadth had passed through the garden in a perfectly straight line, singeing and destroying every green thing in its course. Entering on one side and passing out on the other, its tract was as clearly defined as the course of a river. 2.—At the close of the hot season of 1856, a party of five men were crossing the *pat* (or desert) of Shikārpur, being on their way from Kandahar to that city, when the blast unfortunately crossed their path, killing, if I recollect rightly, three of them, and disabling the remaining two. 3.—A *munshi* (a native clerk or writer) was travelling in company with two others near Chilgeri, the site of a buried city, about seven miles south-east from Bāgh, in Kachhi; they were all mounted, when about two o'clock a.m. the blast struck them. He was sensible of a scorching sensation in the air, like the blast of an oven, but remembered nothing further, as all three were immediately struck to the earth. They were carried to Bāgh, where every attention was afforded them, and they ultimately, after some days of sickness, recovered. 4.—Two *syces* (horsekeepers), with two camels, were sent to

Minuti (20 miles north-west from Jacobabad) for grass. Not returning at the proper time, it was feared that some accident had happened. All four bodies were found lying together in one spot, quite dead. Their deaths had evidently been instantaneous.

From these several incidents Cook gleaned the following items of information concerning the *juloh:* 1st.—That it is sudden in its attack. 2nd.—Is sometimes preceded by a cold current of air. 3rd.—Occurs in the hot months, usually June and July. 4th.—Takes place by night, as well as by day. 5th.—Has a straight and defined course. 6th.—Its passage leaves a narrow, "knife-like" track. 7th.—Burns up or destroys the vitality of animal and vegetable existence in its path. 8th.—Is attended by a well-marked sulphurous odour. 9th.—Is like the blast of a furnace, and the current of air in which it passes is evidently greatly heated; and 10th.—Is not accompanied by dust, thunder, or lightning.

From these several characteristics and effects of the *simum* he has conjectured that it is, as has previously been mentioned, a highly concentrated form of ozone, generated under certain very peculiar conditions.

Towns and Villages.—The chief towns in Kachh Gandāva are Bāgh, Gandāva, Dādar, and Kotri. The first-mentioned, the commercial capital of Kachhi, in about lat. 29° 6′ N., and long. 67° 50′ E., and 650 feet above sea-level, is situate on the route from Shikārpur to Dādar, and is 37 miles south-south-west from the latter place. It is seated on the Nāri river, which *at times* overflows its banks and inundates the surrounding country; but for the greater part of the year it is almost dry, and water, of a brackish and unwholesome character, can then only be obtained from tanks and wells. The neighbouring country is said to be very fertile when irrigated, producing large quantities of *juār* and *bājri*, but otherwise it is a barren, treeless plain of hard-baked clay. The air is here excessively dry. Bāgh was once, it would seem, more populous than at present, and is said 35 years ago to have contained close upon 2000 houses, representing a population of about 8000 persons; now it is believed to possess not more than between 2500 and 3000 inhabitants, and may be considered to be in a decayed and ruinous condition. Near the town are some tombs, serving as monuments of the two half-brothers, Mastapha and Rehim Khān, the sons of Nasir Khān, a former ruler of Kalāt. The transit trade of Bāgh is considerable, owing to its favourable situation; it possessed also the monopoly of the trade in sulphur, derived from the Sunni mines. These mines are situate in the hilly tract west of Suran and Sunni, and are between 14 and 15 miles distant from Bāgh. Though indifferently worked, they yielded, some 30 years ago, a profit of Rs.12,000, but before that time the return was *five* times as great. The ore was taken to Bāgh to be purified, and this was done by boiling the pounded matter in oil until the fluid was evaporated: the stones and other impurities then subsided, leaving the sulphur on the surface.

Gandāva, the political capital of Kachhi, in lat. 28° 32′ N., and long. 67° 32′ E., is situate on a small torrent, running from the Brahuik range, and is on the route of the Mula Pass, distant 40 miles south-west from Bāgh. It is a smaller town than Bāgh, and merely derives its importance from being the winter residence of the Khān of Kalāt, whose palace here, says Bellew, is the only decent edifice in the place. This building was almost wholly destroyed by the great floods of 1874. Here also is the Khān's garden, within a walled enclosure, crowded with a number of fruit-trees of various kinds. The town of Gandāva is fortified, and is built on what is apparently an artificial mound. The number of inhabitants is not known, but it must be fluctuating, owing to the periodical visit of the Khān and his numerous followers.

Dādar, the next town in importance, in lat. 29° 28′ N. and long. 67° 34′ E., and about 700 feet above sea-level, is seated on the Bolān river, about five miles east of the entrance to the Bolān pass, and 37 miles north-west from Bāgh. It is well supplied with pure and good water from the Bolān river for a great part of the year, but for the remainder recourse is had to water from the wells, which is brackish and unwholesome. Cook, who resided here for about three weeks in the month of May, speaks of it as being better provided with trees and gardens than Bāgh, and that the maximum heat was not so great as at Bāgh; but others have written of Dādar as possessing a heat in the summer season probably not exceeded by that of any other place in earth on the same parallel of latitude. The position of the place, surrounded as it is by bare and rocky hills, must of itself be productive of an excessively close and stifling state of the atmosphere, and it is on record that at an early period of the year the thermometer showed a temperature of 130°, with an utter stagnation of air. Even early in March the heat must have been intense, for one authority thus speaks of it:—"There was a hot wind whirling clouds of dust into my tent, and the plague of flies was most intolerable. The heat in the house was such that I fairly staggered, and the mountains for the last two days, though close at hand, had been but dimly outlined through a flickering mist like that over a furnace." About 15 miles east from Dādar is the village of Sibi (or Siwi), of the great heat at which, in summer, the inhabitants themselves have the following saying—"O God! when you had Sibi, why need you have made hell?" Dādar must, from its peculiar position, be just as hot as Sibi, perhaps *hotter*. Masson even observes of

Dādar that the heat there is singularly oppressive, and the unburnt bricks of the old tombs were pointed out to him as having become of a red hue from the fervid rays of the sun.

There is, it is said, a good deal of cultivation around Dādar, and large quantities of wheat are grown in the valley, as also cotton, cucumbers, and melons. The exact number of inhabitants in Dādar is not known, but it is supposed not to exceed 2000. Besides the towns already described, there are a large number of villages in Kachhi, but individually they are small and unimportant. The town of Kotri (or Kotra), or what may more properly be called a cluster of four villages making up this place, belongs to the Eltarzai family, of which the Khān of Kalāt is the head. Bellew remarks that when he passed through this town in 1872 he found the villages to be neat and prosperous, possessing comfortable dwellings, with several walled gardens of fine trees around them; but the number of inhabitants is not known. Kotri is said to be the *entrepôt* of the trade between Kalāt and Shikārpur. There might, no doubt, be many such prosperous villages in this extensive district, were only safety to life and property guaranteed to the people by their ruler; but it will never come to pass so long as the present miserable state of things is allowed to continue, and while marauding bands of Brahuis are permitted to go about and plunder the unhappy Jat villagers of all they possess. It is on this account that there are now so many deserted villages in the province, and their numbers must inevitably increase unless the predatory propensities of the Baloch tribes are put down with a strong hand.

Inhabitants.—A tabular statement of several of the tribes inhabiting the Kachhi country has already been supplied (at page 33), and a notice of the Jat race, who, as permanent residents, are to be found throughout the length and breadth of the province, has also been given. Before, however, saying anything further of this latter people, it will be necessary to give a brief account of two, at least, of the Rind tribes of Kachhi, the Jakrānis and Dumbkis, who, in their day, as border robbers, displayed a very warlike spirit, and gave immense trouble to both the Khān of Kalāt and the British authorities on the frontier.

The Jakrānis are a branch of the great Rind tribe, and formerly resided at Lehri and its immediate neighbourhood. As a tribe they are quite distinct from the Dumbkis, though the two are generally associated, since they were, in days gone by, united in war, under a celebrated robber-chieftain named Bijar Khān, and before the year 1845 were noted for their lawless and predatory habits. In 1839 these two tribes were able, under the leader just mentioned, to muster jointly a force of fifteen hundred well-armed horsemen, and about five hundred able-bodied armed footmen. It is not known whence the Jakrānis originally migrated, but the Dumbkis are said to have come from Persia, and to take their name from a river in that country called Dumbak. The Dumbkis, sometime before the year 1828, had driven out the Kaihiris (originally an Afghān tribe) from their lands at Pulaji, Chattar, and other places in Eastern Kachhi, and had there settled themselves, the Kaihiris eventually fleeing into Sindh, and finding a refuge in that country from the ferocity of their Baloch enemies. The Jakrānis are subdivided into several families, known as (1) the Salivānis (the chief), (2) the Suwanāris, (3) the Shiahpaz, (4) the Majānis, (5) the Solkānis, (6) the Molkānis, (7) the Sudkānis, (8) the Karor-Kānis, and (9) the Dir-Kānis.

Both the Jakrāni and Dumbki tribes came into contact with the British power about the year 1839, when a force under Major Billamore (Bombay Army) was sent specially to punish these hill-robbers of Eastern Kachhi, including also the Bughtis in their number. This force, divided into two

JAKRĀNI CHIEF AND FOLLOWERS. FRONTIER DISTRICT, UPPER SIND.

To face page 108.

detachments, boldly entered the hill country, notwithstanding its very difficult nature and the want of information concerning it, traversed it in every direction, and so terrified the Jakrāni and Dumbki chiefs in their own fastnesses, that they at once surrendered to the political officers in the plains, were imprisoned, but eventually released, and permitted again to take up their lands in the plains of Kachhi.

The Jakrāni and Dumbki tribes did not, however, long remain in peace and quietness, for about 1843, at a time when the conquest of Sindh had denuded the frontier of British troops, these restless robbers resumed their predatory inroads; and, under the chieftainship of Darya Khān and Bijar Khān, laid waste large portions of Kachhi and North Sindh, till, in January, 1845, it was deemed advisable by Sir Charles Napier, then Governor of Sindh, to proceed against these lawless tribes and make a notable example of them. The expedition was in every way successful, and resulted in the Jakrānis, under Darya Khān, and a portion of the Dumbki tribe, under Bijar Khān, being removed bodily into Sindh, where they were located at a place called Jānidēra, a few miles south of the present town and cantonment of Jacobabad, and a commissioner appointed to superintend them. Henceforth they became to all intents and purposes tribes of British Sindh. But these men were for long unable to repress that strong marauding spirit which possessed them, and, unknown to the British authorities on the border, they once more began a series of plundering incursions on a large scale into the Kachhi country, and these they managed for a time to carry on in a very adroit and successful manner. The arrival, about 1847, of Major John Jacob on the border, with the Sindh Horse, soon put a stop to these inroads, and he disarmed every man not a Government servant, and compelled the Baloch settlers to take to manual labour in the shape of field cultivation and public works. At the present time a portion of the Dumbki tribe still resides at Lehri in Eastern Kachhi, where they own a large quantity of land and exercise a considerable amount of influence.

In returning to a consideration of the Jat race of Kachh Gandāva, it may be mentioned that wherever they are found —and they may, it seems, from what Masson states, be seen not alone in the Panjāb and Sindh, and in those countries lying between the Satlej and Ganges rivers, but even at Kābul, Kandahār, and Herat—they preserve their vernacular tongue, the Jatki. Of this language many dialects are believed to exist, and it may well be suggested by Masson, that the labour of reviewing them would not be found altogether unprofitable. It appears to be a fact that the Jats, in some places, pursue the calling of itinerant gipsies, and this more particularly in Afghānistan, and it is not unlikely that some affinity in their language and habits might very possibly be traced between them and the vagabond race of Zingāris which are spread over so large a portion of Europe. The Jats of Eastern Kachhi, the supposed descendants of the ancient Getæ, form the cultivating and camel-breeding classes, and are of industrious and peaceable habits, but are dreadfully harried and plundered by the marauding Balochis of the neighbouring hills. They are, so to speak, the original inhabitants of this district, the Rinds, Balochis, and Brahuis having settled in the country at a comparatively recent period. The Jats are numerously sub-divided among themselves, the sub-tribes amounting, it is said, to nearly 40 in number; some of these are known under the names of Abra, Haura, Kalhora, Khokhar, Machhi, Manju, Palal, Pasarar, Tunia, and Waddera. In religion they are all Muhammadans of the Suni persuasion.

THE BORDER TRIBES OF BALOCHIS—THE MAZĀRIS, GORCHĀNIS, BUGHTIS, AND MARRIS.

As it has been mentioned previously that the province of Kachh Gandāva is at times greatly disturbed by the lawless incursions of the hill people residing on its northern and eastern borders, it has been considered advisable to devote some space to a description and history of these tribes, so far as can be ascertained; and this is rendered comparatively easy by the publication lately of some interesting notes on the various hill tribes living near the Panjāb border by Mr. R. B. Bruce, the Assistant-Commissioner of Rājanpur. The principal tribes of Balochis described by him are the Mazāris, Drishaks, Gorchānis, Tibbi Lunds, Laghāris, Bughtis, Marris, Khetrans, Khosas, Bozdārs, and the Kasrānis; but those which have had most to do with plundering transactions on the Panjāb border and in Kachhi are the Mazāris, the Gorchānis, the Bughtis, and the Marris, and it is to an account of these four tribes that attention will be more especially directed.

THE MAZĀRIS.

The Mazāris occupy a strip of country about 40 miles long by 20 broad, lying between the hills on the west and the Indus on the east, and extending from Umarkot and the Pitok pass on the north to the frontier district of Sindh on the south. The tribe is divided into four principal divisions, and these, again, are sub-divided into 57 sections, or sub-divisions, which are capable of furnishing in the aggregate about 4000 fighting-men, but 800 of these are in the adjoining districts of Sindh and Bahāwalpur. The chieftaincy of the tribe belongs to the Belochāni branch.

Their chief town is Rājhan, about 110 miles from Dēra Ghāzi Khān, along a portion of the boundary line of which district their territory is principally situate. It is 40 miles distant from Rājanpur, in the same British district. The following tabular statement will show the main branches of the tribe, their sub-divisions, and the number of fighting-men each branch is supposed to be able to supply :—

Main branches.	No of fighting men.	Sub-divisions.	Main branches.	No. of fighting men.	Sub-divisions.
1. Belochāni	266	Gulsherāni	2. Rustāmāni (*continued*)	1865	Gulrain
		Nustakāni			Bannu
		Azadāni			Talpur
		Machiāni	3. Masidāni	1469	Selatāni
		Hyderanzai			Lulais
		Saidazai			Dulāni
		Khodadāni			Nukāni
		Hybatain			Sanjrāni
		Radāni			Sehalaf
		Batelāni			Sanidāni
2. Rustāmāni	1865	Pirkāni			Shakija
		Murāni			Wohāni
		Adiāni			Nozkāni
		Hurwāni			Lutāni
		Bungrāni			Haurāni
		Abdulāni			Surija
		Kaisarāni			Gerāni
		Shabarkāni			Tukerāni
		Minglāni			Bhamberāni
		Dharwāni			Murkāni
		Surwāni			Puhitāni
		Nazāni			Esain
		Chaunglāni			Joar Kain
		Zumkāni			Sumlāni
		Meriāri			Rurkalli
		Golāb			Shulain
		Lalāni	4. Sargāni	400	Sargāni
		Gulāni			Jullor
		Esam			

The Mazāris seem to have fought with pretty well all the neighbouring tribes, such as the Bughtis, Bolidas, Drishaks, Gorchānis, Jakrānis, and others. It was in the reign of Mohbat

Khān of Kalāt, that a force was sent by that ruler, under the command of Adam Khān Brahui, to take the Mazāri country, since the people paid neither tribute nor allegiance to any sovereign. Adam Khān was successful, but in a few years the Mazāris made a raid on Kashmor (in the Sindh Frontier District), taking the town and compelling Adam Khān to retreat. After this they were independent till about A.D. 1791, when they became subject to the Mirs of Sindh. They do not seem to have interfered with the Kachhi country till some years after this last event, when their *tomandār*, Bahram Khān, committed a raid on Bāgh, in Kachhi, carrying off a number of cattle. The Mazāris are very adroit thieves, and have, or at least had, years ago, the character of being the most expert cattle-stealers in the whole of the border country. Elphinstone also refers to them as being famous for their piracies on the Indus, their robberies on the highway, and their depredations into the countries of all their neighbours.

THE GORCHĀNIS.

The tract of country occupied by the Gorchānis, like that of the Mazāris, in no way directly adjoins any portion of the Kachhi Province, but this tribe affected Kalāt territory when the Harrand and Dājil districts formed part and parcel of the dominions of the Brahui Khān of Kalāt. The tribe derive their name from their ancestor, one Gorish, and most of the Gorchānis pronounce the word as if spelt "Gorishāni." They are divided into 11 main branches, and have 81 sub-divisions, containing in all 2580 fighting-men. The chieftaincy of the tribe is in the Jellubāni sub-division of the Shikāni main branch. The following table will show these branches and sub-divisions of the Gorchāni tribe :—

Main branches.	No. of fighting men.	Sub-divisions.
1. Shikāni ...	320	Jellubāni, Shikāni, Bukarāni, Mankāni, Dodāni, Mehāni, Babulāni, Mittāni
2. Lishāri ...	420	Jellubāni, Budolāni, Gurkāni, Bangalāni, Jamrāni, Ghoramāni, Mordāni, Gishkori, Nihalāni, Turklāni, Gabol, Sundlāni, Faujlāni, Shahwāni, Hakdadāni
3. Pitāfi ...	240	Jarwāni, Hutman, Kutalāni, Brahmāni, Mutakāni, Janglāni, Surmorāni, Thulrāni, Imegrāni, Gokebawāni
4. Jiskāni ...	120	Dadāni, Fatehyāni, Kiugāni, Funjwāni, Dilshatlāni, Ghuram
5. Durkāni	720	Nokāni, Lingrāni, Zahrāni, Melohar, Gatāni, Zubrāni, Airie, Gundagwalug, Zehadāni, Umrāni, Jundāni, Alkāni, Kahuri, Raulkāni, Purkāni, Seahpagh, Sulemāni, Nehalāni
6. Hutwāni	260	Saujāni, Babulāni, Chutiāni, Manukāni, Kasmāni, Kulaugāni
7. Khulilāni	120	Bakerāni, Bahadurāni, Gorpatāni
8. Bazgir ...	130	Mupurwāni, Pabadāni, Dulalāni, Brahmāni
9. Chang ...	90	Mewāni, Ahmdāni, Kingāni, Kohunāni
10. Surāni ...	110	Harwāni, Mirkam, Musāni, Suwāni
11. Hulwāni	50	Wadāni, Lodāni, Mutakāni

The Gorchāni tribe are only half Baloch in descent, as, from their own traditions, it would appear that they are partly descended from a Hindu Rājāh who formerly ruled at Nerankot (the modern Hyderabad), in Sindh, but on the Arab invasion of that country in about A.D. 711 he was, with his people, forced to embrace Islamism. After a time, 2000 of these converted families fled from Sindh to Makrān, where they found the Balochis settled under Mir Shabuk. With these they joined, and at length, proceeding northward in one of the two divisions of the Mogul Emperor Humayun's army, they passed through their present lands, and, attracted by the country and the climate, resolved to settle there, driving out the Pathāns, who then inhabited them. On the discomfiture of the Mahrattas by Ahmad Shāh Durāni, about A.D. 1760, the districts of Harrand and Dājil were given to Nasir Khān I., the Kalāt ruler, for the great services he had rendered during that campaign; and as many of the Gorchānis had accompanied Nasir to the war, he continued to them all the privileges that had previously been granted them by Ahmad Khān, when they were in charge of the Harrand and Dājil frontier, and he also set apart a sum of money for the construction of a fort at Harrand, called Lālgarh, which was the headquarters of this tribe. After this the Gorchānis fought with the Mazāris, and eventually with the Marris, who at various times seem to have handled them severely. About A.D. 1839 or 1840, the Harrand and Dājil districts were annexed by the Sikh Government to the Panjāb, but to the Gorchānis were guaranteed all the privileges they had enjoyed under preceding governments. After the annexation of the Panjāb to British India, this tribe had the worst name for depredations and robberies of any on the Dēra Ghāzi Khān frontier. The Lishāri branch of the tribe was looked upon as the most daring in this respect, and as nearly always fighting with the Bughtis, Marris, and Khetrans; but about 1867 this portion of them was settled in the plains, and in that same year the Gorchāni tribe did good service in helping to resist a very serious raid made on Harrand by a large combined force, consisting of Marris, Bughtis, and Khetrans.

THE BUGHTIS.

The important tribe of the Bughtis occupy a considerable tract of country, having the Marris and Gorchānis to the north, the frontier district of Upper Sindh to the south, the Panjāb frontier to the east, and the Kachhi Province of Kalāt to the west. Their chief town is Dēra. The tribe consists of six main branches, with 44 sub-divisions, and they are able to furnish a fighting force of 2210 men. The accompanying statement will show these several branches and sub-divisions:—

Main branches.	No. of fighting men.	Sub-divisions.	Main branches.	No. of fighting men.	Sub-divisions.
1. Reheja ...	175	Reheja			Segrāni
		(*Perozanis*)	3. Massuri (*continued*)	[325]	Dihāni
		Rahum			Jeskāni
		Khanzai			Pudlāni
		Pujlur	4. Kalpur...	250	Hulkāni
		Jakrāni			Batilāni
		Shalwāni			Hamzāni
		Dhamgiāni			Shong
2. Nuthāni	810	Mahlāni	5. Phong ...	150	Haijmāni
		Bigrāni			Mundrāni
		Ramuzai			(*Riazı*)
		Rohlāni			Mirzāni
		(*Zumkānis*)			Hamzāni
		Kumkāni			Mehriāni
		Shumbiāni			(*Shumbāni*)
		Mehranzai			Gudai
		Amdranzai			Rahmlāni
		(*Jaffirānis*)	6. Reari (or Shumbani	500	(*Saidāni*)
		Jaffirānis			Tunjwāni
		Noriāni			Tiksur
		Sunderāni			Pujdur
3. Massuri...	325	Gurāni			Riazai
		Surkri			Shungwāni
		Nukāni			Muchobar
		(*Bashkwānis*)			Pabai
		Gulshurzai			

Alum Khan Kalpur, Bughti Baloch.

To face page 116.

This tribe trace their origin from the Rind division of Balochis, and though the Khān of Kalāt claimed sovereignty over them, they paid revenue to no one, and were perpetually at war with the Marris, and plundered their neighbours on every side whenever an opportunity offered. Owing to continued depredations committed by the Bughtis in Kachhi, the Kalāt ruler sent a force under Mian Khān and Abdul Kādir to punish them, but the Brahui troops were completely routed and a large number of them killed.

This tribe first came into contact with the British about 1839, and an expedition was sent in the month of October of that year under the command of Major Billamore to the Bughti hills. In the course of a three months' campaign he captured their chief, their principal town, Dēra, and inflicted great loss on the tribe as a whole. Not till 1843 did the Bughtis recommence their plundering incursions on a large scale; but this was mainly due to the removal of their rivals, the Dumbkis and Jakrānis, from the plains of Kachhi. In January, 1845, Sir Charles Napier's great hill-campaign into the Bughti and Marri country took place; but the Bughti tribe, though denied access to their country by the Marris, managed to find a refuge with the Khetrāns, where they remained till the British force returned to Sindh. In 1846 the Bughtis made a very bold raid into British Sindh, with perfect impunity carrying off an immense booty, amounting, it is said, to as many as 15,000 head of cattle. But in 1847 arrangements were made which very soon put a stop to these disorders on the border. The Sindh Horse were ordered up to the frontier in January of that year, and from that time peace and security of life and property were established along the border.

Though shut out from British Sindh, the Bughtis persisted in making predatory inroads into the plains of Kachhi. In one of these incursions between 600 and 700 men were intercepted by a detachment of about 133 men of the 1st Sindh Horse, under Lieut. (now Colonel Sir W. L.) Merewether, the present Commissioner in Sindh, who at once charged them, and obtained a brilliant and complete victory. It is stated that on this occasion about one-half of the whole of the fighting-men of the tribe were either killed or taken prisoners. Its strength as a tribe was completely broken, and the Bughti chiefs soon came in to the British authorities in Sindh and surrendered at discretion. Large numbers were settled on lands near Larkāna, but in 1848, owing to certain intrigues, the chiefs fled to their hills and began once more to revert to their former predatory habits. Within the last few years they have been at continual feud with the Marris, but are now beginning, it is said, to settle down and cultivate their lands.

THE MARRIS.

Of all the hill tribes hitherto enumerated, there are none which in number and importance equal the Marris. Their country, as at present composed, is bounded on the north by the Makhiānis, the Murēchis, and other Pathān tribes; on the south by the Bughtis, on the east by the Ketrans and Gorchānis, and on the west by the Kalāt province of Kachhi. This country is divided into four separate districts, *viz.*: Kahankhās, Mundahi, Jantalli, Phailawar and Missu. Of these, Kahankhās was all that originally belonged to the Marri tribe; the others have been acquired by the sword. The Marri country is very hilly and barren, though possessing a few fertile valleys. The rivers running through it are the Nāra, Lar, and Lhāri. Kahan is the chief town, and is situate in a valley of the same name, about twelve miles in length by three in breadth. The Marri tribe is divided into three main branches with 22 sub-divisions, and they can muster, in the aggregate, 4000 fighting-men. There is another sub-division of the Marri tribe, known as the Mazarānis, about 700 strong, separated, says Bruce, from the rest of the tribe many years ago, and now living to the west of Siwi (or Sibi), near the Bolān pass. They still continue to acknowledge a *nominal* allegiance to the Marri *tomandār*, and pay him *panjak*, that is, a one-fifth share of plunder; otherwise they are quite independent of him. The following table will show the branches and sub-divisions of this tribe as mentioned by Bruce:—

Main branches.	No. of fighting men.	Sub-divisions.	Main branches.	No. of fighting men.	Sub-divisions.
1. Ghuzeni...	1400	Rahawalzai Mohandāni Langāni Isanāni Tuigeāni Mozundagāni Ladwar Chilguri Alliāni	3. Bijurāni	1500	Kulandorāni Sumrāni Salarāni Rahmkāni Pudi Kungerahi Kilwanni Purdadāni Shaheja
2. Loharāni	1100	Kunderāni Gusarāni Sherāni Mohandāni			

The Marris, though really subjects of the Brahui Khān of Kalāt, pay no revenue to their sovereign, and act independently of him. In the great Nasir Khān's time, his authority was real and not nominal, and he made his power felt among them, and it so continued during a part, at least, of his son Mahmud's reign—so long, indeed, as Mastapha Khān, that ruler's half-brother, was alive; for never were the hill tribes better and more firmly controlled than by this chieftain. After that, with the single exception of Khudadād Khān's campaign against them in 1859, when they acknowledged him to be their lawful prince, the Marris did generally that "which seemed right in their own eyes," and the following remark of Bruce's may very well apply to their present condition :—"The Marris are, like their neighbours the Bughtis, nominally the subjects of H.H. the Khān of Kalāt. They occupy the hills which form the extreme north-eastern frontier of his territory, and hold, with respect to him, more the position which the independent hill tribes on our frontier do with regard to the British Government than that of subjects towards their rightful sovereign. Thus for years they have committed constant raids in his territories, coercive as well as conciliatory measures having been used from time to time to keep them in order."

The British Government first came into contact with the Marri tribe in 1839, when, as mentioned in the account of the Bughtis, Major Billamore's force penetrated into the hill country with the object of punishing the robber tribes for their continued plundering excursions into the low country. Kahan, their chief town, was taken, and a small detachment was sent, under the command of a Bombay officer, Captain Lewis Brown (known afterwards as Kahan Brown), of the 5th Bombay N.I., to occupy it in April, 1840. Notwithstanding the failure of two attempts to relieve him, Brown held out bravely for five months against the Marris, and nobly refused to surrender the fort until the last extremity, and then only after he had secured for himself and his brave comrades a safe retreat with all the honours of war from the Marri chief, Doda Khān. During Sir Charles Napier's campaign in the hills in 1845–46, the Marris sided with the British against their inveterate enemies, the Bughtis; but when the removal of the Dumbki and Jakrāni tribes from Kachhi left that part of the Khān's dominions temptingly open to raids, they at once seized their opportunity, and plundered all over Kachhi as far south as Kanda. In the second treaty concluded in 1854 with Nasir Khān by the

British Government, the Kalāt ruler had specially bound himself to prevent all outrages by his subjects within or near to British territory, and to protect merchants in their transit through his dominions, and for this he was to receive an annual subsidy of Rs.50,000 from the Indian Government. To keep the Marris and others from molesting merchants and traders generally in the passes and elsewhere, the Khān subsidized these hill tribes, and made other arrangements for the protection of the frontier, which might have turned out satisfactorily had not his death occurred early in 1857.

After this event, the conduct of the Marris in the matter of raiding became so thoroughly outrageous that the new Khān (Mir Khudadād) was compelled to fit out an expedition against them in 1858–59, which brought them to their senses for a time; but they speedily returned to their old habits, and this, in 1862, necessitated another campaign against them, which being unsuccessful in its results, the *extra* annual subsidy of Rs.50,000 allowed the Khān by the British Government was withdrawn. The Marris soon after began their plundering incursions against both the Panjāb and Kalāt borders, and though some arrangements were made for the better protection of the Panjāb frontier, the great raid on Harrand in January, 1867, by a combined force of Marris, Bughtis, and Ketrans, showed that the checks placed on the tribes were not of a satisfactory nature. Opportunity was then taken of making other and more efficient arrangements with the Marris, and these, though satisfactory as regarded the Panjāb frontier, unfortunately did not provide for the Kachhi district, which was still plundered at will and with perfect impunity by this lawless tribe. In 1871–72 the Marris joined the Brahui tribes, then in open rebellion against their sovereign, and shortly afterwards the latter assisted the Mazarāni branch of Marris in robbing two caravans in the Bolān pass in April, 1872. To put a stop to their lawless proceedings, the Commissioner in Sindh (Sir W. L. Merewether), who had been desired by the Government of India to suggest measures for preventing this continual raiding, recommended a blockade of the Marri tribe, and that, in case of their continued defiance of the British Government, a small but efficient force should proceed into the Marri hills (now well known to the British authorities) and inflict upon them the punishment they deserved. But these suggestions, unfortunately, did not meet with the approval of the Indian Government, who feared that blockading the Marris would entail more hardship upon British subjects than upon the Marris themselves, and that it would be better to bring about an amicable settlement, if possible.

Up to the end of the year 1875 the report was that no improvement in the behaviour of this tribe had taken place—so far, at least, as Kachhi was concerned—but that, if anything, their conduct in the matter of raiding was worse than ever. To make these tribes respect the Kalāt frontier, and to prevent them from plundering harmless trade-caravans in the passes, is of course the urgent desire of the British Government, and should be also the earnest wish of the Kalāt State; and if it be found that strong punitive measures are absolutely necessary to bring the Marri tribe to reason in this matter, the sooner such are carried out the better will it be for the Khān's subjects in Kachhi, and for the trade which passes through their province. On these points it is impossible not to agree with Bruce where, in speaking more especially of the Panjāb frontier, he says:—"Wherever the remedy lies, imperial interests of great weight demand that it should be applied; and there is little doubt that, if successful, it would add materially to the power of the British Government on one of the most, if not *the most*, important parts of the North-Western frontier, as well as to her *prestige* throughout Central Asia."

CHAPTER V.

A GENERAL DESCRIPTION OF THE PROVINCE OF LAS.

THIS, the smallest of all the five provinces making up Kalāti Balochistan, is bounded on the north by the highlands of Jhalawān; on the east by a portion of the Khirthar range of mountains and the Habb river, which separates it from Sindh; on the west by the Hāra and Hinglāj mountains, and the Aghor (or Hingol) river, separating it from the Makrān province; and on the south it is washed by the Arabian Sea, from the mouth of the Habb river in the east to that of the Aghor river in the west, a distance of not less than 112 miles. It derives its name of Las from a word signifying a *plain* or *level country*, and is in length from north to south about 85 miles, while its average breadth from east to west may be taken at 95 miles, the entire area of this district being estimated in round numbers at 8000 square miles. It does not appear to be divided into any sub-districts, as in the case of the Sarawān and Jhalawān provinces, nor does it possess any fertile valleys of the same kind as are found in those two more highly favoured and extensive portions of Balochistan. The province of Las is indeed surrounded on three sides, that is to say, its northern, eastern, and western, by ranges of dry and arid hills, while another chain moves down in a southerly direction from Jhalawān, through its midst nearly to the coast, dividing it into two unequally sized parts. These mountains are offshoots, or spurs, from the great Brahuik mass which covers so much of the Sarawān and Jhalawān provinces, but in height are very much less than the parent range, decreasing, in fact, in elevation the nearer they approach the sea-coast. They are in both formation and composition similar to the Brahuik range. Of the two large plains into which Las is divided by its mountain system, that to the west is by far the smaller and less productive, much of it being covered by a mass of barren hills with small valleys intervening, the remainder being a level sandy district, in most places barren and almost destitute of inhabitants. The other, or eastern plain, being to some extent watered by the Purāli stream and its numerous tributaries, is productive only where the river water can irrigate its soil. This plain is perfectly flat, except at a spot on the coast some eight miles or so broad, where there is a belt of low broken hillocks.

Of the various rivers, or mountain torrents, of Las, there is but little to be said. The principal stream is the Purāli, of which mention has already been made in the description of the Jhalawān province. This stream enters the Las district at a place some 18 or 20 miles north of the town of Bēla, and leaves the hills about 10 miles south of the border. Here its bed is said to be nearly 300 yards broad, but this at Bēla, near which it flows, is increased to close upon half a mile, the stream when in water having no depth, but merely covering a large superficial area. In its winding course from Bēla it meets with numerous tributaries from the mountains on the eastern border of the district, and its bed has a greater width at the points of confluence with these lesser torrents. At one place, where one of these latter, the Kahto, joins the

Purāli, the bed is nearly a mile across, and when in water must present a fine sight. In the rainy, or inundation, season the surplus water, which at once entirely destroys all *bandhs*, or mounds, raised in the dry season for agricultural purposes, escapes into a level plain bounded on the south by the sand-hills on the coast, and also by another outlet on the eastern side, and thus generates a line of lagoons or swamps in that part where the ground is very low. Some of these lagoons are several miles in length and as much as a mile wide, but decrease considerably in the dry season, when the water becomes salt, and much charged with vegetable matter. Carless states that the water of the Purāli holds in solution a large quantity of saline ingredients. It is through one of these large lagoons that the Purāli reaches the sea on the shores of the Bay of Sonmiāni, a few miles below the harbour of that name. Another of these mountain torrents, the Habb, which forms for about 60 miles a well-demarcated line of frontier between Las and Sindh, differs from the Purāli only in having permanent banks and a regular *embouchure* to the sea *when* in water. For the greater part of the year its bed is dry, and presents only here and there a disconnected series of pools of water. It must, however, be mentioned that at one place on this stream, about seven or eight miles north of the road, or rather camel-track, running from Sonmiāni to Karāchi, in Sindh, there has lately been constructed a substantial *bandh*, or weir, across the river, with the object of collecting sufficient water to irrigate an extensive area of fine level land on the Sindh side, known as the Habb estate. This estate, comprising nearly 34,000 acres, was some years ago granted by the British Government in perpetuity to one Khān Bahādur Murād Khān (now deceased), an enterprising and public-spirited Afghān gentleman, who had been able to render important services to the Government at a time when such were greatly needed. The Khān had long contemplated the construction of a stone weir across the Habb river for purposes of irrigation, but it is only within the past few years that this project has been carried out, under the direction of Mr. A. Molloy, the superintending engineer of the Habb estate. The weir is about 1100 feet in length, from bank to bank, with a height from foundation to low-water line of 23 feet. This foundation is carried through a fine sand down to the solid rock, but it is intended to raise the height of the weir 16 feet above low-water line of river, so as to enclose a still larger water area, a portion of which would no doubt be available for the irrigation of lands on the Las side, provided the cultivators are prepared to pay for the boon. The freshets which come down the Habb after a rainfall in the hills are at times very heavy, as in some places the fall in surface is as much as six feet in the mile. After heavy rains in the Pabb mountains a large expanse of water accumulates just above the weir, where, to the delight of the angler, are to be found a variety of fine fish, amongst them two kinds of barbel, the "kariāh" (*barbus tor*) and the "pitohi" (*barbus titius*).

The Aghor (or Hingol) river, forming a good line of boundary between Las and Makrān, rises, it is believed, in the Hāra mountains, and, unlike the Habb and Purāli, would appear to possess an uninterrupted flow, which at times, on the melting of the snows in the mountains, acquires a considerable volume. In the upper part of its course down to the Hingol mountain it is known as the Hingol, thence to the sea as the Aghor. The water of this stream is not considered to be wholesome, owing to the great quantity of sand it holds in solution. It is on the right, or *western*, bank of this river, and about two days' journey from the port of Ormāra, in Makrān, that the temple of Hinglāj is situate; it is a noted place of pilgrimage for both Hindus and Musalmāns, but especially for the former.

VIEW ON THE HAEB RIVER, LAS, SHOWING MURĀD KHĀṆ'S "BANDH" OR WEIR.

To face page 126.

Climate.—The climate of Las is represented to be very variable. In the cold season the atmosphere is clear, dry, and cool, and in the neighbourhood of Bēla, in the month of January, the thermometer has been known to show as low a temperature as 35° in the mornings, and to rise not higher than 67° at any portion of the day. Carless remarks "that, situated as it is just without the limits of the south-west monsoon, and being nearly encircled by high mountains, which not only reflect the sun's rays but exclude the wind, the heat in the summer season is intense, and although the atmosphere is occasionally cooled by refreshing showers, it is severely felt by the inhabitants." There seem to be two seasons, as in the neighbouring province of Makrān, in which rain is prevalent, *viz.*, in February or March, and again in June, July, and a part of August; but, taken as a whole, Las is said to be less insalubrious in climate than the adjoining province of Makrān.

Towns and Villages.—The chief towns and villages in the province of Las are few, and of but little importance. They are Bēla, the capital; Sonmiāni, a harbour on the coast; and the villages of Utal and Liyāri. The port of Ormāra, in Western Makrān, belongs to the Las State, but an account of it will be given under the heading MAKRĀN in the next chapter. Bēla, the first-mentioned town, is seated on the banks of a confluent of the Purāli river, this latter stream being about a mile distant. The town is built on some slightly elevated ground in lat. 26° 12′ N., and long. 66° 20′ E., and is 70 miles or thereabouts distant from the sea-coast. It is the residence of the Jām, or chief, of the Las province, and is surrounded by a ruinous mud wall, entirely undefended. The palace of the Jām, which is within the walls, is the only brick building in the place; though Masson speaks of it as being of mud, and surrounded by lofty castellated walls, flanked with circular towers at the angles. The houses seem to be all composed of mud, with the usual appliances on the top for the admission of air, such as are in vogue in the large towns of Sindh, and known there as *bādgirs*, or wind-catchers. The streets are narrow, and are said to be clean in consequence of their peculiar situation, which is not the case in Baloch towns generally. Pottinger, in 1810, estimated the number of houses at 2000, or, say, with from 8000 to 10,000 inhabitants; but Masson (in 1841) thought there were not more than 300 houses, of which one-third were occupied by Hindus. Carless, who visited the place a few years earlier, considered it to possess about 800 houses, with a population ranging from 4000 to 5000 souls; what the number of inhabitants is at this present time is not known. There seems to be a good deal of cultivation in the neighbourhood of Bēla. The people get their water from wells, some of which are on a level with the river, while others are found in the old bed of the Purāli, where vegetables, tobacco, and rice are largely grown. The town derives some importance from being on the main road leading from Sonmiāni to Kalāt.

The town and harbour of Sonmiāni is a small and insignificant place, in lat. 24° 25′ N., and long. 66° 35′ E., distant about 70 miles south from Bēla, and 52 miles north-west from Karāchi, in Sindh. It is seated at the northern extremity of a kind of bay, or large inlet of the sea. The harbour, situate also at the northern head of the bay, which, says Carless (who wrote upon this place many years ago), has been formed by the Purāli river, is a large, irregular inlet, spreading out, like that at Karāchi, in extensive swamps, and choked with shoals. It is at the southern portion of the Bay of Sonmiāni, Pottinger believes, that the port of Alexander, so named by Nearchus, was situate, and that here his fleet, according to Arrian, remained for a considerable period. The channel leading into the harbour is extremely narrow, and has a depth of 16 or 17 feet at high water in the shallowest part, but it shifts its position every year, and vessels of any size could not navigate it without great difficulty until it had been buoyed off. Inside there are six, seven, and even ten fathoms in some places; but towards the town the channels become shallow, and the trading boats cannot approach it nearer than a mile.

Sea-going vessels generally anchor outside the bar, their cargoes being discharged into small boats and so brought to shore. Vessels at anchor inside the harbour are constantly aground at low water.

During the south-west monsoon the harbour cannot be entered, for the bar at the entrance is then exposed to the whole force of the swell, and the breakers on it are very heavy. Montrion, who surveyed the harbour in 1842, states the entrance to be between two sandy points; the western of these is not well defined, being a low range of sand-hills, utterly destitute of vegetation; the eastern has some low tamarisk trees on it, and terminates more in a bluff. The breadth between these two points is about 5400 yards, with a bar right across it, and breakers on it at all times. At low water this bar had two fathoms of water upon it, but the depth was noticed to be *diminishing yearly.* The channel through this bar was then 2500 yards or thereabouts in length, the breadth at the narrowest part being about 300 yards. This deepened over into another channel on the eastern shore, some 4¾ miles in length, with an average breadth of 400 yards, and terminated at about 1¾ miles to the eastward of the town of Sonmiāni. Montrion noticed that the rise and fall of the tide at Sonmiāni was about nine feet at the full and change, and that there was more water when the wind blew strong from the southward and westward. The velocity of the tide was very irregular, the greatest observed being two knots per hour. These observations were made, it is true, many years ago; but in the absence of any very recent information on this harbour, the main features here drawn may no doubt, to a great extent, be presumed to apply at the present time.

The town—situate, as has been stated, on the northern side of the harbour—is a very poor place, being simply an assemblage of a number of mud huts with *bādgirs*, or ventilators, on the roofs, open to the sea-breeze, for without these they would not, on account of the excessive heat, in the summer season be habitable. The place, notwithstanding its mean appearance—in the first instance it was a mere fishing village, known among the natives as "Miāni"—had, and may still be held to have, a considerable trade. The number of houses at present is not known, but in Carless's time the place did not possess more than 500, with a population of about 2000 souls. At one time Sonmiāni was surrounded by a mud wall, but this was allowed to fall to decay, and in 1838 scarcely a vestige of it remained. The remains of a small fort in the suburbs, built, it is said, in former times to resist the attacks of pirates, were still visible in 1840, but after the destruction of these pirates by the British it was not kept in repair.

Oil from the *shira* (or *shangruf*) plant is largely made at Sonmiāni, where many mills are worked for this purpose. Some silks, coarse cotton cloths, and carpets were also fabricated in the place.

Drinking-water at Sonmiāni is brackish, and is procured by digging pits in the sand; these pits, or holes, are about four or five feet deep, and are above high-water mark. Wells appear to be scarce. Carless states that he found the water so undrinkable at Sonmiāni as to be compelled to send to Karāchi for a supply for his vessels. The inhabitants of Sonmiāni are mostly Numris and Mēds, or fishermen, with a sprinkling of Hindus; these last are chiefly engaged in trade.

Of the trade of Sonmiāni, the only really authentic details obtainable are those for the years 1840 and 1841, when a British agent (Lieut. Gordon, Bombay Army), was located at that port by the Indian Government. The commerce of this place is believed to have been much more extensive formerly than it is at present, and a large portion of it went by the Kalāt route to the northern provinces of Hindustan. In 1808 it received a severe check, when Sonmiāni was captured and plundered by the Joasmi pirates, and after that from the fact of the Mirs of the neighbouring province of Sindh having issued strict orders to the merchants at Karāchi to cease, under severe penalties, exporting goods to any of the ports in Las. Pottinger mentions that in 1810 the exports from Sonmiāni consisted mostly of grain and some carpets; these went chiefly to Makrān and the Arabian coast, whence they received in return dates, almonds, and slaves. From Bombay were imported metals of various kinds, sugar, betel and cocoa nuts; from Sindh, chintzes, *lungis*, and a little raw cotton. Horses, are known to have formed an important article of export from Sonmiāni; but this fact seems to have been overlooked by Pottinger. The trade, however, gradually declined, though about 1832 or 1833 wool began, for the first time, to be exported from Sonmiāni as a remunerative article. It had previously been used up locally in manufacturing a stuff called *nodi*, then in general use among the people of the Las Province, but, as Gordon remarked in 1841, its value since it became an export to Bombay rose from three rupees to eighteen and even twenty rupees for the Sonmiāni maund, and in consequence the native manufacture was entirely abandoned. During the trading season of 1840–41, Gordon found the total value of the entire export and import trade of Sonmiāni to be about Rs.9,96,000, and that of 1841–42 at Rs.16,21,000. The imports, which were received from Bombay, Maskāt, and Sindh, comprised chiefly piece-goods, beads, metals, sugar, tea, broad-cloth, silks, velvets, and rice from the first-mentioned port; dates and wheat from Maskāt, and rice from Sindh, while the exports to Bombay were chiefly wool, ghi, horses, oil, and fishmaws. To Maskāt were sent indigo, madder, hides, and a little cotton, and to Sindh, a coarse stuff made from goat's hair, called *boris*, mung (*phaseolus mungo*), ghi, and oil.

A summary of this trade for the two years above mentioned, as prepared and placed before the Bombay Government by the British agent at Sonmiāni, is here reproduced. Of the articles mentioned, the exports from the Las State itself are said to have been wool, ghi, and a gum called *gogar* (the "bdellium" of commerce), some oils of various kinds, mung, and large quantities of fish and sharks' fins. Those brought from Kābul and from up-country generally to Sonmiāni for exportation comprised madder, saffron, asafœtida (hing), raisins, almonds, and dried fruits of various kinds. Horses came down in considerable numbers, and sometimes as many as two thousand were exported in the course of a single season:—

IMPORTS.

	Value in 1840–41.	Value in 1841–42.
	Rupees.	Rupees.
By Afghāns from Bombay	6,29,884	12,73,221
By resident traders at Bombay	64,615	93,776
,, ,, Maskāt	42,225	30,275
,, ,, in Sindh	11,403	61,256
Total imports	7,48,127	14,58,528

EXPORTS.

	Value in 1840–1841.	Value in 1841–1842.
	Rupees.	Rupees.
By Afghāns to Bombay	67,061	83,544
By resident traders to Bombay	1,74,718	58,625
" " Maskāt	1,434	5,973
" " Sindh	5,033	14,134
Total exports	2,48,246	1,62,276
Total imports	7,48,127	14,58,528
Total value	9,96,373	16,20,804

The coins current at Sonmiāni are the Kashāni rupee of Ispahān, but there would appear to be a local currency also, consisting of *fulus* and *falvas* (½ and ¼); the first is equivalent to 2½ pies of British Indian currency.

As the office of British agent at Sonmiāni was soon after abolished, no other reliable records of the trade of the port from that time down to the present are available; but so far as the trade of the place with Karāchi (in Sindh) and Bombay is concerned, some items of information are obtainable from the custom-house records of those two ports, though they do not show the trade of Sonmiāni exclusively, but as jointly with that of the smaller ports of Makrān, such as Ormāra, Gwādar, Pasni, etc. With Sindh the trade, though fluctuating, seems to be somewhat on the increase, but with Bombay it has in several articles fallen off very much. The *exports* from Sonmiāni to Sindh comprise chiefly wool, seeds, oils, and a little grain at times; to Bombay, mostly wool and provisions, with small quantities of oils, grain, and pulse. Of what nature these provisions from so poor a province as Makrān may be, it is difficult to say, but the average *annual* value of them during the five years ending with 1874–75 was not less than Rs.70,000. The *Imports* into Sonmiāni from Sindh comprise piece-goods and grain; those from

Bombay are piece-goods, metals, grain, and pulse. The following table will give some idea of the *value* of the imports and exports of Sonmiāni, in conjunction, of course, with the small ports of Makrān, for the five years ending with 1874–75, but neither the export nor import trade with ports in the Persian Gulf, or elsewhere, can be shown, as no available records of this nature are forthcoming:—

Value of the Exports from Sonmiāni (and Makrān Ports).

Year.	To Sindh.	To Bombay.
	Rupees.	Rupees.
1870–71	1,64,543	1,93,900
1871–72	2,14,132	1,83,663
1872–73	76,895	1,84,184
1873–74	84,110	1,64,813
1874–75	1,78,273	1,31,443

Value of the Imports of Sonmiāni (and Makrān Ports).

Year.	From Sindh.	From Bombay.
	Rupees.	Rupees.
1870–71	1,47,907	1,12,330
1871–72	1,16,188	61,163
1872–73	1,52,622	69,368
1873–74	1,46,143	49,335
1874–75	1,33,606	37,662

In the exports from Sonmiāni horses do not now appear to form an item, as they once did, but find their way to Karāchi by the far safer and better route of British Sindh. The trade at Sonmiāni was, and is still, greatly dependent upon the state of that part of Balochistan lying between it and Kalāt. When the Kalāt ruler is able to make his power felt in these intermediate districts, by preventing any undue exactions being levied on the part of the Brahui chiefs from the caravans passing through the country, and, in short, can guarantee the safety of both the persons and property of traders, the commerce of that port flourishes; but when this is not the case, it as a natural consequence declines. In 1840 the customs duties at Sonmiāni were, according to Hart, as follows:—On each bale of piece-goods, 10 rupees; on other articles, at the rate of Rs.3 2 annas to merchants, and Rs.3 8 annas to ryats. On every slave a tax of Rs.5 was taken. Each pilgrim to Hinglāj paid a fee of Rs.2 2 annas to the customs contractor of Sonmiāni, out of which six annas went to the Jām, or native ruler. This was for protection to the pilgrims while in the Las territory. Gordon also mentions that up to 1841 a duty of four per cent. was levied at Sonmiāni on exports and imports of every description, and Rs.4½ on each horse, while in addition to this a transit duty of one rupee was payable at Bēla on every camel-load of merchandise passing it from the northward, but caravans from the coast which had already paid the regular customs dues at Sonmiāni were freed from this additional impost.

In 1841 the port and transit duties in the Las territory were, by order of the then Khān of Kalāt (Shāh Nawāz), reduced to one-half of what they had been formerly, that is, to a percentage of but two rupees at Sonmiāni, and half a rupee transit duty on each camel-load at Bēla. But it was in passing through the country of the Minghal and Bizanju tribes that the caravans were so harrassed with heavy and arbitrary exactions. These varied according to the power or weakness of the reigning Khān, and ranged from one rupee to four rupees per camel-load. The chief of Wadd was at times dreadfully exorbitant in his levies, and often enforced payment at the rate of ten or twelve per cent. These unreasonable duties, accompanied with an occasional pillage of the caravans by the chiefs of these districts, were in themselves quite sufficient to prevent any increase in the commerce of Sonmiāni, and it is only surprising that any Pathān merchants could be found to carry on trade under such depressing and discouraging difficulties.

The only other towns and villages of the Las district besides Bēla and Sonmiāni, excepting Ormāra—which, though belonging to Las, is situate in the Makrān Province—are Liyāri and Utal; but these are insignificant as regards both population and importance, having but from 150 to 200 inhabitants in each. Pottinger, indeed, speaking of the former village (Liyāri), says that in his time it was considered to be the second town in the district, and that Utal was a well-built, clean village, containing about 400 houses, or, say, 1600 inhabitants; but they have evidently both sadly declined since the time he wrote about them.

Inhabitants.—The population of the Las State is supposed not to exceed 30,000 souls, or a little more than three persons to the square mile, and the greater number of these are found on the Purāli river and its confluents. The predominant tribe is the Lumri (or Numri), whose ancestor is said to have been one Narpat; it has a number of sub-divisions, of which the following are the chief:—

1. Jāmhat (or Yamhat)	5. Gadur	10. Sur
	6. Masorah	11. Vahreh
2. Gungah	7. Manghia	12. Runjah
3. Angariah	8. Shekh	13. Bura
4. Chutah	9. Shah-Lokah	14. Dodah

The principal of these is the Jāmhat, and it is of this sub-tribe that the Jām, or ruler, of the province is the head. They held possession of the Las district for some centuries, until dispossessed for a time, about A.D. 1730, by the Burfat (or Bulfat) Numris, who, under their chief, Pahar Khān, seized the reins of government. These retained the sovereignty for not more than ten years, when the Jāmhat tribe again succeeded in asserting its supremacy, and have ever since maintained possession of the province. The Chutah tribe are, by other authorities, said to be descended from the Sumras of Sindh, and not to be a section of the Lumri. They at present occupy both banks of the Habb river, having the Minghals and Kadrānis to the north, and the Pabb hills to the west. The area of country occupied by this tribe is about 1200 square miles. Their personal appearance is not favourable, and they are even worse in character. There are numerous sub-divisions, or clans, and their numbers in the aggregate do not probably exceed 2300 of both sexes. The Gadur tribe is said to be a branch of the celebrated Arab tribe, the Korēshi, and to have settled in Las in the reign of the third Kalifah, Omar. The Shekh and Runjah tribes compose, for the most part, the cultivating classes of this province, and it is from them that the government land-tax is principally collected. The Lumris are said to have consanguinity with the Battis of Jaisalmir, and a similarity in both their appearance and manners goes far to warrant this assertion. Pottinger also saw in them a great resemblance to the Hindu. They are a pastoral race, and possess herds of oxen and buffaloes, as also large flocks of goats, but not sheep, as the country is unsuited to them. In person the Lumris are not a fine race, but both in appearance and bodily strength are inferior to their neighbours, and are also ignorant, indolent, apathetic, and superstitious, and not given to cleanliness in either their persons or dress. The women are very ordinary in features. They are noted, it is also said, for their bold and licentious manners.

The Lumris claim a close affinity with the Burfat and the Jokia tribes of Sindh. The Burfats are divided, according to Masson, into two clans, the Bappahāni and the Amallāni. The Jokias are sub-divided into fourteen families, as follows:—

1. Tebir (the chief)	6. Mohmat	11. Tagia
2. Musa	7. Panda	12. Hamirah-Kah
3. Bardijah	8. Hinghura	13. Shikāri
4. Salarah	9. Ghad	14. Panhwar.
5. Haria-putra	10. Harti	

The Jokias mostly inhabit the mountainous country to the eastward, and were, says Carless, formerly subject to the chief of Las, but when Karāchi was taken by the Sindhians, they threw off their allegiance and acknowledged only the authority of the Talpur Mirs.

The dress of the Las tribes is much the same as it is in Sindh, that of the male portion consisting of a loose *pahiran* or shirt, a pair of trousers, and a small cap. The women adopt much the same kind of costume, except that the shirt is much longer and comes down to the ankles, while some have a small silk or cotton jacket under it. Their food is principally rice and other grains, fish (on the coast), and buttermilk. The better classes use flesh-meat, but this is a luxury which can seldom be afforded. As a rule the people are given to opium-eating. The Lumris speak a dialect common to the kindred tribes of Jokias and Burfats in the west of Sindh; it is known as Jad-gāli, or Jat-gāli, a name which appears to be derived from the Jat tribe, and Masson speaks of a fixed portion of the population inhabiting Bēla and Sonmiāni under the name of Jad-gāl, in contradistinction, it would seem, to the Mēds, or maritime and fishing classes on the sea-coast. In addition to these classes of the people inhabiting the Las territory, there are also Mēmons, who mostly conduct the slave traffic at Sonmiāni, and who are not themselves orthodox Muhammadans. Negro slaves are numerous, too, at Sonmiāni, and there are, besides, a good many resident Hindu traders at both this port and at the town of Bēla.

Productions.—The vegetable productions of Las are confined to but few articles, and these are, comparatively speaking, small in quantity, owing to the barren nature of the country, and the want, at times, of water for irrigational purposes. Agriculture is, indeed, both neglected and despised in the Las Province. A little rice is grown in the bed of the Purāli river, and wheat, barley, *juār*, oil-seeds, cotton, *mung*, and some other grains are produced in small quantities. The gum called *gogar* (bdellium), already mentioned as forming an article of export, is obtained from the *gugal* tree, and the oil-plant (*shira*, or *shangruf*) is largely cultivated for its seed and oil, both of which are exported to other places. The oil is made mostly at Sonmiāni, where the mills for expressing it from the seed are numerous.

The animal productions of Las are of more account, for the Lumris are essentially a pastoral people, and rear and breed cattle, camels, and goats in amazing numbers. Ghi is made in considerable quantities, and much wool is exported annually from the port of Sonmiāni.

Of the mineral productions of Las but little is as yet known. Iron ore exists, it is said, in the hills north of Bēla, and in those between the towns of Liyāri and Bēla copper is reported as being found in large quantities. Hart states that the whole country is, he believes, rich in mineral productions, and would be well worthy the attention of an experienced geologist.

Trade and Manufactures.—The trade of the Las Province, such as it is, has already been partly described in that passing through the port of Sonmiāni, but it may also be mentioned that large quantities of firewood, grass, date leaves, hides, seeds, ghi, and wool, are sent to Karāchi, in Sindh, from Bēla and other places by the coast route on camels, bullocks, and donkeys. Horses are also despatched to Karāchi for sale, by the same route. It has been found impossible to give any idea of the *value* of this portion of the Las trade, but it is believed to be by no means insignificant.

The manufactures are very trifling, and are confined to oils, cotton-cloth of an exceedingly coarse texture, and coarse carpets made at Bēla.

Administration and Revenue.—The government of the Province of Las, which may be regarded as tributary to that of Kalāt, is vested in an hereditary chief with the title of JĀM, who is a vassal of the Brahui Khān of Kalāt, and, as such, is bound to supply, on emergencies, a contingent of troops, said by some authorities to number as many as 4500, but generally supposed not to exceed 2700 or 3000 men. The Las Province was, it is believed, anciently ruled by the Rungah tribe of Lumris, the first chief being one Sappar; but his descendants were deprived of their power by the Gungah tribe under two chieftains—Jām Dinar and Jām Ibrahim. The Jāmhat tribe then gained the ascendency under a leader named Jām Ali, about 1046 of the Hijri (A.D. 1638); to him succeeded Jām Rubāna, of the same tribe, but happening to kill his brother, the son-in-law of Pahar Khān, the Amallāri Burfat chief, this latter usurped the reins of government. The rule, however, of his son, Izzat Khān, was found so oppressive that Jām Ali, a descendant of Rubāna, of the Jāmhat tribe, obtained possession of Las with the aid of the Kalāt Khān, and from this circumstance arose the connection between the two States.

The chieftainship of Las has continued in this line down to the present time. Masson thus wrote of the government of this territory in 1843, at a time when the neighbouring province of Sindh was under Talpur rule:—"The government of the Lumri community of Las is vested in an hereditary chief, with the title of Jām. He exercises within his own territories an independent and uncontrolled jurisdiction, acknowledging, nevertheless, the supremacy of the Brahui chief of Kalāt, to whom, if required, military service is rendered. Although it is understood that the chief of Kalāt may not, on occasions of lapses of authority, disturb the natural order of succession, his concurrence in the selection of the future ruler is deemed necessary, and his deputy performs the inaugural ceremony of seating the new Jām on the *masnad.* The dependence of Las upon Kalāt, while so easy as to be little more than nominal, is likely, however, to become more definite, both because the Government is visibly deteriorating, and that the connection is the only precautionary measure which the inferior State can adopt to secure its independence from being destroyed by its powerful and grasping neighbours of Sindh, who behold with extreme jealousy the harbour of Sonmiāni, and the diversion of a portion of the commerce, which they wish should be confined to Karāchi."

With respect to the revenue of the province, it is impossible to state with any degree of accuracy what it amounts to at the *present* time, owing to the anarchy and dissension which have prevailed there for so long a time past. During the reign of Jām Mehr Ali, before 1840, the annual revenues are said to have exceeded Rs.40,000, raised mostly from customs duties at Sonmiāni; but after that year they dwindled away to about Rs.25,000. Jām Mehr Ali had indeed offered several advantages to merchants trading to Sonmiāni, by waiving the right of searching all caravans, and had attempted in other ways to encourage them to frequent that port rather than Karāchi, this latter place being then in the hands of the Baloch tribe of Talpurs.

In 1836, according to Carless, the revenues reached Rs.35,000, derived from a duty of 3 per cent. on all imports and exports at Sonmiāni, and a bazār toll of 1 per cent., collected at the towns the caravans had to pass through on the road to Bēla. The land-tax comprised *one-third* of the produce from all lands irrigated by the river, and *one-fifth* on those which depended solely on rain for a water supply. In 1854 Preedy reported that the revenues of Las averaged about Rs.33,000, derived chiefly from a land-tax and from customs duties, and that it was collected as follows :—

	Rupees.
From the customs at Sonmiāni	6,000
From the customs at Ormāra	4,000
Land-tax from the Bēla district and other parts of the province	23,000
Total	33,000

Mud-volcanoes.—Before referring to the antiquities of the Las district, it will be necessary to devote some attention to certain singular productions of nature known as the *Kups*, or basins, of Rājāh Ramchandar, situate near the Phor stream, on the road to the temple of Hinglāj, and between the greater and less Hāra mountain ranges. By other authorities the term "Kup" is said not to mean basin, or well, but "anger," and that it is derived from the following legend:—"In the 'Sat Jug,' or golden age, Suda Shiwa, or Siva, and Parbatti, his wife, visited the Makli hills, near Tatta. The former resolved to proceed onward to Hinglāj, and Parbatti was ordered to prepare his provision of boiled *juār* for the journey. He arrived at Hinglāj, but could not find the Devi there. It is said that she took the shape of a fly, and so remained on the ball of ashes which Siva held in his hand. For twelve years he searched for her, but in vain, when, in a paroxysm of rage, he dashed the ball to the ground, where it lay broken in eighty-four pieces. These eighty-four parts of the ball became the hills known as 'Chandra-Kups.' Chandra-Kup is explained to mean 'Chandar' or 'Chandra,' the moon (on the head of Siva) and 'Kup,' anger, from this circumstance." These "Kups" are found on hills of extremely light-coloured earth rising abruptly from the plain. The hills are from 200 to 400 feet in elevation, and are conical in form, with flattened and discoloured tops, and somewhat precipitous sides, streaked with what would appear to be water-channels. They all have at the base numerous fissures and cavities, which reach far into their interior. These mud-volcano hills are also found in the neighbouring province of Makrān. Those in the Las territory are said to be only seven in number, and are not all situate near one another; one of them lies close to the great Hāra range, and three others are among the mountains.

Captain Hart, who visited these mud-geysers nearly forty years ago, thus describes what he saw of them:—"On ascending to the summit of the highest of these hills, I observed a basin of liquid mud about one hundred paces in circumference, occupying its entire crest. Near the southern edge, at intervals of a quarter of a minute, a few small bubbles appeared on the surface. That part of the mass was then gently heaved up, and a jet of liquid mud, about a foot in diameter, rose to that height, accompanied by a slight bubbling noise. Another heave followed, and three jets rose, but the third time only two. They were not of magnitude sufficient to disturb the whole surface, the mud of which, at a distance from the irruption, was of a thicker consistency than where it took place. The pathway round the edge was slippery and unsafe, from its being quite saturated with moisture, which gives the top a dark-coloured appearance. On the southern side a channel a few feet in breadth was quite wet from the irruption having recently flowed down it. The entire coating of the hill appeared to be composed of this mud, baked by the sun to hardness. No stones are to be found on it, but near the base I picked up a few pieces of quartz. Crossing the ridge which connects this hill with the least elevated of the three, I climbed up its rather steep side. In height or compass it is not half the magnitude of its neighbour, and its basin, which is full of the same liquid mud, cannot be more than twenty-five paces in diameter. The edge is narrow and broken, and one jet only rose on its surface, but not more than an inch in height or breadth; but a very small portion of the mass was disturbed by its action, and although the plain below bore evident marks of having been once deluged at a short distance with its stream, no irruption had apparently taken place for some years. At times the surface of this pool sinks almost to the level of the plain; at others it rises so as to overflow its basin; but generally it remains in the quiescent state in which I saw it. Two years previous it was many feet below the edge of the crest. On my way to the third hill, I passed over a flat of a few hundred yards which divides it from the other two. The sides are much more furrowed with fissures than theirs are, although their depth is less, and its crest is more extended and irregular. The ascent is very gentle, and its height about 200 feet. On reaching the summit, a large circular cavity some fifty yards in diameter is seen, in which are two distinct pools of unequal size, divided by a mound of earth, one containing liquid mud and the other clear water. The surface of the former was slightly agitated by about a dozen small jets, which bubbled up at intervals, but in the latter one only was occasionally discernible. A space of a few yards extended on three sides from the outer crust to the edge of the cavity, which was about 50 feet above the level of the pools. Their sides are scarped and uneven. On descending the northern face I remarked a small stream of clear water flowing from one of the fissures into the plain, which had evidently only been running a few hours. The mud and water of all the pools are *salt*. By the Hindus these 'Kups' are looked upon as the habitation of a deity, but the Muhammadans state that they are affected by the tide (the sea is not more than a mile distant from the large one); but this I had reason to doubt, as of the many persons I questioned who had visited them at all times, not one remembered to have seen the pools quiescent, although several had been on the large hill when the mud was trickling over the side of the basin. In order to ascertain this fact I placed several dry clods of earth in the bed of the channel on a Saturday, as I expected to return by the same route the following week. Nine days after this I again visited the 'Chandar Kups.' The appearance of the one which had fallen in was the same in the muddy pool, but that of water, instead of being *clear* as before, was quite discoloured. The stream also had ceased flowing for some time, as the plain bore no marks of moisture. On reaching the summit of the large one it was very evident that an irruption had taken place the day before (Monday), for the channel on the western side was quite filled with slime, which had oozed down the side of the hill, and had run some thirty yards into the plain below. The dry clods I had placed when there before were covered, and it was not safe to cross where the mud had found an issue, whereas my whole party had, when with me, walked round the edge of the basin. The jets rose as usual. So tenacious is the mud of this one, that even cocoa-nuts, which the Hindus threw on it, do not sink, but in the others it is more liquid. No alteration had taken place in the appearance of the small 'Kups.'"

Ruins and Antiquities.—Among the ruins and antiquities of the Las Province, an ancient excavated city, about nine miles north of the town of Bēla, known as "Shahr Roghan," requires some notice. It was visited by Carless, who gives the following account of it:—"About nine miles to the northward of Bēla a range of low hills sweeps in a semicircle from one side of the valley to the other, and forms its head. The Purāli river issues from a deep ravine on the western side, and is about 200 yards broad. It is bounded on one side by steep cliffs, 40 or 50 feet high, on the summit of which there is an ancient burying-ground, and the water runs bubbling along it in two or three small rivulets among heaps of stones and patches of tamarisk jungle. Having crossed the stream we pursued our way up its bed amongst the bushes, until we gained the narrow ravine through which it flows, and then, turning into one of the lateral branches, entered Shahr Roghan. The scene was singular. On either side of a wild, broken ravine the rocks rise perpendicularly to the height of 400 or 500 feet, and are excavated as far as can be seen in some places where there is footing to ascend up to the summit. These excavations are most numerous along the lower part of the hills, and form distinct houses, most of which are uninjured by time. They consist in general of a room 15 feet square, forming a kind of open verandah, with an interior chamber of the same dimensions, to which admittance is gained by a door. There are niches for lamps in many, and a place built up and covered in, apparently to hold grain. Most of them had once been plastered with clay, and in a few, where the form of the rock allowed of its being done, the interior apartment is lighted by small windows. The houses at the summits of the cliffs are now inaccessible, from the narrow, precipitous paths by which they were approached having been worn away, and those at the base appear to have been occupied by the poorer class of inhabitants, for many of them are merely irregular shaped holes with a rudely constructed door. The rock in which these excavations have been made is what I believe is called by geologists a conglomerate, being composed of a mass of rounded stones of almost every variety of rock, imbedded in hard clay. It contains a large quantity of salt (natron, I think), which is seen in a thin film on the walls of all the chambers and at two or three spots in the upper part of the ravine where water drops from the overhanging crags. It would be singular if such a place as Shahr Roghan existed among a people so superstitious as the Lumris without a legend of some kind being attached to it, and they accordingly relate the following story:—In the reign of Solomon this excavated city was governed by a king celebrated all over the East for his wisdom and the great beauty of his only daughter, Badal Jumāl. She was beloved by seven young men, who, from the great friendship existing among them, were called, by way of distinction, the seven friends; but they perished one after the other in defending the object of their admiration from the designs of half a dozen demons, who, attracted by her surpassing beauty, made repeated attempts to carry her off. At this interesting period of her history, Saif-ul-Malik, son of the King of Egypt, arrived at Shahr Roghan, who, being the handsomest man of his time, and as brave as he was handsome, had been despatched by his father on his travels, in the hope that by the way he might conquer a few kingdoms for himself. The princess, as a matter of course, fell in love with him. The demon-lovers were in despair, and made frantic efforts to carry her off at her devotions, but they were all slain in the attempt by the prince. The father of the fair princess rewarded him for his gallantry with the hand of his daughter, and the happy couple lived to reign for many years in peace and security over the excavated city.—A short distance above the entrance of the city, the broken, precipitous ravine in which it is situate decreases in width to 10 or 12 yards, and forms a deep natural channel in the rock. For about half a mile the cliffs are excavated on both sides to a considerable height, and, taking the remains of houses into account, I think there cannot be less altogether than 1500. In one place a row of seven in a very good state of preservation was pointed out by the guides as the residence of the seven friends, and further on we came to the grandest of all, the palace of

Badal Jumāl. At this part the hill, by the abrupt turning of the ravine, juts out in a narrow point, and towards the extremity forms a natural wall of rock about 300 feet high and 20 feet thick. Halfway it had been cut through and a chamber constructed about 20 feet square, with the two opposite sides open. It is entered by a passage leading through a mass of rock, partly overhanging the ravine, and on the other side of the apartment two doors give admittance to two spacious rooms. The whole had once been plastered over, and from its situation must have formed a safe and commodious retreat. At the summit of the hill near it there is another building, which my attendants said was the mosque where the princess was rescued by Saif-ul-Malik when the demons attempted to carry her off. Having seen everything worthy of notice in this trogloditic city, we quitted it and returned to Bēla."

Temple of Hinglāj.—Another celebrated place in the Las territory, and which, as a sacred spot, is much visited by natives from all parts of India, is the Hindu temple of Hinglāj, seated on the Hāra range of mountains, and near the Aghor (or Hingol) river, distant about two days' march from the small seaport of Ormāra, and over 150 miles from the town of Karāchi. Its position is somewhat romantic, and is described by Hart, who visited the place, as being situate in a narrow gorge, with mountains on either side rising perpendicularly to nearly 1000 feet in height. The temple is a low mud edifice built at one end of a natural cave of small dimensions, and contains merely a tomb-shaped stone, called the goddess Māta, which is the object of idolatrous adoration. It is noted as a place of pilgrimage in consequence of its being one of the fifty-one *pitas*, or spots, on which the dissevered limbs of Sati, or Darga, were scattered. But its sanctity does not appear to be confined alone to the

Hindus, for Masson states that it is revered also by the Musalmāns as a *ziārat*, or shrine, of Bibi-Nāni, that is, the Lady Nāni. He further remarks that it is possible they have preserved the ancient name NANAIA, that of the goddess of the old Persians and Bactrians, now so well known by coins. Close by is a large circular tank, or well, which is said by the natives to be unfathomable, and into this those of the pilgrims who can swim jump from an overhanging rock, proceeding through a subterranean passage to another part of the mountain, an act which they believe purifies them from their sins. There is also, says Carless, a species of divination practised by throwing a cocoa-nut forcibly into the water, and according as the bubbles rise in a larger or less quantity, the individual will be either happy or miserable. Goldsmid refers to the practice that evidently exists at Hinglāj of sacrificing animals to the goddess Kāli, and states that he observed a hollow in the hill smeared with the blood of those that had been so slaughtered.

Another place of sanctity, but far less so than Hinglāj, is the tomb of Shāh Bilāwal, a reputed Muhammadan saint, situate near a hamlet of the same name, in about lat. 25° 49′ N., and long. 67° 5′ E., and in close proximity to a mountain stream called the Virāb river. The shrine stands embosomed among the Pabb hills, in the eastern part of the Las district, and the water from a fine spring which flows through the narrow valley is said never to fail, and as the soil is comparatively speaking fertile, there is a fair amount of foliage in and around this spot. Close at hand also is a mosque with a cemetery attached to it, and the Balochis have an idea that peculiar blessings attend the souls of those who lie buried there.

Between the same Pabb hills and the Habb river, on the road from Karāchi to Sonmiāni, Masson noticed on a large fragment of rock certain symbolic characters in red and black colour on a white ground, as here shown :—

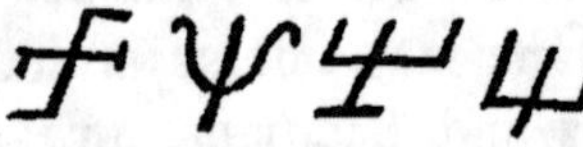

These he believed to be curious, and supposed them to be Budhist emblems. The first character on the left he considered was the *swastika,* or sanctified cross, but what the others referred to he was unable to tell, but thought they might possibly be literal combinations of mystical or secular import.

CHAPTER VI.

A GENERAL DESCRIPTION OF THE KALĀTI MAKRĀN PROVINCE.

UNDER the name of Makrān is included that vast and extensive, though as yet comparatively little known, region having Persia on its west, the Las State and a portion of the Jhalawān Province on its east, a part of Persia, Afghānistan, and the Kharān district on its north, and the Arabian Sea washing its entire southern border. In this description is included that part of Makrān forming a part of Persian Balochistan; but, as an account of this tract, comprising a large slice out of the western portion of the province has already been given in Chapter III., it only remains to speak of what is now known as "Kalāti Makrān," or that territory which is more or less under the rule of the Brahui Khān of Kalāt. The western boundary of Kalāti Makrān, as laid down by the mixed commission of 1872, has previously been minutely described at pages 57 to 59 (Chapter III.), and it has also been mentioned that the boundary thence up to the Kharān district is undefined, though the Washati (or Mach) mountains may no doubt be considered as the proper natural frontier. The extreme northern limit of Kalāti Makrān would appear to be in lat. 28° N., and long. 65° 27′ E., at a spot not less than 160 miles in direct distance from the sea-coast. The boundary line thence runs south, skirting the Jhalawān Province, and afterwards follows the course of the Hāra mountains and the Aghor river, in the Las State, down to the sea. In area Kalāti Makrān may be *roughly* estimated at 32,000 square miles, with a population of, say, not more than 110,000 souls, or a little over *three* persons to the square mile.

As to the origin of the word "Makrān" there seems to be some divergence of opinion, but the meaning given to it by St. John is no doubt the true one, and has, as he himself remarks, the authority of history to back it. He considers the word to be derived from "Mahi-Khorān," that is to say, *fish-eaters*, or *ichthyophagi*, such as the inhabitants undoubtedly were in Alexander's time, and are still. The term "Makrān" is evidently not in favour with the inhabitants themselves of the province so called, who nearly all differ as to the particular districts which should pass under this obnoxious appellation, and St. John states that the Brahui Balochis of Kalāt comprehend in Makrān all that country west of the Kharān desert; but this is repudiated by the people of Dizak and Panjgur, for whom Makrān means the districts between the water-parting and the sea, thus including Sarbāz, Kasrkand, and Bolida. The Greek name of the present province of Makrān was "Gedrosia;" it was also known to the ancients under the name of "Karmania Altera." This latter term still exists in the Persian province of "Kermān," which borders on Persian Balochistan.

In physical aspect the Makrān Province may be said to consist of alternate hill and valley. Barren and arid chains of hills, long and narrow, running parallel to the coast—that is to say, from east to west—cover much of the country. A part of the north-western border and a very large portion of the middle of this province are to this day marked on the maps as "unexplored," so that it is impossible to say what is really their physical aspect. They are believed, however, to contain the same kind of dry and barren ranges of hills, with intervening valleys which, from the absence of rivers, are little better than deserts. A portion of what is now known as the Baloch plateau covers much of western Makrān; this elevated tract has already been described in the first chapter of this work. On the coast the hills and cliffs form promontories and headlands dividing shallow bays. These promontories often run out into bold capes, such as those of Gwādar and Ormāra, being connected with the mainland only by narrow sandy isthmuses.

Those peculiar natural productions, mud-volcanoes, or *chandra-kups*, as they are locally called, are also found on several parts of the Makrān coast. They are similar to those which have already been mentioned as occurring near the sea-coast in Las. The largest of them rises to a height of quite 300 feet, and on the top is a small crater, about 20 yards in diameter, filled with liquid mud, which at times throws up jets and overflows its sides. It would appear, says Ross, that these craters have communication with the sea, as the state of the tides has some influence on the movements of the mud.* By the natives these volcanoes are called "*dariya cham*," signifying the "eye of the sea."

There are, so to speak, no rivers in the Province of Makrān, but, as in Las and other parts of Balochistan, simply torrents, which after a heavy rainfall fill rapidly with water and become for a time impassable, but for the greater part of the year show only dry beds. The most important stream in Makrān is the Dasht, known in the upper part of its course as the Nihing, and this, in conjunction with the Kēj river, drains the southern slopes of the Baloch plateau, falling, after a course of about 170 miles, into the sea at Gwattar Bay. It is this great want of rivers with a perennial water-flow that makes Makrān the dry, barren, and in

* Compare, however, Hart's account of those in Las, *ante* p. 144.

parts uninhabitable wilderness it is at present found to be. Another stream, or torrent—the Bhasul—has its rise in the Kolwah hills, in eastern Makrān, and falls into the sea in the Ormāra district. The Shadi-Khor (or river) is another which finds its way into the sea at Pasni; it is tidal for three miles only from its mouth, and is dry at low water. The bays and creeks on the coast are numerous, and afford tolerably safe harbours for native craft. These harbours, or ports, are found at Ormāra (which belongs to Las), at Kalamat, where is a large river creek, about 50 yards wide and always containing water, and at Gwādar and Jiuni; these two latter are said to have good anchorages in sheltered bays.

About 18 miles south of the coast from the Kalmatti creek lies the island of Astola, called by the Balochis "Habtala," but by the Hindus "Satadip." It is in length not more than three miles, and its southern side is bleak, and has the appearance of a barren rock of whitish sandstone. The shoals and inlets on the north side abound in turtle. There is, it is said, a safe channel, about eight miles broad, between the island and the mainland, with soundings of from five to eight fathoms. This place is much resorted to by pilgrims who visit Hinglāj; and Goldsmid mentions the following portion of a verse having reference to it, which he believes makes the island more venerated than the Hinglāj mountain:— "*Sat pahar Satadipmen; athon pahar Hinglāj*," that is—"Seven divisions of time in Satadip, the eighth in Hinglāj."

Climate.—The climate of Makrān, at least in the interior, has an unenviable notoriety for heat and unhealthiness, and is in this respect unlike Persia, where the coast climate is far inferior in salubrity to that inland. "The seasons in Makrān," says Pottinger, "are four in number, consisting of two wet, one hot, and one cold; this latter is very moderate, especially on the sea-coast. The wet seasons are in February or March, and in June, July, and a part of August; the former comes from the north-west, and only continues for a fortnight or three weeks, but the latter comprises all the fury of the south-west monsoon. The hot season begins in March and lasts till October (the south-west monsoon intervening), and in it occasionally the heats are so excessive as to prevent even the inhabitants from venturing abroad during the days called "*Khurma-paz*," or date-ripening, which take place in August. The months of November, December, January, and February are looked upon as the cold season; but even then it is much warmer than at any period of the year in the upper parts of Jhalawān and Sarawān. North-west winds prevail at this time, and are particularly strong towards the close of the cold weather; during the remaining eight months the hot winds blow continually inland, and, though they are seldom known to be fatal to life, they destroy every symptom of vegetation, and will, even after dusk, scorch the skin in a most painful manner. Makrān is considered by the people of the adjoining countries to be peculiarly unhealthy, except on the immediate coast, where the atmosphere is tempered by the sea breezes." This opinion of Pottinger's is borne out by the remarks of other European travellers who have visited this part of Balochistan; and Ross, speaking of the climate, states it to be like that of Lower Sindh, not receiving the rains of the south-west monsoon, and, again, not coming within the range of the Persian monsoon. The greatest rainfall, he considers, takes place during the *winter* months. Cook also, who had an opportunity of visiting the Mushki district in north-eastern Makrān, remarks that the climate of Makrān generally, but especially of the level tract south of the mountains, is very unhealthy. Fevers of a peculiarly bad type, and accompanied by great hepatic derangement, are rife, particularly at the season of the date-ripening in August.

The province of Kalāti Makrān is broken up into numerous districts or divisions, which it will perhaps be considered more convenient to distinguish under the terms "inland" and "coast." Thus the latter may be said to comprise the following, viz. :—(1) Ormāra, (2) Pasni, (3) Kolānch, (4) Gwādar, and (5) Jiuni. Of the former, such as are at present known are, (1) Kolwah, (2) Dasht, (3) Panjgur, (4) Kēj, (5) Tump, (6) Mand, and (7) Mushki; but there are, no doubt, others concerning which all details are at the present time wanting. The following tables give a list of these coast and inland districts, together with such other information regarding them as may be considered fairly reliable:—

COAST DISTRICTS.

District.	Tribes inhabiting.	Chief Towns and Villages.	Remarks.
1. Ormāra	Bizanjus Mēds (or fishermen)	Ormāra (about 1000 inhabitants)	Though in Makrān, this narrow strip of coast, extending from Ras Malān to the Kalamat Creek, belongs to the Jām of Las Bēla.
2. Pasn ...	Kalma ttis ...	Pasni	This small tract of coast has barely 500 inhabitants in all—extends from Kalamat Creek to Shemāl Bandar. Revenue paid by the chief to Naib of Kēj.
3. Kolānch	Puzh Bunds Zad-gāls (or Jat-gāls) Bizanjus Wardilis	Bān Nogbar Kalag	Situate between Pasni and Gwādar, and is about 30 miles long; a mountain range intersects this district. Is productive and populous: the number of inhabitants in all about 2000. Grain and cotton produced, and large herds and flocks reared; water only is needed for extensive cultivation.
4. Gwādar	Reganis Kalmattis Mehdizais Mēds	Gwādar, with about 4500 inhabitants	Extends easterly from Barambāb Khor to Cape Pishin in the west, a distance of 40 miles, and is 14 miles wide. Belongs to the Maskāt government. Much of the land is fit for cultivation, and there are many date-tree groves.
5. Jiuni ...	Shahzādeh Balochis Raises	Jiuni	A small district extending from Gwādar to Bahu. Is a subordinate division of the Dasht.

INLAND DISTRICTS.

District.	Tribes inhabiting.	Chief Towns and Villages.	Remarks.
1. Kolwah	Bizanjus Homarāris Mirwānis Kaudāis Nushirvānis Rakhshānis	Balor Rodah Khān Siggak Gushānak and Madag	An extensive valley south of Mushki, in eastern Makrān. Ross speaks of Kolwah as being out of Makrān. Large quantities of grain grown; neighbouring districts draw off it for supplies. Trade with Ormāra, to which it sends wool, *roghan*, hides, and bdellium (*gogar* gum), receiving thence dried fish.
2. Dasht ...	Kaudāis Rinds Hōts Buris Shahzādahs Bīrdis	None of any importance.	Extends from Gwattar Bay to near Kēj (about 100 miles), but breadth is inconsiderable. Is one of the most fertile districts in all Makrān, owing to alluvium brought down by the river (Dasht). Total number of inhabitants not accurately known. Cotton, barley, wheat, juār, and other grains, cultivated. Revenue about Rs.2000 per annum. This district is divided into a number of "reses," or sub-collectorates.
3. Panjgur	Gitchkis Nushirvānis	Panjgur Tasp Khoda Badān and Soridu	One of the richest and most fertile districts in Makrān. Is situate north-east of the Kēj division, and was once subordinate to it, but has now a governor of its own. Noted for its fine dates; grows corn and grapes in abundance; considerable trade in wool. Annual revenue from this district about Rs.20,000. The people of Panjgur are reported to be the most civilized throughout Makrān.
4. Kēj ...	Gitchkis Mullāis Raises Sanguris Dorzādehs Ketwaris Loris	Kēj, made up of several forts and villages	This can hardly be considered a single district, but rather a collection of such, comprising the Dasht, Kolānch, and others which have here been treated as separate districts.
5. Tump ...	Gitchkis Hōt	Tump and Nasirabad	A small district in western Makrān, north of the Dasht and east of Mand.
6. Mand ...	Rinds	Mand	Another small district, west of Tump; inhabited by Rinds, who profess to be independent of both Persia and the Khān of Kalāt.
7. Mushki ...	Mehmasanis Nushirvānis Mirwānis	Mushki Shahr Kalāt and Gajar	Is situate in the extreme east of Makrān, having Jhalawān on its east, and Kolwah to the south. But little is known of this division, and it seems even doubtful whether it ought to be considered as a part of Makrān or of Jhalawān.

Towns, Harbours, Forts, etc.—The principal towns and villages in this province are Kēj (the capital of Makrān), Gwādar, Ormāra, and Panjgur; all the others are merely insignificant villages and hamlets. Kēj, the so-called capital of Kalāti Makrān, in about lat. 26° N., and long. 62° 50′ E., is situate in a valley on what is known as the Kēj river, about 65 miles north-west from Pasni, and 80 from the port of Gwādar. It has communication also, by road or track, with Pishin, in Persian Balochistan, through the villages of Tump and Mand. Kēj is not a town of itself, but is made up of a cluster of forts and villages, some of the names of which are Miri, Kālatok, Killa-i-Nau, Gushtang, Turbat, and Absir. According to Pottinger, the fort is built on a high precipice on the left, or eastern, bank of the river, and is considered by the natives impregnable. The town is said to have been at one time (during the reign of Nasir Khān I.) very populous and flourishing, and to have contained 3000 houses. It had then an extensive trade with Kandahār, Kalāt, Shikārpur, and the seaport towns of Gwattar and Chāhbār, but this has long since fallen off, and the place has of late greatly declined in importance. An agent, or Naib, of the Khān of Kalāt is stationed here to collect the revenue, which, after deducting expenses, is not supposed to exceed Rs.10,000 annually. The Naib resides at Turbat, one of the villages making up the town of Kēj. Formerly, says Pottinger, the governor supported, as an officer of the Kalāt Government, 4000 or 5000 men, but "has not now-a-days" (1810) so many hundred Arabs in his pay.

Gwādar is a seaport in the district of the same name, in lat. 25° 8′ N., and long. 62° 10′ E. The town is situate on a sandy isthmus about three-quarters of a mile in width, at the foot of a promontory rising to a height of 400 feet, and hammer-shaped in configuration. The long flat strip of rocky land on the top, which shows the remains of some fortifications, is called the "*batel*," very probably from its fancied resemblance to a *batēlo*, or flat-bottomed boat. From the top of this hill there is a fine view of the surrounding country. The inhabitants, numbering between 4000 and 5000, consist of Arabs, Hindus, Khwājahs (known here as Lotahs), Mēds, Korwas, and several Baloch tribes, such as the Regānis, Kalmattis, and Mehdizais. The Hindu community are mostly Lohānos, with a few Bhatiyas among them. The slave population is tolerably large, and they follow generally the calling of fishermen. There is a fort in the centre of the town, which has a well-built tower of masonry, but the streets of the place are filthy, and the stench from putrid fish disgusting. Both the town and district, as previously mentioned, are in the possession of the Sultan of Maskāt, and how this came about is thus described by Ross :—"During the reign of the Imām Said-bin-Ahmad at Maskāt, his younger brother, Sultān, ambitious and restless, aimed at usurping his power. Being at first unsuccessful, Sultān was compelled to fly, and crossed the sea to Gwādar, recently annexed by Nāsir Khān I. From Gwādar he performed a journey to Kalāt, and besought the aid of Nasir in his undertakings. The Khān dismissed him with a present of the port of Gwādar, then an insignificant fishing village, a grant in which there will appear nothing extraordinary or unusual to those familiar with the usages of Oriental princes. Sultān resided some time at Gwādar, and eventually, in the year 1797, succeeded in usurping the sultanate of Maskāt. Thenceforward he and his successors retained their hold of Gwādar, which was fortified and improved. Subsequent efforts on the part of the Balochis to regain the village were unavailing."

A British resident is stationed at Gwādar; it is also a station of the Indo-European Telegraph Department. The revenue of this port would seem to be farmed out to a native contractor on a three years' lease. Goldsmid mentions it as amounting to no less than Rs.10,000 annually. The exports comprise wool, sent to Bombay and Maskāt; *ghi*, to Bombay, Karāchi, and Maskāt; and mats and mat-bags, to Bombay, Basreh, and Maskāt. Among the articles imported are metals, rice, sugar, and sugar-candy from Bombay; silk, indigo, *juār*, and *sarsaon* oil from Karāchi; silk, almonds, and perfumes from Maskāt; timber, cocoa-nuts, bamboos, and rice from Malabar; and dates from Basreh. With the exception of certain dues on the export of fish, mats, and mat-bags, the tax on imports and exports generally is said to be four per cent.

The small port and district of Ormāra, belonging to the Jām of Las, is situate to the west of the Hingol river, in about lat. 25° 12′ N., and long. 64° 45′ E. The place was given to a former Jām by the Kalāt ruler in return for services rendered to the latter by the Jām in Makrān. The port and town are seated under a lofty promontory, and the latter is inhabited chiefly by mēds, or fishermen, and a few Hindu and Khwājah traders. The bay of Ormāra is very shallow at low water; it is well sheltered on the north, south, and west, but is open to easterly gales; large boats can approach quite close to the town at high-water. The population is reckoned by Ross to number 1000 souls, and the amount of annual revenue sent to the Jām by the resident *naib*, or governor, is estimated at about Rs.6000, though Masson puts it down at but Rs.1000. Nothing is known of the quantity or value of the trade at this place, but it is believed to be small and insignificant, and to comprise mostly shipments of wool, fish, and fish-roes. The imports are rice, wheat, cocoa-nuts, sugar, sugar-candy, and metals from Bombay; rice, wheat, *juār*, oil, and cloth from Karāchi; rice, *gūr*, and nuts from Malabar; and dates from Maskāt. The rocky promontory of Ormāra is said to be about 650 feet in height, and both the air and water are described to be better on the top of this plateau than in the town below. There is a telegraph-station at Ormāra belonging to the Indo-European Telegraph Department; the distance by telegraph-wire from Karāchi is 205 miles exactly.

Panjgur is the chief town of the district of the same name, and is said to be about 100 miles north-east of Kēj, with which place it has communication by camel-track. It is not one town, but, like Kēj, is made up of a cluster of villages amid groves of date-trees. A governor of the Brahui Khān of Kalāt resides here, and Panjgur is in this respect on the same standing towards the Khān as Kēj. The trade of the place is good, and wood and seeds are sent to Gwādar, *viâ* Kēj, for export elsewhere. The number of inhabitants is not known, but the Gitchkis are numerous here, and the governorship of the district is generally held by a member of this tribe.

All other places in the Makrān Province are small and unimportant. Pasni, an insignificant seaport, but the chief place in the district of that name, is seated upon a few low sand-hills, distant 75 miles from Kēj, and having not more than 70 houses, with a population of 200 souls, principally Kalmattis. The houses are mostly constructed of mats held together by poles. There is a mud fort, and in Goldsmid's time two mud houses only in the place. The trade of this small port is very inconsiderable, and the people are wretchedly poor.

There are no roads, in the proper sense of the word, in Makrān, but simply tracks practicable for camels, which is, indeed, all that is needed, in the present state of the country. There is, however, one sign of modern civilization to be seen in both this province and in the Las State, and this is the land-line of the Indo-European Telegraph Department, which runs from Karāchi, in Sindh, to Jāshak (Jask), in Persian Balochistan, a distance in all of 697 miles by wire, having intermediate stations at Ormāra, Gwādar, and Chāhbār. From Jāshak it is placed in connection with the Persian port of Bushir by a submarine cable. The land-line portion runs from Karāchi to Sonmiāni, in Las, a distance of 49 miles, thence to Ormāra, 205 miles from Karāchi; from Ormāra it proceeds to Gwādar and Chāhbār (this latter place distant 277 miles from Ormāra), and thence on to Jāshak, 215 miles from Chāhbār. The line was constructed in 1863, and has, with few or no interruptions, been worked ever since.

Inhabitants.—The population of the large district of Kalāti Makrān are, as a rule, known under the name of Balochis, but, as Ross remarks, in comparison with their neighbours, the Brahui Balochis, the difference of their appearance, their language, and their character, is so marked as to carry conviction of a dissimilarity of origin. He further states that many of the most important tribes, or clans, of Makrān, while calling themselves Baloch, claim to be of Arâb extraction; and their appearance and habits seem to bear out the assertion. It is pretty certain that several families, originally of Arab descent, came to Makrān from Sindh, where they had in the first instance settled. The various tribes of Makrānis, differ much in physical appearance from one another. Those of Arab descent, both men and women, are generally speaking well-made and good-looking, but the fishing classes—the inferior tribes, in fact—present usually a squalid and disgusting appearance, and much of this may no doubt be attributed to their poor food and very low standard of morality. As a rule all classes of the people are prone to hospitality, which, indeed, is with them a prescribed duty. Ross, whose residence among them makes his opinion valuable, thus bears testimony to the character of those with whom he came in contact:—"Makrānis are faithful in performing a duty of trust which they may undertake for hire. Though not a bold and daring race, they are usually courageous in danger; and though not eager about running into peril, they are not over-careful of their persons. In their own internal conflicts they generally avoid close fighting, and the bloodshed is consequently inconsiderable. Though not powerfully built, the Makrāni is capable of enduring much fatigue and privation, and it is not an uncommon thing for a man to travel on foot at the rate of 50 miles and upwards a day, subsisting by the way on a few dry dates carried in a bag by his side." The same authority has divided the various tribes of Makrān into four classes: the first comprising those who have at times furnished the ruling chiefs of Makrān, the second including the great or powerful tribes, the third the tribes of respectability, and the fourth those of an inferior description. These four classes it has been thought desirable to tabulate, and to give such reliable information regarding each as is available. The different districts in which these several tribes are to be found have already been mentioned at page 156, *et seq.*:—

CLASS I.

Tribes.	Remarks.
1. Gitchki ...	Are of Sikh origin, and settled in the valley of Gitchki, in Makrān, early in the 17th century. Have two branches, one residing at Kēj and Tump, the other at Panjgur. Have intermarried with the Bolidas and Bizanjus. Frequent strife and contention has occurred between the Gitchkis and the Bolidas.
2. Bolida ...	Are said to be of Arab extraction, and take their name from the Bolida district, near Kēj. They were the ruling family in the 18th century, but were afterwards displaced by the Gitchki tribe.

CLASS II.

Tribes.	Remarks.
1. Nushirvāni ...	Claim to be of Persian descent. The head-quarters of this tribe are in Kharān ; they possess property in Kolwah and Panjgur, and are found also in Mushki.
2. Bizanju ...	Settlements of this tribe are to be found at Kolānch and in other parts of Makrān, as also at Ormāra, Kolwah, etc.
3. Mirwāni (or Mirwāri)	Are settled in Kolwah, Mushki, and Jau. The Brahuis are said to acknowledge the superiority of this tribe among themselves.
4. Hōt	This tribe is the most numerous in all Makrān, and is held in high consideration. They reside in the Tump and Dasht districts, and have many sub-divisions. As a rule they are exempt from all taxation by the State.
5. Rind	This tribe is a branch of that residing in Kachhi, and they state themselves to be of Arab descent. They are to be found at Mand, near Tump, in Western Makrān. They also are very numerously sub-divided, and pay no tribute or dues of any kind. They are noted for their lawless propensities, and are a source of disquietude to their more peaceably disposed neighbours.

CLASS III.

Tribes.	Remarks.
1. Mullāi	A tribe of the Kēj district, not numerous, but respectable.
2. Kaudāi ...	Have two principal divisions, one residing in Kolwah and the other in the Dasht.
3. Zod-gal (or Jod-gal, perhaps more correctly Jad-gāl, or Jat-gāl).	Are settlers from Sindh, and reside at Kolānch in Kalāti Makrān, and at Bahu and Dashtiyāri, in Persian Makrān.
4. Shahzādah	An orderly and well-behaved tribe, originally Arabs, and settled in Sindh, whence they migrated to Makrān. They inhabit Jiuni and the Dasht, and are also found at Bahu, in Persian Balochistan. They are few in number.

CLASS III (*continued*).

Tribes.	Remarks.
5. Kalmatti ...	This is a tribe also found in Sindh, where they are known as Karmātis. They are said to have come originally from Halab, on the frontiers of Persia. They claim affinity with the Rinds, are few in number, and reside mostly in the Pasni district.
6. Ketwāri 7. Sanguri 8. Sujodi	Are said to be all of Brahui origin. The Ketwāris are settled at Kēj, but the Sanguris, an agricultural tribe, together with the Sujodis, are widely scattered over the province, both inland and on the coast.
9. Mehdizai	Are found at Gwādar, and take their name from a hill at that place.
10. Loguri (or Nohāni)	Came originally from Sindh. They inhabit Bahu, in Persian Makrān.
11. Wardili ...	Originally from Sindh, and were carpenters by trade. They are found in the Kolānch district.
12. Puzh ... ... 13. Bund	These tribes state themselves to be off-shoots of the great Rind tribe of Kachhi. They are found residing mostly in the Kolānch district.
14. Bīrdi ...	Originally Brahuis ; inhabit the Dasht and Bahu.
15. Shēhi ... 16. Kosagi 17. Zisht Khāni 18. Latti 19. Buri	These five tribes are found principally in the Bahu and Dashtiyāri districts of Persian Makrān.
20. Raise ...	This tribe is numerous and is widely dispersed. They are found at Kēj, and also on the sea-coast.

CLASS IV.

Tribes.	Remarks.
1. Korwah ...	Came to Gwādar originally from Jiuni, at which latter place they were in the position of slaves, or at least servants, to the Shahzādeh tribe. At Gwādar they are sea-faring people.
2. Mēd	Are fishermen and sailors, and are found at all places on the sea-coast. Both the Mēds and Korwahs have peculiar religious customs, and in character are superstitious and immoral.
3. Lundi ... ... 4. Lutti ... . 5. Behāri ... 6. Dorzādeh ... 7. Lori	These inferior tribes are found in various parts of Makrān following humble and menial employments, such as smiths, carpenters, tailors, tinkers, etc., etc.

The dress of the Makrāni male is a long tunic and *paijāmas*, or trousers, with a small red cap for the head when not travelling, otherwise a turban is used. This, with a *lungi*, or scarf, and sandals made from the *pish* plant, completes the attire. The dress of the women consists of a long loose gown reaching to the ground, and a *chadar*, or cloth for throwing over the head. The commonest description of ornaments in use are nose and ear rings, but others are also indulged in, according to the means of the wearer. As a rule the women are not particular in concealing their faces from strangers.

The food of the people of Makrān comprises bread made from the grain of the juār (*sorghum vulgare*), rice, dates, and salt fish. Meat is rarely eaten, as it is a luxury in which few can afford to indulge. Their habitations are mostly mat-huts, such as have already been described in treating of Baloch dwellings generally. There are but few permanent structures to be seen, and these only in the seaport towns and in and around forts. Their forms of address and salutation with each other are as long, formal, and tedious as those that have already been mentioned in the first part of this work as occurring in the northern parts of Balochistan (see page 41, *et seq.*).

Religion.—The Makrāni Baloch is in matters of religion a Suni Muhammadan of the Hanifite division, and is usually remarkably observant of the forms prescribed by his religion. Of the different *unorthodox* Musalmān sects in Makrān, such as the Zikris, Rafāis, and Khwājahs, mention has been made in Chapter II., but a sect of Muhammadan heretics, or "Kharējites," found among the Arab population of the towns of Gwādar and Chāhbār requires some brief notice. The sect—which is locally known as the "Biādhiah," indicating either spiritual purity, or having reference to the colour of their clothes—is thus described by Ross :—"One account of the origin of this sect is that they are descended from the survivors of a party who quarrelled first with the Khālifah Othman and afterwards with Ali also. By the latter they were all exterminated but three, or, as some say, seven persons, one of whom fled and reached Oman. The sect accordingly deny both Othman and Ali, and are consequently adverse to both Sunis and Shias, who on their part unite in despising them as 'Kharējites,' or heretics. Like the Shias, the Biādhiahs practise *takiyah*, that is, dissimulation in religious matters. They are free from bigotry, drink wine freely, and are more disposed for the society and friendship of Europeans than the generality of Muhammadans."

Language.—The Makrāni Balochki is the dialect, says Pierce, spoken by the people living in the eastern and southern parts of Balochistan. Its limits on the sea-coast are the Malān mountains on the east, and a line drawn about 50 miles west of Chāhbār on the west. Inland it is spoken generally over the large provinces of Kēj, Kolānch, and Kolwah, with the adjacent districts. The Makrāni Balochki, he further remarks, appears to be a dialect of Persian mixed up with a great many words of Indian origin, which have probably been introduced by the Jad-gāls. The Jad-gāls, or as they may perhaps be more properly called Jat-gāls, are a Sindhi tribe settled in Makrān, and occupying the Perso-Makrāni districts of Bahu and Dashtiyāri; their language is consequently believed to be a dialect of the Sindhi. Ross considers the Makrāni Balochki language to be a dialect or *patois* of the Persian, the points of difference being attributable, not so much to a *gradual* change and deterioration from the original tongue, as to the extensive admission of Arabic words and phrases into modern Persian, and the elegant finish and polish, which in the course of the last few centuries the latter language has received. He is of opinion, also, that the spoken-tongue changes by imperceptible gradations from Persia to the frontier of Las, commencing with the sonorous Persian and finishing up with the rough and harsh-toned Balochki dialect, but that this latter is evidently derived from the Persian of a past age, as in the Makrān Province words and expressions are in frequent use which have long been obsolete in Persia.

Productions.—Of the animal kingdom of Makrān, the domestic portion consists chiefly of camels, oxen, buffaloes, sheep, and goats. Camels are bred in large numbers along the coast between Gwādar and Jāshak (Jask), and are capable of enduring much fatigue. In the western districts a hardy species of pony is reared. The sheep are for the most part of the fat-tailed kind known as the *dumba.* Poultry are everywhere procurable. Among the wild animals common to this province are the hyena, bear, wolf, jackal, fox, hare, porcupine, hedgehog, and others. Ibex and wild sheep are found in the hilly portion of the country, and antelopes in the plains. Field-rats are exceedingly numerous and very destructive to the crops. On the whole, small game is not abundant, but varieties of the partridge are to be met with.

The vegetable productions of Makrān comprise wheat, barley, and *juār*, large quantities of which are raised in the Panjgur, Dasht, Kolānch, and Kolwah districts. The wheat harvest in Kēj takes place as early as February, but that of Kolwah, which stands higher, in the month of March, while in Panjgur, which is more elevated than either, and has a more genial climate, it is not gathered in till May. Cotton is also cultivated in several places, and is at times exported from Gwādar. Rice, mung (*phaseolus mungo*), and tobacco are grown, but in comparatively small quantities. The date is most extensively cultivated in several parts of the province, those of Panjgur being generally considered the finest throughout Makrān. To the culture of this important fruit the greatest attention seems to be paid in Makrān, as will be evident from the following description given of it by Pottinger:—"The trees, both male and female, generally begin to blossom about the end of February or early in March. The flower grows out of the stem between the topmost leaves or branches, and has much the appearance of a bunch of wheat-ears, except that it is larger and quite white. The male flower is sweet and palatable, but that of the female bitter and nauseous to the taste. As soon as the trees are completely in flower they are pruned of all exuberant branches, besides which it is often found advisable to remove a certain quantity of the blossoms from the female, otherwise the fruit will not come to the same perfection. When this has been done a stalk of the male flower is inserted into a small incision made in the core of the top of the female tree, and the dates gradually increase in size till the *khurma-paz*, or date-ripening, which is a term applied to a period of extremely hot weather, seldom exceeding three weeks, that occurs in August or September. Without this agency the female blossoms will form into the shape of dates but never ripen, and those of the male tree are of no other use, unless I may add that the Balochis eat them as bread, either in their green state or roasted. One tree of the latter sex is sufficient to fecundate many hundred females, as the minutest particle of farina will answer for that purpose, and I was even assured that the same portion might be removed in case of necessity from one to another with equal effect. When the *khurma-paz* is past, the dates are pulled and appropriated according to the views of the owner. Some are dried on mats in the sun in the state they come off the tree; the same method is pursued with others after extracting the stones, and they are then strung on small lines made of goats' hair. Those that are intended to be kept in a moist state are immediately packed into baskets made from the palm-leaf, and the abundance of saccharine matter that they contain preserves them from spoiling. There are numerous kinds of the tree and fruit, as the conjunction of any two varieties forms a third, distinguished by another name; yet a person, to be deemed well versed in the cultivation of dates, must be capable of pointing out and mentioning, on seeing each tree, the name and description of the fruit it bears. Those most esteemed in Balochistan are called Lur, Pappu, Mujwatti, and Shingaskand." Other fruits grown in the province are the mango, the *ber* (or jujube), a kind of apple, and melons of various sorts. Of the trees, those most frequently met with are the bābul, the tamarisk, and the camel-thorn bush. There is, however, a dwarf-palm, called by the Balochis "*pish*," and by the Arabs "*gudhaf*," supposed to be the *chamœrops Ritchiana*. It is a bush with fan-shaped leaves, and, according to Ross, peculiar to Makrān, growing luxuriantly among the hills. This tree is put to a great variety of uses, as from it not only houses and mats are made, but it furnishes also shoes, ropes, pipes, and drinking-cups. Tinder is obtained from its pith, and an edible stalk between its topmost leaves.

Of the *mineral* productions of Makrān nothing would appear to be known.

Trade.—The trade of Kalāti Makrān is very small and insignificant when the great area of the province is considered, and what there is of it is conducted mostly by Hindus and Khwājahs, who are pretty numerous on the coast. The principal roads, or rather tracts, on which the produce of the interior is conveyed to the sea-coast, and *vice versâ*, are those between Panjgur, Kēj, and Gwādar, between Kolwah and the port of Ormāra, between Bahu and Gwādar, Kolānch and Gwādar, and Dizak and Gwādar, and between Panjgur and Karāchi, *viâ* Las Bēla. The import and export trade from the ports of Gwādar and Ormāra has already been noticed in the description of those towns. The insecurity of both person and property experienced by merchants when travelling through the interior of Makrān is a great impediment to commerce, and trade cannot be expected to increase while this obstruction lasts. Were but safety guaranteed to caravans by a strong and energetic government—one that would make its strength felt throughout Balochistan—the encouragement it would give to both exports and imports would be something marvellous, as the export trade, especially of Makrān, is capable of very great expansion under a wise and strong rule.

The currency in circulation in Makrān consists of gold coins, mostly Venetians, called *putlis* in Western India, but which are here known as *sitarāmis* by the Hindus, and *surs* by the Balochis. Silver coins, such as dollars, rupees, and *paulas*, or four-anna pieces, are also in general use. The Indian *pie*, three of which go to a pice, is current, but not the pice. The weights in force, according to Ross, are *kiasses*, *krars*, and *mian;* but they vary very much in different districts. The value of the several coins in circulation is contained in the following table:—

32 pies (or gaz)	=	1 muhammadi (or zur).
6 muhammadis	=	1 rupee (or kildar).
11¾ ,,	=	1 rial (or dollar).
5½ rupees	=	8 sitarāmi (or sur).

At Gwādar one kiass weighs Rs. 17, or 3060 grains (Troy); this is within a small fraction of seven ounces avoirdupois. This weight differs, however, in the following places:—

Weights.	Gwādar.	Kēj.	Panjgur.	Pasni.	Chāhbār	Mand.	Kasr-kand.	Dizak.
1 Kiass ..	7 oz.	14 oz.	3½ oz.	$6\frac{5}{12}$ oz.	7⅓ oz.	2⅞ oz.	2⅓ oz.	2⅓ oz.
1 Maund (24 kiasses)	10½ lbs.	21 lbs.	5¼ lbs.	9⅝ lbs.	11 lbs.	4⅓ lbs.	3½ lbs.	3½ lbs.

Revenue and Administration.—It is almost impossible to state with any degree of accuracy what is the *probable* annual revenue derived by the Khān of Kalāt from that portion of the Makrān Province under his authority. The Panjgur and Kēj districts are those which seem to be more directly under his sway; but at times, when the Khān's rule is weak, the inhabitants, under their chiefs, not unfrequently throw off their allegiance, and pay no revenue until compelled to do so by force of arms. Ross states that the Khān's naib has the general supervision of the Kēj division, and is held responsible by the Khān for the proper collection of the revenue, while Panjgur is under a Gitchki chief. They, however, interfere but slightly with the administration of justice, etc., in the sub-districts, which are left to the control of the local chiefs, who exercise unlimited power within their respective limits.

Upon the system of taxation in force, Ross remarks that it is as bad as it can well be. The agriculturists bear the burden almost alone, and of these only the poorer, the rich and powerful being usually exempted. One-tenth of the produce of the fields and groves is the property of the State, added to which is a tax on inheritances. These, with the exception of occasional fines, are the only sources from which the State derives any revenue. Trade and manufactures escape free. The land-tax would, no doubt, Ross thinks, produce a considerable income, were it not that whole classes have been exempted by grants from its incidence, and these include the *wealthiest* of the people. In Kēj it is estimated that four-fifths of the land property is owned by Gitchkis, Sangurs, and others, who claim absolute immunity from all taxation. Under these circumstances the amount of income actually realized is ridiculously small compared with the produce of the country. From the Kēj Province, after payment of expenses, the balance sent to the

Khān's treasury seldom exceeds Rs. 10,000 annually, while from Panjgur it is believed to be not more than Rs. 20,000, and this from a province some 30,000 square miles in area. The seaport and district of Gwādar, being under Arab domination, yields nothing to the Kalāt Khān's treasury, and the same may be said of the port of Ormāra, which belongs to the Las State.

History and Antiquities.—As the history of the Makrān Province is, at least in modern times, much mixed up with that of the other districts making up Balochistan, it will be unnecessary to dwell minutely on those parts of it which will be considered in a separate chapter, when treating of the history of Balochistan itself. The history of its present race of inhabitants is traceable, indeed, to no distant period, and is at best involved in much doubt and conjecture; but, as Masson has justly observed, the voyage of Nearchus, the admiral of the great Alexander, has conferred an interest on the dreary shores of Las and Makrān which goes far to redeem them in the eyes of the historian; while the passage of the great conqueror himself through its arid, inhospitable wastes, with a European army, nearly 2,000 years ago, has of itself an interest which no lapse of time is calculated to either weaken or destroy. Whether Makrān in a by-gone age was a province independent in itself, or belonging to some other power, or whether broken up into a number of petty dependent or independent states, it is impossible to say, for no authentic information is available to judge of its condition at so distant a period of history. It is, indeed, well known that about the beginning of the eighth century, when an Arab force, under the command of Muhammad Kāsim Sakifi, invaded Sindh, at least part of Makrān became an Arab conquest, and that Arab colonies were from that date formed in the province; but how Arab rule prospered there, and whether the natives, as is the custom of Oriental peoples, frequently revolted when they saw the paramount power was weak and powerless to enforce its authority, are matters which can only be surmised. About the early part of the eleventh century it is known that Sultan Masāud, the son of the great Māhmud of Ghazni, reduced the province of Makrān, then, it would appear, a maritime appendage of Persia, among his other conquests; but what was subsequently done with this acquisition history does not record. From this time down to the early part of the seventeenth century, the history of Makrān is involved in total obscurity. At this latter period the province is presumed to have been governed by several rulers known as "Maliks," the Arabic term for prince or governor. It is at this time that the Bolida tribe are found occupying a prominent position, and they seem to have, in some way or other, dispossessed the Maliks of power, and to have reigned themselves as independent princes. The names of some of the chiefs of this family, says Ross, writing on this subject in 1868, are still familiar to the inhabitants, and old men may be met with whose fathers remembered the time when Shāh Bilar, who was the last to hold extensive authority, reigned at Kēj. It has been ascertained that Shāh Bilar was in power some time about A.D. 1729, and when Persia was in the grasp of its Afghān conquerors. Ten years later on, however, the authority of the Bolidas was subverted by another revolution, and by a family or tribe called the Gitchkis, who still hold high authority in various districts of Makrān, and who are, moreover, now closely allied to the Bolidas by marriage. These Gitchkis are the descendants of a Sikh chieftain, one Panna-Singh, of Lahore, who settled in a part of Balochistan, the Gitchki valley, in the Panjgur district, in the early part of the seventeenth century. It was in consequence of a blood-feud, most probably between this tribe and the Bolidas, that the latter were dispossessed of power, and were succeeded by Malik Dinar Gitchki, who became the chief of Kēj and its dependencies. Soon after Nādir Shāh ascended the throne of Persia, and in his foreign expeditions, Makrān, as well as other portions of Balochistan, which, no doubt, had previously been tributary states of Persia, were singled out for reconquest. Malik Dinar seems to have resisted, but to no purpose, as he was ultimately compelled to submit, and he was then permitted to keep the government of Kēj Makrān, holding it as a tributary to Persia. About the year 1736 the two sons of Abdula Khān, the ruler of Kalāt, Mohbat Khān and Eltarz Khān, presented themselves, says Ross, at the court of Nādir Shāh, where they were kindly received, and the former confirmed anew in the government of Balochistan.

From this date the history of Makrān becomes inseparably connected with that of the Kalāt State. Malik Dinar Gitchki, who was left by the Persians, as has been mentioned, Governor of Kēj and its dependencies in 1739, retained his authority for some years, but ultimately fell a victim to the stratagems of a Bolida chief, and, though resistance was made by his son, Shāh Omer, he was ultimately compelled to submit to the Kalāt ruler, then the great Nasir Khān I., who had superseded his brother, Mohbat Khān, and then sat on the throne of Kalāt. Thenceforward the Gitchki chief became a vassal of the Brahui Khān, on the condition that he would not be disturbed in his possessions on the payment of half his revenue to the Khān's Naib, who was appointed to reside at Kēj. The blood-feud between the rival tribes of the Bolidas and Gitchkis still continued, resulting in the death of Shāh Omer, who was slain in one of the encounters that took place between them. After Nasir Khān's death, in 1795, the Gitchkis threw off the yoke of Kalāt, but were in 1831 speedily reduced to obedience by his grandson, Mehrāb

Khān, and from this time down to 1872, when the Kēj district once more revolted, there were no serious outbreaks against the Khān's supremacy. From 1872 to the present time the Kēj district, which may be said to be only nominally governed for the Kalāt Khān by the Naib, Fakir Muhammad Bizanju, has sent little or no revenue to the Kalāt treasury; the fact being that, in the present state of anarchy and confusion into which Kalāti Balochistan is plunged, the governors of remote provinces either see no necessity for collecting revenue for their sovereign, or are really and truly unable to do so. Nor, without recourse to an armed force, which these distant feudatories can see pretty well is not likely in the present state of things to be sent against them, is it probable that any revenue will be collected till a stronger and better government is established, that shall compel all its subjects, whether near or distant, to pay their just dues to the State.

CHAPTER VII.

HISTORY OF BALOCHISTAN FROM THE EARLIEST PERIOD DOWN TO THE DEATH OF MIR MEHRĀB KHĀN OF KALĀT, IN 1839.

THE early history of the country of Balochistan, before the march of Alexander the Great through its two southernmost provinces, Las and Makrān, is involved in the greatest obscurity. It is presumed that Balochistan may very probably have been among the one hundred and twenty-seven provinces over which the great king Ahasuerus, as mentioned in the sacred writings, ruled, "from India even unto Ethiopia." Arrian's account of the Macedonian monarch's march from India, through the country of the Oritæ and the Gedrosii, clearly shows the former to have comprised the present district of Kolwah, with the tract adjacent to it on the west in the Makrān Province, and this has contributed in some degree to invest these poor and wretched places with no small interest and renown. Alexander is, by his historian, said to have left Pattala, in Sindh (presumed to be Tatta, on the Indus), some time either in the months of March or April, and to have proceeded in the direction of Bēla, crossing in his route the lower ranges of the Brahuik mountains. Thence he marched in the direction of Jau, in Makrān, forcing a very difficult pass some distance south-east of the ancient town of Gwajak, and here it was that the natives of the country had assembled in considerable numbers to oppose his progress. He is then supposed to have kept somewhat nearer the coast, traversing the present Kolwah district, where mention is made of the difficulty experienced in procuring water. The great conqueror's admiral, Nearchus, about the same time, under the direction of Alexander and for purposes principally of discovery, coasted along the shores of Balochistan, and his account of the natives he met with, and the difficulty he found in obtaining supplies, is as credible as if the voyage had been carried on under similar circumstances at the present day. The severest privations of fatigue, hunger, and thirst had to be endured by all, from the highest to the lowest, and both the fleet and army suffered extreme hardship, until the latter reached the fertile and cultivated valley on the western border of Gedrosia, the present Banpur; thence it passed into Karmania, now known as the Persian Province of Kermān. It would appear that another detachment of the Greek army marched from India to Persia by a higher route, through Arachosia and Drangiana, the modern Kandahār and Sistān districts. This was the force under Kraterus, which does not seem to have met with so many difficulties and obstructions as that immediately under Alexander's command in the country of Gedrosia (Makrān).

The tract occupied by the Oritæ, as mentioned by Arrian, would no doubt include the present district of Kolwah and the tract adjacent to it on the west. Sixty days after leaving the country of the Oritæ, Alexander is reported to have reached Pura, the capital city of the Gedrosii. This name, unchanged even at the present day, belongs to a town near Banpur, between Aibi and Kalagān, and about 500 miles west from the town of Bēla, in Las. From this expedition of Alexander's down to the commencement of the eighth century of the Christian era, nothing *certain* seems to be known of the history of any portion of Balochistan. It is surmised that it was at times intimately connected with the Persian empire, as a dependent province or provinces, though at other periods exercising, it is presumed, an independence of its own, divided possibly among a number of chiefs of greater or less power and influence. In A.D. 711, or about a thousand years after Alexander's march through the country, the army sent by the Governor of Basreh, Hejāj, under the command of the celebrated Arab general, Muhammad Kāsim Sakifi, is supposed to have effected the subjugation of Makrān on its route; and from this date may no doubt be traced the colonization of much of the country by various tribes of Arabs. Between this period and the early part of the eleventh century little seems to be known of any part of Balochistan; but about A.D. 1030 it is recorded that Musāud, the son of Māhmud of Ghazni, extended his conquests up to Makrān, but did not penetrate into the mountainous portion of Balochistan. His inroad seems to have been confined almost entirely to the level districts, and without any attempt at a permanent retention of the country. Nor can this be wondered at, since neither the country nor its people were able to offer sufficient inducements for their conquest, though it would seem to be an ascertained fact that its wilds and fastnesses were often resorted to by defeated or disappointed competitors for the thrones of neighbouring States as places of temporary refuge.

After this there is another great gap in the history of Balochistan, and nothing at all definite is known till the period of the Brahui conquest, under the direction of one Kambar, a chief of the Mirwāri tribe, which is believed to have occurred towards the latter end of the seventeenth century. Before this period there is a tradition that a Muhammadan family, the Sehrais, ruled at Kalāt, and their burial-ground, says Masson, is still shown immediately south of the town walls of the capital of Balochistan. This reigning family seems to have been displaced by a Hindu caste, the Sewāhs, but when they began to wield supreme power in the country, and how long their rule lasted, history does not record. This much, however, is known, that the Sewāhs in their turn were ousted by the Brahui tribe, under the leader already mentioned, and Pottinger thus relates the story of the revolution :—" Kalāt had previously been governed by a Hindu dynasty for many centuries, and the last Rājāh was either named Sewāh, or that had always been the hereditary title assumed by the princes of his race on mounting the *gadi.* This last surmise seems to be the best founded, because the city of Kalāt is at this hour very frequently spoken of as Kalāti Sewāh, an appellation it is more likely to have derived from a line of governors than from one individual, unless, as was the case with Nasir Khān, he was distinguished for great talents and virtues. Sewāh himself resided principally at Kalāt, while his only son, Sangin, officiated in the capacity of a Naib, or lieutenant-governor, at Zehri, in Jhalawān. The administration of both these princes is allowed to have been very equitable, and to have afforded every possible encouragement to merchants or other sojourners in their territories. Sewāh was at length obliged to invite to his aid the mountain shepherds with their leader, against the encroachments of a horde of depredators from the western parts of Multan, Shikārpur, and Upper Sindh, who, headed by an Afghān chief, with a few of his followers and a Rind Baloch tribe called the Mazāris, still famous for its robberies, infested the whole country, and had even threatened to attack the seat of government, which was then nothing better than a straggling village. The chief who obeyed the summons was Kambar; his ancestors were believed to have been originally Abyssinians, and he was considered to be the lineal descendant of a famous *pir*, or saint, who had worked many miracles in his time. This gave Kambar and his adherents a weight and respectability amongst their countrymen which would have been due neither to the numbers of the latter nor to the hereditary possession of the former, whose paternal property was very trifling indeed, and lay in the district of Ṗanjgur, in Makrān. On their first ascending the lofty mountains of Jhalawān and Sarawān, these auxiliaries were allowed by Sewāh a very small pittance, on which they could scarcely support life; but in a few years, having either extirpated or quelled the robbers against whom they had been called in, and finding themselves and their adherents the only military tribe in the country, and consequently masters of it, Kambar formally deposed the Rājāh, and, assuming the government himself, forced numbers of the Hindus to become Musalmāns, and, under the cloak of religious zeal, put others to death. Sewāh, the Rājāh, with a trifling portion of the population, fled towards Zehri, where his son Sangin was still in power; but their new enemies daily acquired fresh strength by the enrolment of other tribes under their banners, and at length succeeded in driving them from that retreat, whence they repaired to the cities of Shikārpur, Bakhar, and Multan, and obtained an asylum among the inhabitants there, who were principally of their own creed. Sewāh is said to have died during the latter part of this rebellion, and his son Sangin, being made a prisoner, abjured his faith and embraced Islamism, which example was adopted by a good number of his followers, who still retain evidence of their former religion in the name of their tribe, that of Guruwāni."

On the accession of Kambar to supreme power, which it was decided by the tribes should be hereditary, two counsellors, whose dignities also were hereditary, taken from the Raisāni and Zēhri tribes, were appointed Sardārs, the one of Sarawān and the other of Jhalawān. It was arranged, says Masson, that these two Sardārs, on all occasions of *darbār*, or council, were to sit, the Sardār of Sarawān to the right, and the Sardār of Jhalawān to the left, of the Khān. Matters of public interest, or which concerned the welfare of the Brahui community, were first to be submitted to the consideration of the Sardār of Sarawān, who had also a priority in the delivery of his opinion. In the second instance the Sardār of Jhalawān was to be consulted. Nothing of importance was to be undertaken without the concurrence of these two Sardārs, who, possessing an influence amongst their tribes independent of the Khān, could at pleasure withhold their support. This system of rule, whether suggested by the notion of promoting a union between the Khān and his tribes, or of effectually counteracting any attempt on his part to assume despotic authority, placed the head of the government in too dependent a state, and subject to the caprices of chiefs, often, it may be presumed, restless and contrary.* The Khān had besides, says the same authority above quoted, a special adviser, or *vazir*, whose office was alike made hereditary, and this minister was selected from the Dehwar, or Tājik, population, thus showing a desire to conciliate that class of his subjects from whom revenue was to be principally derived. The resources of the Khān must have been very scanty, for he derived then, as now, *no revenue* from the tribes, whilst the provinces of Kachh Gandāva and Dājil to the east, and of Panjgur, Kēj, etc., to the west, were either under other authority or independent. The scanty revenues of Kalāt and of the villages of Sarawān and Jhalawān must have furnished him with the means of keeping his court, paying his troops, etc.

To Kambar succeeded his son, Sambar, of whose reign

* As events have since shown, not *presumed* merely; they are now well known to be but too often unruly, disobedient, and even in open rebellion against their sovereign.

nothing appears to be known, and he was followed in the Khānship by his son, Muhammad Khān, of whose doings history is also equally silent. From all oral accounts of these rulers it is believed that, contrary to the policy of their ancestor, Kambar, they gradually laid aside their enmity to their Hindu subjects, and persuaded many of them to reside and trade within their territories. They are also credited with the plan of incorporating the wandering Brahuis into tribes, granting them tracts of land free from all dues to the State, but requiring them to furnish certain quotas of troops when the exigencies of the reigning sovereign might need their aid.

The fourth ruler in descent from Kambar was Abdula Khān, an enterprising chieftain, whose lawless exploits and marauding excursions still form a stirring theme for the wandering minstrels of Balochistan, one to which the Brahui still loves to listen. He is believed to have succeeded to the Khānship about the commencement of the eighteenth century, but, at all events, he was the ruler of Kalāt some time before the celebrated Nādir Shāh of Persia invaded India in 1739. Abdula Khān, who was a brave and ambitious man, had about this time occupied himself in subjugating the large province of Kachh Gandāva, then held by a number of petty chiefs, the majority of whom paid tribute to the Kalhora princes of Sindh. This tract of country was so utterly laid waste by the Brahui leader that its *naffas*, or vital principle, is said by the Brahuis themselves to have become extinct. He also made marauding excursions to Kēj and Panjgur, in the Makrān Province. Nādir Shāh, when at Kandahār, is reported to have sent a portion of his forces under experienced commanders to effect the reduction of Balochistan, and this seems to have been attended with success, since the two sons of Abdula Khān were forwarded to the Persian monarch as hostages for their father's good behaviour, Abdula Khān being confirmed by Nādir in the government of the Kalāti kingdom. In another inroad made by this ruler into Kachh Gandāva, he, with but 1500 men, ventured to attack a large Sindhi force of 8000 men at a place between Dādar and Mittri, in that district, and was there slain with 300 of his followers.

His son, Mohbat Khān, one of the hostages in the camp of Nādir Shāh, having received the usual *khilat*, on honorary dress, from that monarch, at once proceeded to Kalāt and assumed the government of Balochistan. He seems to have been very different in character from his father, being both tyrannical and licentious, and holding the Hindu portion of his subjects in such utter detestation that he did everything possible to prevent their remaining in his dominions. It was during this prince's reign that the invasion of India by Nādir Shāh occurred (A.D. 1739), and, as a necessary consequence, the whole of the provinces west of the river Indus were annexed to the Persian Empire by the treaty which followed the submission of the Indian monarch, Muhammad Shāh. Nādir, according to Masson, also appears to have ceded Kachh Gandāva to the Baloch ruler as an equivalent or atonement for the blood of his slaughtered father, Abdula Khān; but it is thought that the services rendered by Mohbat Khān to the Persian King by engaging in hostilities with the Ghiljis, the inveterate enemies of the latter, had more to do with this cession than anything else.

After Nādir's death in 1747, Mohbat Khān made an incursion towards Kandahār, but the active successor to the Persian throne, Ahmad Shāh Durāni, soon revenged this insult by invading the Baloch province of Sarawān and taking away with him the two brothers of the Kalāt ruler, Eltarz Khān and Nāsir Khān, as sureties for his future good behaviour. The tyrannical conduct of Mohbat Khān had incensed the chiefs of the country, and the Sardār of Sarawān put himself in communication with both Nasir and Ahmad Shāh Durāni, the latter of whom summoned Mohbat to his capital, and kept him captive till his death; his brother, Nasir Khān, being sent to Kalāt to rule in his stead.

Pottinger, however, gives quite another version of this change of sovereigns by stating that Nāsir Khān was sent to Kalāt by Nādir Shāh with the express object of deposing his brother Mohbat, in consequence of the ill-government of the latter. Nasir Khān is then said to have expostulated with his brother, but this proving of no effect, he next despatched him with his dagger, the guards not making the slightest opposition, but declaring the murderer to be their chief, who, amid universal joy and rejoicing, assumed the reins of government. After sending an account of this transaction to Nādir, then at Kandahār, he received back from him, in due course of time, a *firmān* nominating him "Beglerbeg" of all his Baloch possessions.

Whichever be the true account—though perhaps Masson's version, from his longer residence in the country and better knowledge of Balochistan, is likely to be the correct one—Nasir Khān at all events justified the choice of his subjects, and he soon began to initiate large and enlightened schemes of policy, such as no ruler either before or after him has ever done. He had had the misfortune, when a hostage at Kandahār, to kill *accidentally* his brother Eltarz Khān, from whom the Eltarzai families of Baghwāna and Kotri are descended; but on his accession to power he took the best steps to secure both the fidelity and esteem of his subjects. The great desire of this ruler seems to have been the firm union of the Baloch community, and with the view, says Masson, of engaging the hearty co-operation of his tribes, and to secure the recent acquisition of Kachh Gandāva, he divided its lands and revenues into four equal portions, making over two shares to the tribes of Sarawān and Jhalawān, assigning another to the Jat population of the country, and retaining the fourth to benefit his own revenue. A fifth portion occupied by the Rinds and Maghzis was not interfered with, grants to them having been made by Nādir Shāh. These two tribes, however, were included within the political system of the Brahuis—the Rinds by being attached to Sarawān, and the Maghzis by being united to Jhalawān. No arrangement could have been more popular, and it is worthy of observation that, while intended to provide against the recovery of the province by the Kalhora princes of Sindh, it was not only effectual, but has proved the means of exciting the tribes to a strenuous opposition to the measures adopted by the British political authorities.

Nāsir Khān, in order to foster trade in Balochistan, is said to have remitted many of the taxes imposed on merchandise by his brother, fixing them at a moderate rate. He was also extremely solicitous to induce Hindus to reside in his towns, and he revived an old grant formerly made by one of his predecessors, which empowered them to levy, for the maintenance of a Hindu temple and its priests at Kalāt, one quarter of a rupee on every camel-load of goods entering the bazar. He also recalled a colony of Bābis who had been expelled by his brother. It is to Nasir Khān also that may be attributed the planting of the numerous gardens in the valley close to the town of Kalāt; he stocked them with fruit-trees brought from Kābul and Persia, and offered rewards for the finest specimens of fruit, grain, etc.

In his warlike expeditions he was also fairly successful. Furnished by his chiefs with their respective quotas of troops, he got together a very large force, with which he penetrated into Makrān, annexing Kēj and Panjgur, with the intermediate districts, proceeding even as far west as the town of Kasrkand (now included in Persian Balochistan), and returning to Kalāt by a northern route through Dizak and Kharān. Though by treaty he had acknowledged himself to be a dependent of the Durāni monarch, he had nevertheless so ingratiated himself in Ahmad Shāh's good graces as to obtain from him the districts of Shāl (Quetta) and Mastung. He also strengthened his connection with the maritime province of Las, and managed to obtain possession of the port of Karāchi from the Kalhoras of Sindh. But in an evil hour he was induced, about the year 1758, on some pretext or other, to declare himself independent of his suzerain, Ahmad Shāh, who, highly provoked at his conduct, engaged his troops near Mastung and defeated Nasir Khān, who fled to Kalāt, where he had made the necessary preparations for a vigorous resistance. Negotiations, however, took place, ending in a treaty between the Durāni King and the Brahui Khān, in which it was mutually agreed that Nasir Khān should pay no tribute, but should furnish, when called upon, a contingent of troops, sending them at his own cost to the royal camp, he receiving a cash allowance equal to half their pay. The chief stipulation in this treaty was carried out in 1761–62, when the Khān was called upon with his troops to accompany Ahmad Shāh on his second expedition into Hindustan, and again in 1759, when a combination of Persian chiefs took place with the object of attacking the Afghān territory on the west. Twice in this latter campaign the judgment and bravery of Nasir Khān were conspicuous, and as a reward for his services Ahmad granted him the Harrand and Dājil district, as well as Shāl and Mastung, to hold in perpetual and entire sovereignty.

During the latter part of his reign Nasir Khān had to quell some disturbances in Balochistan fomented by his relative Bahram Khān, the grandson of Mohbat Khān, who sought an equal share of the government of the country with Nasir Khān. This question was decided by the sword, when Bahram Khān was defeated and had to return to Kābul. He did not again trouble the country during the reign of Nāsir, who died in June, 1795, after a long and prosperous reign of forty years.

His character, as drawn by Pottinger, is here given *in extenso*, and were but half of what is said of him true, his reign must be unanimously admitted to have been the Augustan age of Balochistan :—"If we contemplate the character of Nasir Khān, whether as a soldier, a statesman, or a prince, and call to mind the people among whom he was placed, we shall find in him a most extraordinary combination of all the virtues attached to those stations and duties. He began his career under the odium of having put his own brother to death, and yet such were the pangs he suffered when he had leisure to reflect on that act, that even his enemies pitied him, and his conduct throughout life proved that he believed it to be a duty incumbent upon him to sacrifice his brother in order to save his country.* He could not have been dazzled by the hopes of wealth, as he never lived in any better style than his attendants when in the field, and showed a total disregard to riches except as the means of rewarding merit and improving the condition of his subjects. He seldom made presents in money, and frequently said he had remarked that by doing so he encouraged idleness, but when any artizan brought him a specimen of his handiwork, he would order him ten or twelve times the value of it in cloth and other necessaries. As a statesman he reconciled to his authority in a few months an immense kingdom bestowed upon him by a cruel conqueror, and what proves his address was that the most *distant* districts were always equally alert in obeying his orders with those near at hand. His justice and equitable discharge of his duties as a prince were so con-

* As mentioned in this chapter, there is some doubt as to his having assassinated his brother. Masson in no way confirms this.

turbed that part of the Brahui Khān's dominions; and had induced thereby a sense of security to both person and property such as had never before been felt in that lawless borderland. He it was who demanded the restitution of the port of Karāchi from the Talpur Mirs, and was prepared, in case of refusal, to get it back by force of arms. The Mirs, evidently frightened at the menace of so energetic a man, offered at first simply to restore it, then to refund *three* years' revenue collected from it, and finally to give up *all* the revenue they had drawn from the place while under their control. The fact seems to have been, that an intended partition of Sindh by Mastapha Khān and the ruler of Bahāwalpur, Sādat Khān, had about that time been seriously considered, the treaty which had been concluded between these two chieftains providing, in the event ot success, that all the country west of the Indus should fall to the Brahui Khān of Kalāt, while Sādat Khān was to have that to the east of that stream.

But the tragic death of Mastapha Khān put an end to these schemes and the restitution of Karāchi to Kalāt never took place. Masson's account of this occurrence is interesting, and serves to illustrate in a striking degree the peculiarities of character so common among Orientals generally, but especially so among the Baloch race:—"Mastapha Khān and Rehim Khān, who, it should be noted, were half-brothers, were in Kachh Gandāva when news arrived from Kalāt of the death of Rehim Khān's mother. As customary with Muhammadans on the decease of their relatives, the bereaved son sat, as it is expressed, on the *gillam*, or carpet. Supposing, as a matter of course, that Mastapha Khān would be a visitor, Rehim Khān, to distinguish him, had, on the first day of sitting on the *gillam*, prepared an entertainment for him. Mastapha Khān did not appear, neither did he on the second or third day, which induced Rehim Khān to send a message. Mastapha Khān excused himself, but promised to attend on the morrow. Rehim Khān, persuaded that his brother would now become his guest, ordered a due repast to be provided. On the morrow, seated at a balcony of his house, he beheld Mastapha Khān quit his residence, which was contiguous, and mount a camel. Instead of taking the road to Rehim Khān's abode of grief, Mastapha Khān took one in the contrary direction. It became evident that he was gone on a hunting excursion, accompanied by four or five attendants. Rehim Khān, incensed at the neglect or premeditated insult of his brother, determined upon desperate and unlawful revenge. With fifty or sixty armed men he followed Mastapha Khān during the day, but at such a distance as not to be recognized by him, awaiting an opportunity to assail him. This did not present itself until evening, when Mastapha Khān, on his return homeward, alighted from his camel and seated himself on the ground. Rehim Khān, with his retinue, then appeared, and he fired a shot at his brother, which took effect. Mastapha Khān exclaimed, 'Ah, Rehim! do not destroy me from a distance; if thou art a man, close with me.' Rehim Khān rushed upon his brother, and after a violent struggle, both being on the ground, Mastapha Khān was despatched. Rehim Khān also was wounded. The corpse of Mastapha Khān was interred near Bāgh, and a *makbara* was erected over his remains a little to the north of the town. Although the resentment of Rehim Khān was the immediate cause of the assassination of Mastapha Khān, it is pretended by some that the rulers of Sindh, fearing his designs, had promised a considerable sum of money to an aunt of Rehim Khān, residing at Kotri, in case she should despatch Mastapha Khān, and that the nephew, at her instigation, committed the atrocious deed. Rehim Khān, indeed, immediately fled towards Sindh, and he received from its chiefs a sum of money, but whether the reward of perfidy, or the proceeds of a private sale of jewels and swords, must remain doubtful.

"Mastapha Khān had the character of an undaunted soldier. Of a commanding stature, his fine person and noble aspect were well fitted to ensure the respect of his rude countrymen, as his liberality and valour were calculated to win their esteem and admiration. He was a man of violence but of justice, and the innocent had nothing to fear from him. Powerful to chastise an enemy, he was prompt to reward a friend, and his generosity of sentiment and action had often converted to a friend a worthy enemy. He retained in his pay a body of 800 well-equipped Afghān horse, which, while it made him competent to carry any of his measures, also left him but little dependent on the tribes. Robbers he chastised with the utmost severity, and although his punishments were barbarous, as impalement, etc., he proved that it was possible to restrain the licentious habits of his subjects. It had ever been the custom in Kachh Gandāva, and in most Muhammadan countries, for a Hindu, in passing from one village to another, to put himself under the protection of a Musalmān, for which he presented a fee. Mastapha Khān, during his administration, abolished this system, punishing by fine the Hindu who paid a Muhammadan for protection, and by *death* the Muhammadan who accepted a protecting fee. In his progresses among the hill tribes he was wont to throw on the road rolls of cotton cloth. If on his return, or at any subsequent time, he found them *in situ*, he rejoiced, and would observe, 'I almost fancy that Mastapha Khān's authority is respected as it ought to be.' So fearful were the natives of the hills of exciting the attention of their terrible chieftain, that on seeing a roll of linen on the ground, they would run away from it, and pray that Mastapha Khān might never know that they had even seen it."

O

Such was the fate and character of a Brahui chief who, had he lived, might perhaps have greatly changed the destinies of the province of Sindh, or at least a part of it, by adding that portion westward of the Indus permanently to the dominions of the Khān of Kalāt.

After the murder of his brother, Rehim Khān fled, as has been mentioned, to Sindh, whence he returned with an armed force and took possession of the eastern districts of Harrand and Dājil. But he soon after met with his deserts, for, upon entering Kachh Gandāva, accompanied by a few followers, with the view, as it is thought, of gaining the western hills, he was met by the troops of Mastapha Khān's sister near Gandāva, overpowered, and slain. He was buried by the side of the brother he had assassinated. The then reigning prince of Kalāt, Māhmud Khān, seems to have taken but little notice of these proceedings, allowing matters to go on as they would. He was too indolent and irresolute to follow his father's vigorous footsteps, and at the latter end of his reign is said to have become devoted to wine, and to have spent the greater part of his time in the society of Sindhi dancing-girls. His death, about the year 1821, is commonly reported to have occurred from over-indulgence and intemperance, but it is also thought that he was carried off by poison, administered to him by one of his wives, the mother of his successor, Mehrāb Khān, who was disgusted at the predilection shown by her husband for the dancing-girls of Sindh.

Mehrāb Khān, the son of Māhmud Khān, showed at first some vigour in his administration. He caused his authority to be again recognized at Kēj, in Makrān, and remedied, for a time at least, other disorders in different parts of his kingdom. But he was soon troubled with the pretensions of Mohbat Khān's family, and the son of Bahram Khān, Ahmad Yār Khān, rose in arms against him. Three several times was this rebel defeated by Mehrāb Khān, and on two occasions the expenses he had actually incurred to carry on the rebellion, amounting in all to about Rs.12,000, were refunded to him by the Khān, a foolish and idiotic proceeding (though by some, perhaps, deemed a chivalrous act), since it simply induced Ahmad Yār Khān to try his fortune once more in another revolt. This he did by raising the standard of rebellion among the tribes of Sarawān; but he was again defeated, and this time made a prisoner and conducted to Kalāt, where, at the instance of one Dāud Muhammad Ghilji, a man high in favour with the Khān, he was assassinated, leaving his two sons, Shāh Nawāz and Fati Khān, in confinement at the same place.

It will here be necessary to give some account of this individual, Dāud Muhammad Ghilji, who had already obtained a great ascendancy for evil over Mehrāb Khān. He was of low extraction, and to keep himself secure in his master's favour, had found it necessary to sacrifice a good many of the more influential Brahui chiefs, who regarded him as an interloper, and, detesting his pride and insolence, desired his removal from power. At length a general combination was organized against Dāud Muhammad, and it was resolved to remove him by force of arms. The malcontents marched on to Kalāt with this intention, where they were joined even by some of those about the Khān, who, in this extremity, had to rely for the most part on his *khānazadehs*, or household slaves, of whom he possessed a large number. Another Khān had even been nominated by the insurgents, namely, the Arkhund Muhammad Sadik; and Mehrāb Khān, who was at the time in tents outside the citadel of Kalāt, was thus placed in a situation of no small danger. Negotiations were, however, set on foot by the merchants and others of Kalāt, by which Mehrāb Khān managed to enter the town about the same time that the Arkhund left it, and, once inside the citadel, a musketry fire was opened upon the insurgents, who had to retire to a distance. Disputes afterwards occurring among them, the confederacy was broken up, and the favourite Dāud Muhammad still remained in the ascendant. But the tribes had not yet given up all hope of procuring his dismissal. The above-mentioned pretender, the Arkhund Muhammad Sadik, visited the Kandahār chiefs for the purpose of selling his master, Mehrāb Khān; but he met with the treatment he so well deserved from one of them named Kohān Dil Khān, who, to quote Masson's own words, "inquired if he were not a *mūlla*, and, being answered affirmatively, asked why he wore a military Baloch cap, and why he suffered his hair to grow so profusely. Commenting upon this inconsistency he called for the barber, and ordered the Arkhund's head to be shaved, and then replaced his cap with a white muslin turban. The Arkhund was so mortified that he did not reappear in public life until his head was again covered with the honours of which the unnatural Durāni barber had deprived it. Kohan Dil Khān knew well how to treat such men."

It was during the reign of Mehrāb Khān that the provinces of Harrand and Dājil were lost to the Kalāt State through a course of treasonable intrigue said to have been carried on by one Saiyad Muhammad Sherif, who, although a subject of the Khān's, was employed in the interests of the British Government. Harrand and Dājil are situate in the present Jampur "taluka," in the Panjāb district of Dēra Ghāzi Khān, but at the time above mentioned (1830) they were annexed by Ranjit Singh, the Sikh prince, to his territory. During the two following years Mehrāb Khān was busy endeavouring to reduce several of the Baloch tribes and their chiefs to obedience. With the Minghal and Bizanju tribes of Jhalawān he was unsuccessful, but a force sent against some of the western tribes, under his brother, Mir Muhammad Azem Khān, was more fortunate, though the chief of Gwajak, on the extreme eastern border of Makrān, held out for a long time, and only saved his stronghold and followers by a twofold action of deception and impudence, such as would seem to be common among the Balochis. Hard-pressed for want of fuel, the besieged offered to surrender the place, but it was agreed that the beleaguered garrison should give an entertainment to the victors, and as large quantities of fuel, which was all they needed for further resistance, were for this purpose introduced into the fort, the former at once closed the gates and resumed the defensive. When again reduced to extremity, the leader of the besieged, Mohan Khān, produced a peremptory order from Kandahār to raise the siege, as he was a vassal of, and would be protected by, the Durānis; this the Khān's army seem to have done, and to have returned to Kalāt as quickly as possible, without accomplishing anything.

It was soon after this event that the two sons of Ahmad Yār Khān—that is, Shāh Nawāz and Fati Khān—escaped from confinement at Kalāt and immediately raised the standard of rebellion. Their cause was espoused by the Sarawān tribes, but Mir Azem Khān, the brother of Mehrāb Khān, met and defeated them, Shāh Nawāz Khān fleeing to Kandahār, and Fati Khān to Sindh. Following this, came the flight of Shāh Sujah-al-Mulkh, the ex-king of Kābul, who had been desirous of recovering his dominions; but, being defeated at Kandahār, arrived a fugitive at Kalāt, closely pursued by the Kandahār chief, Rehim Dil Khān, with more than 2000 men. The Kalāt Khān at once accorded to the fallen monarch that protection and hospitality for which his nation is proverbial.

It would seem to have been the misfortune of Mehrāb Khān to be surrounded in succession by men who merely sought to make a tool of him for carrying out their own selfish ends, and this was fully exemplified in the case of the favourite, Dāud Muhammad, and his rival, one Mūlla Muhammad Husain, who both, from the year 1833, began mutually to plot against each other. The latter was the son of the Vakil, Fati Muhammad, whom Dāud had, in the early part of Mehrāb Khān's reign, seen the necessity of sacrificing in order to maintain his own position. Latterly Dāud's influence had been so much on the decline, that to save his credit he thought it necessary to invite an invasion of his master's kingdom from Kandahār, but his correspondence with this object was intercepted, and his treasonable views stood revealed. From that moment Muhammad Husain determined to destroy his rival, and both men intrigued with the Khān for each other's removal; but the Khān, though ostensibly approving the design of each, would commit himself to neither. At length the wished-for opportunity occurred to Muhammad Husain, who, finding his enemy had retired to a chamber in the palace to perform certain ablutions before prayers, despatched him by two sword-cuts, and, as a natural consequence, at once occupied the post of chief minister which the murdered man had so long enjoyed. From this time may be dated the more serious misfortunes of Mehrāb Khān—misfortunes which in the end led to his own death, the sack of his capital, and the partition of his country.

It had been determined in 1838 by the Indian Government, in connection with the intended restoration of Shāh Sujah-al-Mulkh to the Afghān throne, that a British force should march from the sea-board through Sindh, and thence up one of the mountain passes to Kandahār, through the dominions of the Khān of Kalāt; and the first intercourse between the Khān and the Indian Government took place in the early part of that year, when a Lieut. Leech was instructed by Captain (afterwards Sir Alexander) Burnes, after the failure of the mission to Dost Muhammad Khān, to proceed from Kandahār to Shikārpur to lay in supplies, it is supposed, for the large force then entering upon the Afghān campaign. This officer in due time reached Quetta, and by *invitation*, says Masson, continued his journey to Kalāt. He appears to have been received with respect by the Khān, but a mutual dislike eventually sprang up between them, fomented, as it subsequently turned out, by the unprincipled and intriguing minister, Muhammad Husain. At all events, the British officer left Kalāt with anything but friendly feelings towards the Khān, who, on his part, was glad to witness the departure of his guest. It was soon after this that Mehrāb Khān was accused by Captain Burnes of confiscating the stores of grain which had been collected by Lieutenant Leech's agents in Kachh Gandāva for the British army—an unjust accusation, as it afterwards appeared, if the following explanation, given by Masson, be considered the true version of the matter :—"It seemed that Muhammad Azem Khān, the brother of Mehrāb Khān, was despatched to Kotri, in Kachhi, with a party of horse, to see that no impediments were thrown in the way of the march of the British troops, and to take care that none of the inhabitants committed themselves in quarrels with the soldiery or camp-followers. When there, Muhammad Àzem Khān, in need of money, and acting on his own counsel and authority, demanded a sum from a Hindu of the place, and on his refusal to comply, seized his property, amongst which was a parcel of grain. The Hindu pretended, whether truly or not, that he had purchased the grain for the English; his fellow-traders, as is usual with them when an act of tyranny is practised towards one of their body, closed their shops and ceased to transact business. A compromise was speedily effected, however, and Muhammad Azem Khān, receiving a consideration of Rs.400, the Hindu shops were reopened and business conducted as before. In this case the report, probably, of the British native agent at Kotri wonderfully exaggerated the affair, and the English officers to whom he made it were, perhaps, too eager to listen to any complaints against Mehrab Khān, and the consequences of an attempt at extortion by Muhammad Azem Khān from one of his own subjects were construed into an undisguised and wanton confiscation of the grain collected by British agents in Kachhi, which even Muhammad Azem, worthless as he was, never dreamt of." It is also said that when the Khān heard of this transaction, he severely reprimanded his brother on his unbecoming conduct. But this was not the sole charge brought against Mehrab Khān by the British politicals. Captain Burnes, when at Quetta with the English army, had proceeded, at Sir W. McNaughten's request, to Kalāt, to negotiate a treaty with Mehrāb Khān, with the view of removing ill impressions, and of keeping the communications through Kachhi safe and open. This was done in conformity with the envoy's wishes, and it was further settled that the Khān should proceed to Quetta, there to pay his respects to Shah Sujah-al-Mulkh; but there were two persons who saw plainly that this treaty, if carried into effect, would secure Mehrāb Khān's stability, whereas it was their object to bring about his ruin. These were Muhammad Husain and Saiyad Muhammad Sherif, the latter being in the pay of the British Government. They persuaded the Khān that the English were anxious to decoy him to Quetta for the purpose of making him a State prisoner, while to Captain Burnes they represented that their master had repented signing the treaty, and had commissioned a party to intercept him. Deceived by this intelligence, the envoy placed the treaty, together with a sum of Rs.2000, in the hands of Muhammad Sherif, who accompanied him; but this traitor arranged that some robbers should attack their baggage and abstract both the treaty and the money. This was carried out without any suspicion on the part of Captain Burnes, and the odium of this nefarious transaction was, as a natural consequence, assigned to the innocent Mehrāb Khān. This unfortunate prince heard of the robbery, and, to use Masson's own words, "set inquiries on foot, and particularly called his Naib, Rehimdād, located at Quetta, to account, as it happened within his jurisdiction. The Naib informed him that Saiyad Muhammad Sherif was the offender, and that his nephew and gardener were the leaders of the band, to whom he had paid as fee and reward the sum of Rs. 1400. The Khān, aware that the Saiyad was in the pay and interest of the British Government, did not deem it necessary to take further measures, regarding the matter as one which interested the Feringhis rather than himself, all the while ignorant that *he was suspected or accused* of it."

A third charge preferred against Mehrāb Khān, was that he *instigated* the opposition offered to the passage of British troops through the Bolān pass, and also the serious depredations committed on the baggage. In this instance, also, says Masson, the character of Mehrāb Khān stood the test of inquiry, for it proved that not only did he never promote or recommend such aggressions, but they, likewise, were in a great measure owing to the enmity of his own faithless subjects, and these, again, were the bribed and trusted agents of the British political authorities. The criminals in this case were Ghulam Khān and Khān Muhammad, brothers of Dāud Muhammad, the late Ghilji adviser of Mehrāb Khān, who had been assassinated by the prime minister, Mūlla Muhammad Husain. They had, with a view of avenging their brother's death, and in order at the same time to ruin Mehrāb Khān, offered their services to the British authorities, and these had, it seems, been eagerly accepted. It was these men who had set the Bangulzais, the Kurds, and other tribes adjacent to the Bolān pass in motion. Masson declares that Mehrab Khān had no *real* control over the Bolān pass, which was generally infested by Marris and Khākas, the latter not being even subjects of Kalāt, and that had the Khān to traverse the pass himself with an army, he would have been just as liable to petty plunder as Sir John Keane or any other general. He had been urged by the Kandahār Sardārs and some of his own chiefs to defend the pass against the advance of the British troops, but he adhered to his determination not to offer any obstacle to its march.

But there still remains a fourth charge against the Khān, that he had stored up large quantities of grain at Kalāt, had issued secret orders forbidding its sale, and had diverted all the grain into his own magazines, with the express object of destroying, or at least starving out, if possible, the British forces by want of supplies. Here again the explanation is forthcoming that this collection of grain had no reference whatever to the march of the British army, but that the Khān's Hindu agent, Diwān Bacha, had recommended it as a financial scheme, with a view of making a profit out of the drought, and that it had already been in operation for three years.

Now these are the principal charges made against the Khān of Kalāt, and the explanations here given are mainly taken from Masson, who was himself in the country shortly after the death of Mehrāb Khān and the capture of his capital. As a kind of last resource it seems to have been admitted, even at Kalāt, that a mission should be sent to the British envoy and minister to remove any misunderstanding that might have occurred; and here, again, the extreme imprudence of the Khān was shown by his permitting the selection of Mūlla Muhammad Husain as a proper representative of his interests. With this latter individual went Muhammad Sherif, the other traitor, and the two met the envoy at either Shikārpur or Bāgh. Mehrāb Khān was accused by Muhammad Husain of the most mischievous plots and intentions, and these accusations were credited by Captain Burnes. At the same time he led the British functionary to believe that he himself was an ardent friend of the English, and this, too, was readily credited, with the assurance that such service should not go unrequited. He was desired on his return to Kalāt to urge the Khān to abandon his evil course; but the first thing he did on his arrival there was—to quote Masson's narrative—to assure the Khān that the English were faithless, that their intentions were to send him to Calcutta, and that he had nothing to hope from them; that they had sought, by bland speeches and the lure of money, to secure *him*, but, God be praised! *his* devotion to the Khān was unalterable! He consoled the Khān by representing that the British were comparatively weak, that the amount of their real force was small, and that there was little to fear from them. Nor was this all. To cap his duplicity, and to make the Khān still more obnoxious to the English, he addressed a number of letters in Mehrāb Khān's name to different parties throughout the country, directing them to molest the English troops by every means in their power. As some of these letters, authenticated by the Khān's seal, which the intriguer had in his possession by virtue of his office, fell into the hands of the British (in accordance, doubtless, with Muhammad Husain's intentions), this circumstance more than ever convinced the British envoy and minister of the treachery of Mehrāb Khān, who really knew nothing whatever about them.

Such was the state of affairs when the English army, in 1839, passed through Kachh Gandāva and up the Bolān pass to Quetta. It was on the arrival of the force at Quetta that Captain Burnes, as previously mentioned, proceeded to Kalāt as envoy, to effect, if possible, a reconciliation with the Khān, selecting Saiyad Muhammad Sherif to accompany him. It is believed that a treaty was signed and sealed, by which, for a certain money payment made by the British, the Khān undertook to keep the road open from Shikārpur to Quetta. But all the entreaties of the envoy to induce Mehrāb Khān to pay his respects to Shāh Sujah were ineffectual, owing, no doubt, to the representations of Muhammad Husain, who declared that the journey would cost the Khān his liberty, if not his life.

From this time forth it was considered by the British authorities "that the conduct of Mehrāb Khān was so treacherous, hostile, and dangerous, as to require the exaction of retribution from that chieftain, and the execution of such arrangements as would establish future security in that quarter." An opportunity for carrying this out soon presented itself. Ghazni and Kābul had both been captured by the British army, and a brigade under Major-General Willshire was detached from it to assault Kalāt. It is said that the Khān did not think of making any preparations for defence till he heard of the advance of the troops from Quetta. He then appealed to the chiefs of the Baloch tribes for assistance, but a few only responded to the call. On the 5th of November, 1839, the English force arrived before Kalāt. It consisted of 1261 men and six horse-artillery guns. The garrison comprised mainly the inhabitants of the villages near Kalāt, but the greater part of them, says Masson, dropped from the walls and made off when the assault commenced. One of the gates was speedily knocked in by the fire of two of the horse-artillery guns, and the town and citadel immediately stormed, and Mehrāb Khān, with several of his chiefs, fell fighting, sword in hand, the loss of his troops exceeding

400. Of the rest, about 2000 men were made prisoners; the British loss was 31 killed and 107 wounded. In an upper apartment of the "Miri," or citadel, were found Mūlla Muhammad Husain, the Naib Rehimdād, and Arkhund Muhammad Sadik, together with some 30 others, who at once surrendered. It was only in the search for documents made by the political officers after the capture of Kalāt that the letters of Muhammad Husain to Mehrāb Khān were found under the pillow of the fallen prince, and these, by the disclosures there made, at once condemned the treacherous minister. He was immediately arrested and sent with the Naib Rehimdād, to the fortress of Bakhar, on the Indus, and this discovery was some testimony, at least, to the innocence of the deceased chief.

The Khān's personal property, says Masson, excepting cash and jewels, fell into the possession of the captors, and, to save them the trouble of collecting it, he had already packed it as if for removal. The Khān being reported rich in jewels, inquiries were made for them, and in a few days information was given which led to their discovery in the house of Mūlla Muhammad Husain; so it proved that the wily traitor had been sufficiently adroit to have them deposited there, of course intending to reserve them for his own benefit. Nor was this all; in the same house about 100 blank sheets of paper were found sealed and ready to be filled up at discretion. They explained the origin of the missives by which the tribes were inflamed and incited to action, the odium of which had been unjustly, as it is feared, ascribed to the Brāhui chief.

After the discoveries here made, which, to say the least, must be considered as greatly extenuating the guilt (if any) of Mehrāb Khān, it might be thought that an act of justice would have been done by admitting the claim of his eldest son, then a youth of about 14 years of age, to succeed him as ruler; but here another mistake was committed, for the political authorities raised to the throne, on the plea of legitimacy, Shāh Nawāz Khān, a descendant of Mohbat Khān, the elder branch of the family, at the same time utterly ignoring the claims of Mehrāb Khān's eldest son, afterwards Mir Nasir Khān II. The Indian Government subsequently found it necessary to revise everything that had been done in this matter by the British political officers, including the dismemberment of the country which took place on the accession of Shāh Nawāz Khān; but the circumstances which led to this wholesale reversal of arrangements which ought never, indeed, to have been even contemplated, much less carried out, will be fully considered in the following chapter.

CHAPTER VIII.

HISTORY OF BALOCHISTAN FROM THE ACCESSION OF MIR SHĀH NAWĀZ KHĀN DOWN TO THE YEAR 1876.

THE accession of Shāh Nawāz to the Khānship of Kalāt was at once taken advantage of by the British political authorities to introduce several new arrangements with reference to the kingdom of Balochistan. One of these was the dismemberment of the country, by which the districts of Mastung and Quetta, in the Sarawān Province, and the province of Kachh Gandāva, were made over to his Majesty Shāh Sujah-al-Mulkh. The Harrand and Dājil districts had already, in the lifetime of the late Khān, been quietly annexed to Sikh dominion by Ranjit Singh. The condition, therefore, of Balochistan generally, soon after the elevation of Shāh Nawāz Khān to the throne, was as follows: The son of Mehrāb Khān was a fugitive, and it was pretty well known that both he and the *Daroga* (chamberlain), Gul Muhammad, were the guests of Azad Khān, the chief of Kharān, and that they only awaited a suitable opportunity for disturbing the present state of things at Kalāt. Certain chiefs, who prior to Mehrāb Khān's death were either in revolt or had for years past been disaffected towards that ruler, were *now* the friends of Shāh Nawāz and of the

British; these were Isa Khān of Wadd, Kamāl Khān of Baghwāna, and Rashid Khān of Zēhri. An English political officer was appointed to reside at Kalāt, the first incumbent of this post being the afterwards unfortunate Lieutenant Loveday, who had previously been an assistant to Captain Bean, in political charge at Quetta. Muhammad Khān, chief of the Sherwāni tribe, had been appointed as governor (on a monthly salary of Rs.200) of the district of Mastung, recently given to the Kābul State, and the government of the Quetta district, under the British political officer there, was with Muhammad Ṣidik Khān. The Kachhi province was likewise entrusted, under Mr. Ross Bell, the political agent, to the traitor, Saiyad Muhammad Sherif, who had, conjointly with the unprincipled prime minister, Mūlla Muhammad Husain, done his best to ruin his late master, Mehrāb Khān. To this it must be added that the majority of the Balochis regarded the new order of things with aversion, and only awaited time and opportunity for putting the son of Mehrāb Khān on the throne of his fathers.

Such was the state of affairs in Balochistan, and it was evident that, with Mehrāb Khān's son at large and so many elements of discord already at work, a general insurrection throughout the country might occur at any moment. It was on this account the great object of Shāh Nawāz to secure, if possible, the person of this youth, and with this view he proceeded into the western districts to effect his capture; but secret intelligence of this design seems to have saved the exile from danger. It was not, however, long before the dreaded outbreak took place. The guard placed at the disposal of Lieutenant Loveday at Kalāt numbered some 60 *sipāhis* of one of the Shāh's regiments. Captain Bean, at Quetta, had requested the return of 25 of these, and they left for their destination, accompanied by Loveday's munshi, Ghulam Husain; but on reaching Mastung they were set upon and slaughtered by the Sarawān tribes, who at once raised the standard of revolt, and sent to the son of Mehrāb Khān to join them and thus countenance their proceedings. On this news reaching Kalāt, Shāh Nawāz called in his levies without delay, and took precautionary measures for the safety of the capital; while the insurgents, after destroying the detachment, had gone on to Quetta, which, it appears, had at that very time been almost denuded of troops by the order of the British envoy and minister. But in their intended attack on this place they were anticipated by the Khāka tribes of the neighbouring hills, who, believing the small force located there could make no resistance, had at once assaulted the town. They were, however, repulsed, and, as Quetta was speedily relieved by troops sent from Kandahār, the place was saved; the siege was raised and the rebels retreated, though in order, southwards; the son of Mehrāb, who had accompanied them, retiring to Mastung.

The Khān, who was at Kalāt, heard with delight of the rebels having raised the siege of Quetta, never expecting that they would march upon his capital and besiege him. Of the levies he had called in, only a few chiefs joined with their quotas of troops. They were nearly all Jhalawān men, while their opponents, the insurgents, were men of Sarawān. The walls of the town of Kalāt were just then in a bad state of repair, and, according to Masson, who was in the place at the time, there were, as regards ammunition, certainly sixty barrels of European gunpowder and a large quantity of lead, but *no bullets*, while the few cannon on the walls were very old and altogether unserviceable. In place of vents, says Masson, were apertures as large as the palm of one's hand, and the chambers were so honey-combed that it startled one to think how they would stand to be fired. Had there been even *one* serviceable gun in the place, the insurgent band could never have stayed in the valley. With provisions in case of a siege Kalāt was ill supplied. Shāh Nawāz had not more than 100 *kharwārs* (say about 75 tons) of grain, while Loveday had only a three months' supply for his own small military force and establishment. In addition to these drawbacks, plots and intrigues broke out among the several chiefs then in Kalāt, and these never-ending causes of dissension quite distracted the attention of the Khān from those measures which were imperatively called for to put the town into a proper defensive condition.

The rebel chiefs, on their side, had not been idle at Mastung. Fortunately for them they were not followed up in their retreat from Quetta by Captain Bean, and as the Sarawān tribes had again assembled at Mastung, it was determined to assault Kalāt without loss of time. In a few days the insurgents appeared before the town, and at once made an attack, which was, however, repulsed. In number they were estimated at from 1000 to 1200 men only, armed and unarmed — a mere rabble as it subsequently turned out. On the fifth day after their arrival the insurgents began another attack by escalade—evidently, as was afterwards proved, in collusion with a portion of the garrison—upon that part of the wall defended by the village levies and the Zehri Jataks; and it was soon discovered that about 50 of the enemy had got into the town, *assisted over the walls*, says Masson, by the *lungis* of those stationed to defend them. It was here that Loveday's *sipāhis*, by their steady firing, restored the fortune of the day, and the rebels once more retreated; otherwise Kalāt would soon have been captured by Mehrāb Khān's son. Masson further on remarks that it was proved that the enemy were *unprovided with ammunition*, and that the garrison lowered down supplies to them, while they (the besieged) themselves fired blank. After such wholesale defection as this it is not astonishing to find the defenders stating it was dangerous to continue the defence of the place, and that negotiations, the usual resource of the Balochis, had better be employed. Treachery, in short, was rampant both within and without the walls, and Shāh Nawāz seemed disposed to submit to his fate with that composure which became an Oriental. The British political officer at Kalāt, at one time boisterously elate, at others abjectly despondent, was evidently, from the character that has been drawn of him, altogether unsuited for his post, quite as much so, indeed, as Captain Bean at Quetta. Under such a state of things it is not surprising that negotiations did take place, at first by means of *vakils*, or representatives. They resulted in the production of an *ikrār-nāmeh*, or engagement, between the Sarawān and Jhalawān Sardārs, by which it was mutually agreed to invest the sovereignty of Kalāt in the son of Mehrāb Khān, who was henceforth to be called Mir Nasir Khān. Shāh Nawāz was to leave Kalāt within three days, and to have the districts of Baghwāna, Zidi, and Khozdār ceded to him, while the British political officer was, with his *sipāhis*, to be escorted in safety to Quetta. As no relief was expected from either Quetta or Shikārpur, Shāh Nawāz abdicated, resigning his authority to Mehrāb Khān's son in the rebel camp, and, after in vain urging Loveday to accompany him, he left the town. It was here that Loveday's troubles really began. Deserted by his guard and servants, his letters to Captain Bean at Quetta intercepted by the insurgents, he soon lost all freedom of action, and both he and Masson, the latter of whom has given an interesting account of this revolution with its attendant miseries, were conveyed to the citadel and there imprisoned for some time. They were both afterwards removed to Mastung, whence Masson was sent on to Quetta; but Loveday remained behind with his captors, going with them ultimately to Dādar, in Kachhi, where, in an engage ment which took place in December, 1840, between a British detachment, under Colonel Marshall, and the levies of Nasir Khān, some 4000 in number, the latter were routed, and, in the pursuit which took place, the unhappy officer was barbarously put to death, his headless body being found chained to a *kajāwa,* or camel seat. An English force, under General Nott, soon after entered Kalāt, but speedily returned to Kandahār, leaving Colonel Stacey, who had accompanied it, in political charge of the place. This officer was mainly instrumental in inducing Mehrāb Khān's son to come into Quetta about the month of July, 1841, and tender his allegiance and submission, upon which he was acknowledged by the British authorities, and by the King of Kābul, as Khān in his father's stead. Afterwards, on the 7th October of the same year, he was formally installed by Major (afterwards Sir James) Outram, then in political charge of both Sindh and Balochistan, in the presence of a number of British officers and many of the Baloch chiefs.

The treaty concluded between the new Khān and the Indian Government on this subject is dated 6th October, 1841, and runs as follows :—

"WHEREAS Mir Nasir Khān, son of Mehrāb Khān, deceased, having tendered his allegiance and submission, the British Government and his Majesty Shah Sujah-al-Mulkh recognize him, the said Nasir Khān, and his descendants, as Chief of the Principality of Kalāti-Nasir on the following terms :—

"ARTICLE I.—Mir Nasir Khān acknowledges himself and his descendants the vassals of the King of Kābul, in like manner as his ancestors were formerly the vassals of his Majesty's ancestors.

"ARTICLE II.—Of the tracts of country resumed on the death of Mir Mehrāb Khān, namely, Kachhi, Mastung, and Shāl, the two first will be restored to Mir Nasir Khān and his descendants, through the kindness of his Majesty Shāh Sujah-al-Mulkh.

"ARTICLE III.—Should it be deemed necessary to station troops, whether belonging to the Honourable Company or Shāh Sujah-al-Mulkh, in any part of the territory of Kalāt, they shall occupy such positions as may be thought advisable.

"ARTICLE IV.—Mir Nasir Khān, his heirs and successors, will always be guided by the advice of the British officer residing at his *Darbār*.

"ARTICLE V.—The passage of merchants and others into Afghānistan, from the river Indus, on the one side, and from the seaport of Sonmiāni, on the other, shall be protected by Nasir Khān as far as practicable, nor will any aggression be practised on such persons, or any undue exactions made, beyond an equitable toll to be fixed by the British Government and Mir Nasir Khān.

"ARTICLE VI.—Mir Nasir Khān binds himself, his heirs and successors, not to hold any political communication, or to enter into any negotiations, with foreign Powers, without the consent of the British Government and of his Majesty Shāh Sujah-al-Mulkh, and in all cases to act in subordinate co-operation with the Governments of British India and of the Shāh; but the usual amicable correspondence with neighbours to continue as heretofore.

"ARTICLE VII.—In case of an attack on Mir Nasir Khān by an open enemy, or of any difference arising between him and any foreign Power, the British Government will afford him assistance or good offices, as it may judge to be necessary or proper, for the maintenance of his rights.

"ARTICLE VIII.—Mir Nāsir Khān will make due provision for the support of Shāh Nawāz Khān, either by pension to be paid through the British Government, on condition of that chief residing within the British territory, or by grant of estates within Kalāt possessions, as may hereafter be decided by the British Government.

"Done at Kalāt this 6th day of October, A.D. 1841, corresponding with the 30th Shaban, A.H. 1257.

(Signed) "MIR NASIR KHĀN.
(Signed) "AUCKLAND.

"* Ratified and signed by the Right Honble. the Governor-General of India in Council, at Fort William, in Bengal, this 10th day of January, 1842.

(Signed) "T. H. MADDOCK,
"Secretary to the Government of India."

Mir Nasir Khān II., as he may henceforth be called, to distinguish him from his great-grandfather, Nasir Khān I., might now be considered as firmly fixed on the throne of Kalāt. It was but a short time after his accession to power that the terrible reverses of the British occurred in Afghān-

* This treaty was subsequently annulled in favour of another entered into between the same parties in the month of May, 1854.

istan, and though large reinforcements and stores had to be despatched through the Khān's territories in 1842 for the campaign, Nasir Khān remained true to his engagements, and assisted the British Government to the best of his ability. At the end of that year the English troops were removed from both Afghānistan and Balochistan, a large force, being for a time concentrated at Sakhar, in North Sindh. With this, early in the following year (February, 1843), the province of Sindh itself was conquered and annexed to British territory by Sir Charles J. Napier, when the troops were removed from the frontier. The robber tribes on the Kachhi border, that is to say, the Dumbkis, Jakrānis, and others—ever on the watch to make plundering inroads into the low country—at once took advantage of the Sindh frontier being unprotected, and resumed their lawless proceedings, sacking and destroying large villages in open day, and rendering both life and property everywhere unsafe. This lasted till 1845, when the Governor of Sindh (Sir Charles J. Napier), collecting together a large force, with the assistance of Mir Ali Murād Khān of Khairpur, the only independent Talpur chief then remaining in Sindh, penetrated into the hill fastnesses of these robbers, and reduced them to submission. On his return from the hills, Sir Charles Napier met Nasir Khān, the Kalāt ruler, by appointment, at the town of Shāhpur, in Kachhi, but nothing was then done, it would seem, to strengthen the Khān's hands and enable him to establish good government throughout his dominions. It was, however, noticed at the time that the influence of Mūlla Muhammad Husain, whose treachery as prime minister, it will be remembered, was the chief cause of Mehrāb Khān's downfall, was, strangely enough, paramount at the court of his son, Nasir Khān, and it was evident, as will be seen further on, that he was once more engaged in his old scheme of self-aggrandizement, and was as ready, by his treason and intrigue, to sacrifice the son, as he had been to destroy the father.

And so matters progressed up to the year 1847 without any event that requires special notice. The influence of Mūlla Muhammad Husain in the Kalāt *darbār* was evidently very great, and the time had no doubt nearly arrived when, as he supposed, he could bring matters to a crisis. It will be necessary here to mention that the post of Political Superintendent and Commander of the Upper Sindh Frontier, in connection with the preservation of peace on the Kalāt and Sindh borders, was created in 1847, and Major (afterwards General) John Jacob was the officer appointed to it, with permission to make his headquarters at Khāngarh, the present Jacobabad (so named after this very clever and energetic officer), which, as being nearer to the Kachhi desert than Shikārpur, allowed of hill marauders being followed up with greater certainty and despatch than would have been the case from the latter town. Here it was that Muhammad Husain, in the first instance, sent his brother, Muhammad Amin, the Governor of Kachhi, to feel the way, as it were, before he himself went there to sound the Political Superintendent as to his own treacherous intentions. Having obtained the necessary permission, he arrived at Jacobabad early in March, 1851, but in his interviews with Major Jacob he only affected the greatest concern and zeal for the welfare of his sovereign, the Khān of Kalāt, without in any way touching upon his own ambitious project; and, after about a fortnight's stay, he left Jacobabad, the Political Superintendent being much struck with the man's noble bearing and great mental powers. Early in the following year he again called upon Major Jacob, and during his interview with him he *now* explained his real intentions, which were that he desired the consent of the British Government to seize for himself the Khānship of Kalāt, of which he already possessed the real power. Finding himself thwarted in his treacherous scheme, and denounced as a traitor by the officer whose countenance in the matter he had hoped to obtain, he at once left for Kalāt, became desperate, intrigued with the Marris, and did all he could to sow the seeds of contention between the Khān and the British Government. The views of his minister were fully explained by Major Jacob, in 1853, to the Khān, who could hardly credit what had been reported of his vazir. He was, however, removed from office, and died shortly afterwards in prison, from *poison*, it is said. Next year (1854) Nasir Khān was induced to meet the Commissioner in Sindh, Mr. (afterwards Sir Bartle) Frere, at Jacobabad, where all doubts and misunderstandings that might previously have existed were at once removed, and a death-blow given to the power and influence so long wielded for evil purposes by his traitorous minister, Mūlla Muhammad Husain. It resulted also in another treaty being concluded between the Khān and the British Government (annulling that of October, 1841), which was effected on 14th May, 1854, and ratified on the 2nd of June following.

The text of this treaty, which, it is to be remembered, holds good at the present day, is at follows :—

Treaty between the British Government and Mir Nasir Khān, Chief of Kalāt, concluded on the part of the British Government by Major John Jacob, C.B., in virtue of full powers granted by the Most Noble the Marquis of Dalhousie, K.T., etc., Governor-General of India, and by Nasir Khān, Chief of Kalāt.

"WHEREAS the course of events has made it expedient that a new agreement should be concluded between the British Government and Mir Nasir Khān, Chief of Kalāt, the following articles have been agreed on between the said Government and his Highness :—

"ARTICLE I.—The treaty concluded by Major Outram between the British Government and Mir Nasir Khān, Chief of Kalāt, on the 6th October, 1841, is hereby annulled.

"ARTICLE II.—There shall be perpetual friendship between the British Government and Mir Nasir Khān, Chief of Kalāt, his heirs and successors.

"ARTICLE III.—Mir Nasir Khān binds himself, his heirs and successors, to oppose to the utmost all the enemies of the British Government, in all cases to act in subordinate co-operation with that Government, and to enter into no negotiation with other States without its consent, the usual friendly correspondence with neighbours being continued as before.

"ARTICLE IV.—Should it be deemed necessary to station British troops in any part of the territory of Kalāt, they shall occupy such positions as may be thought advisable by the British authorities.

"ARTICLE V.—Mir Nasir Khān binds himself, his heirs and successors, to prevent all plundering or other outrage by his subjects within or near British territory, to protect the passage of merchants to and fro between the British dominions and Afghānistan, whether by way of Sindh or by the seaport of Sonmiāni, or other seaports of Makrān, and to permit no exactions to be made beyond an equitable duty to be fixed by the British Government and Mir Nasir Khān, and the amount to be shown in the schedule annexed to this treaty.

"ARTICLE VI.—To aid Mir Nasir Khān, his heirs and successors, in the fulfilment of these obligations, and on condition of a faithful performance of them year by year, the British Government binds itself to pay to Mir Nasir Khān, his heirs and successors, an annual subsidy of fifty thousand (50,000) Company's rupees.

"ARTICLE VII.—If during any year the conditions above mentioned shall not be faithfully performed by the said Mir Nasir Khān, his heirs and successors, then the annual subsidy of 50,000 Company's rupees will not be paid by the British Government.

"Done at Mastung this 14th day of May, 1854.

(Signed) "JOHN JACOB, Major,
"Political Superintendent and Commandant
"on the Frontier of Upper Sindh."

"Schedule showing the amount of duty to be levied on merchandise passing through the dominions of the Khān of Kalāt, referred to in Article V. of this Treaty.

"On each camel-load, without respect to value, from the northern frontier to the sea, either to Karāchi or other port, Company's rupees 6.

"On each camel, as above, from the northern frontier to Shikārpur, Company's rupees 5.

"The same duties to be levied on merchandise passing in the contrary direction from the sea, or from Sindh to the Kalāt territory.

(Signed) "JOHN JACOB, Major,
"Political Superintendent and Commandant
"on the Frontier of Upper Sindh."

"The foregoing articles of treaty having been concluded between the British Government and the Khān of Kalāt, and signed and sealed by Major Jacob, C. B., on the one part, and Mir Nāsir Khān on the other, at Mastung, on the 14th of May, 1854, A.D., corresponding with 16th Shaban, 1270, A.H., a copy of the same will be delivered to his Highness, duly ratified by the Governor-General in Council within two months from this date.

(Signed) "DALHOUSIE,
"J. DORIN,
"J. LOW,
"J. P. GRANT,
"B. PEACOCK."

"Ratified by the Most Noble the Governor-General in Council, at Fort William, this 2nd day of June, 1854.

(Signed) "G. F. EDMONSTONE,
"Secretary to the Government of India."

In the year 1856 the plan of having a British Resident at the court of the Khān of Kalāt was put forward by Major Jacob, and received the approval of the Indian Government. The first officer appointed to this post was Lieutenant (afterwards Colonel Sir Henry) Green, second in command of one of the Sindh Horse regiments; but as his services were required during 1856 in the Persian campaign, Lieutenant Macaulay, of the same force, was nominated to act for him, which he did till November, 1857. It was in the month of May of that year that Mir Nasir Khān died suddenly at Anjira, while on his way from Kachhi to Kalāt, not without a strong suspicion of his death having been hastened by poison administered to him by the *Daroga* (or chamberlain), Gul Muhammad. That the latter hated everything connected with Europeans will be readily understood from the account Masson has given of him, when he and Loveday were both in confinement at Kalāt. He represents him to be "a tall, spare, aged, and harsh-featured man, blind of one eye, and his head affected with palsy." Again, in his interview with the Daroga, he thus speaks of him:—"The old man prefaced his discourse by the declaration that he never saw a Feringhi, or even thought of one, that blood was not ready to gush from his eyes, by reason of the wrongs and injuries he had endured. He dwelt much upon them, some concerning the late Mehrāb Khān, others relating more particularly to himself. He told how Sikandar (Captain Alexander Burnes), in that very room, had sworn by Hazrat Isa (or Holy Jesus) that no designs were entertained upon the country. He enlarged upon the service Mehrāb Khān had rendered to the army on its march, and of its requital, and expressed his horror that the corpse of his late master had been exposed in a *masjid* unhonoured and unburied. In like manner he pointed to a hole in the apartment made by a cannon-ball at the time of the assault." From this description of the man it will at once be readily understood that his feelings towards the English were anything but amicable; and it is supposed that, believing Mir Nasir Khān was becoming too much attached to the British Government, he had him carried off by poison, so as to allow of his younger brother, Khudadād Khān, succeeding him, and this youth he believed he would be able to manage as he pleased. The early death of Nasir Khān II.—for he was not much more than 31 years old at his decease—was generally considered to be a great misfortune for his country, for besides being readily amenable to good advice, he would seem to have possessed an influence over his unruly chiefs such as they had not known since the days of his great namesake, Nasir Khān I.

Mir Khudadād Khān, the brother of the deceased ruler, succeeded quietly to the Khānship, and his selection was approved by the chiefs of Balochistan; but, though no obstruction was offered to his elevation to supreme power, there were two parties in the State who were anxious to obtain an undue influence over him for their own selfish purposes. The one was Gul Muhammad Daroga and his friends, who already had the young Khān with them in the "Miri," or citadel, of Kalāt; the other included the Sarawān and Jhalawān Sardārs, with Mir Khān, the Jām of Las Bēla, who, on Khudadād Khān's accession, endeavoured to secure his person by main force, but were fired upon and dispersed by the Daroga. Late in 1857 an insurrection against the Khān and the Daroga's party was instigated by the Sardārs, and serious disturbances were only averted by the timely arrival at Kalāt of Lieutenant Macaulay, with a few of the Sindh Horse, who seems with great tact to have settled matters in such a manner as to prevent any hostile collision. In November, 1857, Major H. R. Green resumed his duties as Political Agent at Kalāt, and found that Gul Muhammad and a native banker named Gangaram—both of whom were very hostile to the British name and power—were at the time the Khān's most trusted counsellors, but not for good. These two men he induced the Khān to dismiss, and to take in lieu, as his *vazir*, or prime minister, the Shahgassi Wali Muhammad, a trusted servant of the late ruler, Nasir Khān, concerning whom all parties were unanimous in speaking very favourably; he was accordingly installed into office in a formal manner, both at Jacobabad and at Gandāva, in 1858–59.

The capricious and unstable character of the new ruler, and the insolent and inordinate demands made upon him by the Sardārs, were, however, in themselves great obstacles to that firm and stable government which Balochistan so urgently needed, and it was readily perceived that they would give rise to endless strife and contention in the future. In consequence of some daring raids which had been committed by the Marri tribe in Kachhi and elsewhere, at the urgent request and with the assistance of Major Henry Green, a force was fitted out by the Khān to punish these robbers in their own strongholds. Some delay occurred in the advance of this expedition, owing to the lamented death of General John Jacob on 8th December, 1858, at Jacobabad. The great experience of this very talented officer in all matters connected with Kalāt and its border tribes, his correct and thorough appreciation of the character of these tribes, and his bold yet discreet method of dealing with them, made his loss at such a time doubly felt, both in Balochistan and in British India. It was he who in 1847, when sent up to command the frontier of Upper Sindh, at a time when nothing but terror and desolation prevailed on the border, at once gave up the plan of *defensive* operations, and substituted the system of posting detachments in the *open* plain, with no defensive works whatever, patrols from these detachments constantly passing and re-passing each other in places where it was thought any of the robber tribes might appear, and when they did appear, attacking them on the spot, no matter how superior in numbers the enemy might be. The success of such bold proceedings as these was marvellous, and this, conjointly with the exercise of that great administrative ability which distinguished General Jacob, soon produced a state of affairs on the border very different indeed from that which had hitherto prevailed there; and perhaps no juster tribute can be rendered to the memory of this great man than the following recorded description of the condition of the frontier in 1854, which he himself had laboured so strenuously to bring about:—"Good roads have been made all over the country; means of irrigation have been multiplied four-fold, and everywhere on the border life and activity with perfect safety exist. Where formerly all was desert solitude or murderous violence, not an armed man is now ever seen save the soldiers and police, and persons and property are everywhere perfectly protected."

The force at length entered the hills early in 1859. It

consisted of a collection of the different tribes amounting to about 4000 men on foot, and a similar number mounted, exclusive of a squadron of Sindh Horse, the escort of the political agent, commanded by his brother, Major Malcolm Green. It must not, however, be supposed that the Khān was himself able to collect this large levy with the object of operating against the Marris. To Major H. Green, the then political agent, who, as has been well observed, gradually drew around him all the real strength of the State, and who had united the Khān and his nobles in this, the first step towards a lasting settlement of the country, is due not alone the conception of the plan and the organization of the large Baloch force, but also the successful carrying out of the whole campaign. Under the prudent guidance of Major Green, the Marri strongholds were taken one after the other and destroyed, and the tribe themselves were eventually forced to submit, and beg for mercy at the hands of their lawful ruler.

After this expedition into the hills the Khān took some of the Marris into his pay, and gave them a small concession of land in the eastern part of Kachhi, on the proviso that they abstained from making lawless incursions into that province. Owing, however, to some misunderstandings, or, as has been said, to ill-treatment of the Marri hostages left with the Khān, raids were again committed by that tribe, and the *jagir* was in consequence resumed.

In the following year another expedition was undertaken by the Khān, with a view to bringing under subjection his western provinces, situated on the borders of Makrān, and the chiefs of which were at the time in open revolt against his authority. This expedition was brought to a successful conclusion, and many of the revolted chiefs accompanied the Khān in his return to Kalāt.

That the Khān was capricious and unstable in character

was soon shown by the insult he passed upon the leading Sardār of Jhalawān, Tāj Muhammad Zēhri, to whose daughter he had been betrothed. Utterly ignoring the betrothal (or *sang*), which among the Brahuis is always looked upon as a very serious undertaking, he married that chief's sister, the widow of his deceased brother, the late Khān, and who was, besides, a determined enemy of her brother. This deep affront precipitated, it is said, the revolution which took place in March, 1863, when the Sardārs suddenly attacked the Khān, then encamped at Gandāva, in the province of Kachhi. In this affair the Khān was wounded, and he fled to the border of Sindh, his cousin, Sher Dil Khān, being made the ruler of Kalāt in his stead. Khudadād Khān remained a fugitive in Sindh till some time in May, 1864, when Sher Dil Khān was assassinated by the commandant of the body-guard, and Khudadād reinstated on the throne of Kalāt, mainly through the assistance of the Sarawān Sardār, Mūlla Muhammad Raisāni. Affairs remained quiet till 1865, when Tāj Muhammad Zehri and Malla Muhammad Raisāni combined endeavoured not alone to provoke an insurrection in the Kachhi Province, but even to assassinate Khudadād Khān and place his infant son on the throne. Here was seen another instance of the strange feeling which at times seems to actuate Balochis in their dealings with one another, for the same Sardār who had taken so active a part in restoring the ruling Khān to his throne in 1864, was now found plotting his destruction in 1865. The project was unsuccessful, and the latter Sardār fled to Kandahār; but his co-conspirator, Tāj Muhammad, was not so fortunate. He was captured and confined at Kalāt, where he died in August, 1867.

In July, 1865, another rebellion took place, instigated this time by Mir Khān, the Jām of Las Bēla, and assisted by the Minghal Sardār, Nuradin of Wadd. The former individual had previously been engaged in several conspiracies against his suzerain, and had as often been pardoned. He was related to the Khān, having married his eldest sister, and this fact no doubt gave him expectations of one day being able to secure the Khānship for himself, though, as a Lumri by origin, he could hardly hope to find himself accepted for such a high office by the Baloch tribes. In this disturbance of 1865 the Khān's troops defeated the insurgents, both leaders being taken prisoners, but they were soon after pardoned by the Khān. After this attempt nothing further of any importance happened till late in the year 1868, when the Jām of Las and Nuradin of Wadd, aided by the arch-intriguer, Azad Khān of Kharān, ventured upon another trial of strength with the Khān. The Marri and Sarawān tribes, though urged to join the insurgents, refused to do so, but the state of affairs was considered sufficiently threatening to call the Khān himself in person into the field. Negotiations were ultimately resorted to, when the rebels retired for a time with their forces.

This disturbance might never have occurred had Sir Henry Green, the Political Superintendent of the Sindh Frontier, remained at Jacobabad. He had in the early part of the year been made, by the mutual consent of the Khān and the insurgent Sardārs, an arbitrator for both parties, his decision being final; but he found it necessary, on account of ill-health, to leave Jacobabad for Europe in May, 1868, and so the adjustment, which it was hoped would have been permanent, never took place. Sir Henry had since 1862 been doing the duty of Political Superintendent of the Sindh Frontier, while the important post of Political Agent at the court of the Brahui Khān was ably filled by his brother, Major Malcolm Green, from May of that same year till the latter end of 1867, when he was compelled to leave on account of ill-health. The great influence exercised

MIR KHUDĀDAD, KHĀN OF KALĀT, AND ATTENDANTS.

SON OF GUL MUHAMMAD DAROGA. — H.H. THE KHĀN. — WALI MUHAMMAD SHĀHGASSI. — A CHIEF OF THE KHĀN'S HOUSEHOLD.

by this officer over the Baloch chiefs was due mainly to his firm, determined, and manly character, and his fearless spirit won for him the respect and confidence generally of the people of Balochistan. Some delay seems to have occurred in the appointment of his successor, Captain Harrison, of the Bombay army, who did not enter upon his political duties at Kalāt till February, 1869.

In the month of May of that same year another rebellion took place, the Jām of Las being, as usual, the prime mover, aided this time by both the Jhalawān and Sarawān Sardārs, and, collecting a force of 4000 men and three guns, they marched on Kalāt, where a hostile collision was only averted by the tact and skill displayed by the newly appointed British resident in bringing about a reconciliation between the belligerents. But the Jām still refused to pay allegiance to his sovereign, and, after calling upon the different Baloch tribes, by means of circular letters, to rise in the autumn, he, together with Nuradin of Wadd, again appeared in open rebellion in the month of October, 1869. His pretext at that time for thus opposing his sovereign was said to be the unjust seizure by the Khān of certain of the Jām's lands at Baghwāna; but the circular letters altogether disprove this. The Jām's forces were met by those of the Khān under the Vazir, Wali Muhammad, and were utterly defeated, the Jām fleeing, together with his son and family, to Karāchi, which he reached on the 8th of December, and where he was granted an asylum on the express condition that he would not mix himself up with either the affairs of the Khān of Kalāt or of his old possession, Las. He had previously permitted the mercenaries attached to *his* own force to plunder the town of Bēla before the Khān's Vazir could get there. As at Karāchi he was discovered to be intriguing with the people at Bēla, he was removed to Hyderabad (Sindh), where, however, he still persisted in his communications with Balochistan, and even meditated an escape to Bēla. At the end of 1871 he was removed to Amadnagar, in the Dakhan, where he still remains. Mūlla Muhammad Raisāni judged it advisable to seek the protection of the Marri tribes at Kahan, while Azad Khān, of Kharān, proceeded to Kandahār in the hope of interesting the ruler of Afghānistan in his behalf.

In 1868 the Marri tribe gave some trouble to the Khān by plundering a caravan when passing through the Kachhi country. For this the Khān had to pay Rs.4000 as compensation to the merchants; but he protested against the payment on the plea that the Marris were favoured and even employed by the British Government elsewhere. This was true, in so far as an arrangement between the Panjāb Government and the Marris was concerned, by which the latter engaged to respect the Panjāb frontier, but it left them at full liberty to plunder elsewhere with impunity. The consequence was that they committed numerous raids in Kachhi, but left the Panjāb border in peace. It was to discuss this matter in its various bearings, and to take such measures on the subject as might seem most desirable, that a conference was held in February, 1871, at Mittankot, in the Panjāb, between the Lieut.-Governor of that province and the Commissioner in Sindh. It resulted mainly in their jointly recommending that the Marri and Bughti tribes should be subsidized to the extent of Rs.30,040 annually, and that a certain number of horsemen should be raised from among them, with the view of inducing them to abstain from committing raids in Kachhi. The experiment was to be tried for one year only, but it had to be indefinitely postponed in consequence of a serious rebellion breaking out in the Sarawān Province in September, 1871, instigated, it is thought, by Mūlla Muhammad Raisāni, and aided by many of the Brahui chiefs of that part of Balochistan. The rebels had captured Mastung, but the

Khān's Vazir, Wali Muhammad, moved rapidly down on them, and compelled them to retreat by the Bolān pass and other routes into Kachhi, where, in consequence of a bad wound, he was unable to follow them up. Here they looted the towns of Dādar, Bāgh, and Gandāva in succession, but the Khān's troops, under one Muhammad Khān, were sent down into the low country in October to pursue the rebels and crush the rebellion. This Muhammad Khān, who was the Khān's *vakil* at Jacobabad, was, from all accounts, a man perfectly unfitted for the work entrusted to him; and this was shown in the way he patched up a kind of inglorious peace with the disaffected chiefs in Kachhi, instead of acting vigorously against them. Another engagement took place between the forces of the Khān and those of the rebels, resulting in the defeat of the latter, who then retired to the hills near Sibi, whence they infested the Bolān pass, looting two caravans, and killing some of the merchants.

The troubles of the Kalāt ruler were indeed fast thickening around him. Early in 1872 Ali Khān, the son of Mir Khān, the exiled chief of Las, escaped from the surveillance of the police at Hyderabad, in Sindh, and rejoined his countrymen at Bēla, while the people of Kēj, in Western Balochistan, were said to have almost entirely thrown off their allegiance to Kalāt. The disturbances in Balochistan had, indeed, assumed such serious dimensions, that a proposition was made to the Khān of friendly intervention on the part of the British Government, to remedy the disorders prevailing in his dominions, and bring about, if possible, a reconciliation between himself and his Sardārs. To this end Khudadād Khān, who decided not to attend the meeting personally, gave plenary powers to the Commissioner in Sindh (Sir W. L. Merewether) to act for him, and his Vazir, Wali Muhammad, was desired to attend and represent the Khān's interests. The meeting took place at

Jacobabad in March, 1872, the only rebel chiefs appearing there being those of Sarawān. After a careful hearing of both sides of the question, the Commissioner, on the 28th of the same month, delivered his award to the following effect:—That in the event of the Sardārs who were implicated in the late rebellion tendering proper allegiance to the Khān, as their lawful sovereign, their lands would be restored to them, and all allowances accorded, as was the case during the reign of the Khān's late brother, Nasir Khān II. At the same time the Sardārs were to restore all property plundered by them during the late rebellion to its rightful owners, and all caravan property that had been robbed was to be given up as well. To these terms the Sardārs readily assented. To the Khān the Indian Government granted a lakh of rupees (about £10,000) to assist him in meeting all immediate pressing demands, at the same time approving the patience and good judgment shown by Sir W. Merewether in his proceedings in so difficult a case. The Jām of Las Bēla had been altogether left out in this meeting, as his repeated acts of rebellion had shut out all hope of his being permitted to return to his own country.

But from the time this decision was given it was remarked that a change came over Khudadād Khān, who, though he had in the first instance accorded full powers to the Commissioner in Sindh to act on his behalf, was very far indeed from being satisfied with the result arrived at, though this, it must be observed, was very favourable to him. To his able minister, Wali Muhammad, he began to show marked displeasure, and his manner to the political agent at Kalāt (Major Harrison) was altogether altered. A month or two only after the Jacobabad meeting plundering in the Bolān pass recommenced, and a body of Samalāni Minghāls suddenly attacked in the same pass some Mazarāni Marris who had settled there, and were engaged as a kind of police by the Khān.

This last outrage, it was strongly suspected, had been connived at by the Khān himself, to allow of his evading the terms entered into on his behalf at the Jacobabad meeting. In June of the same year the Vazir, Wali Muhammad, found it necessary to fly for protection to the British political agent, as he considered his life in danger from the Khān's resentment.

Khudadād Khān was evidently in this business under the domination of others, and it was found that his chief advisers were his own mother and sister, two munshis, and the commander of his troops. The Khān was remonstrated with in writing on the foolish course he was pursuing; and as Major Harrison's position, in this untoward aspect of affairs, was by no means safe, his military escort was strengthened. For a short time a change for the better then took place; the Vazir (Wali Muhammad) was reinstated in office, and the evil advisers, the two munshis and the commander of his forces, were removed to Sindh and confined in the fort of Umarkot, in the Thar and Parkar District. The Khān was induced also to meet in November, 1872, the then Viceroy of British India, Lord Northbrook, who was on his way through Sindh from the Panjāb. The meeting took place at Sakhar, but it was noticed that the Khān appeared to be in great apprehension of some danger happening to him, notwithstanding that he had been received with great kindness and courtesy by the Viceroy. This was subsequently accounted for by the fact of Muhammad Khān, the Jacobabad Vakil, the same individual who had so disgracefully mismanaged the Khān's affairs in the rebellion of 1871–72, having persuaded him that the meeting in question was simply got up that he might be deposed, and his eldest son put on the throne in his stead.

It was during 1872 that the commission under Sir Fredk. Goldsmid, for laying down the Persian and Kalāt frontier, with representatives from those countries, carried out their labours, and thus put a stop to any further advance of the Persian frontier to the eastward.

Early in the following year (1873) compensation to the amount of between Rs.50,000 and Rs.60,000 was paid by the Khān to those merchants whose caravans had been robbed in the Bolān pass; and late in the month of February the Commissioner in Sindh met the Khān by appointment at Shāhpur, in the province of Kachhi. With the Khān were his Vazir, the Sardārs of Balochistan, and, among these latter, Mūlla Muhammad Raisāni. The chief object of this interview was, if possible, to carry out the arrangements previously sanctioned at the Mittankot conference in 1871; but the Khān would discuss no subject save that of the confinement of his three evil advisers previously mentioned. A general sort of assent was given by him to the proposals put forward by Sir W. Merewether, but it was clearly evident that no trust could be placed upon any of his assurances. The Sardārs were warned as to repeating the disturbances of 1871–72, and the Commissioner received their solemn assurance that they on their part would not henceforth disturb the peace of the country; but the interview was plainly a failure so far as the Khān was concerned, and this was soon made manifest by his subsequent conduct.

In the following month (March), before the Khān's return to Kalāt from the low country, it was perceived that he had taken a *personal* dislike to the British Resident at his court, and was altogether indifferent to everything connected with the well-being of his country. He had, besides, allied himself to three other bad characters: the ex-vakil, Muhammad Khān, being one, and Muhammad Hyat, the Kāzi of Bāgh another; the third was one Abdul Aziz, an inferior official; and he would listen to the counsel of none but these men. Under these circumstances, and after repeated written remonstrances from the Commissioner in Sindh on his conduct and to what it would ultimately lead, the political agent was withdrawn from his court; Wali Muhammad resigned his vazirship and accompanied Major Harrison to Jacobabad; and the yearly subsidy of Rs.50,000 allowed to the Khān was withheld. It was now deemed advisable to let the Khān see how he could manage to get on with his turbulent chieftains without the moral as well as the pecuniary aid hitherto afforded him by the Indian Government.

That matters were rapidly going from bad to worse was soon made patent by an event that occurred in February, 1874. This was the perpetration of a most impudent raid within British territory by a band of 200 armed men of tribe of Brahuis, for the ostensible purpose of recovering some fugitive slaves. Having accomplished their object they returned to their own country. The Khān was requested to give up the perpetrators of this outrage, but he either could not or would not do so. The Commissioner in Sindh accordingly recommended the despatch of a small but efficient force to Kalāt to demand reparation and enforce a better observance of the treaty. It was also recommended that opportunity should be taken of afterwards coercing the Marri tribe, whose persistence in plundering the province of Kachhi deserved, the Commissioner considered, condign punishment. But these suggestions did not meet with the approval of the Indian Government, who feared that an armed intervention in the affairs of Kalāt might compel the Government to a military occupation of the country, and might, in fact, produce ulterior results of a very serious kind. In short, all active measures against either the Khān or the Marri tribe were to be deprecated. No reference or communication of any kind was to be made to the former until such time as he manifested both a willingness and ability to perform the duties of a good neighbour, though at the same time reasonable endeavours were to be made to render the trade routes safe, and to cultivate friendly intercourse with the tribes and states on the British borders. But how these trade routes were to be made more secure without any vigorous remedial measures on the part of the Indian Government was an enigma which, it was believed, nothing short of a military demonstration could solve. In the place of the able and trustworthy vazir, Wali Muhammad, the Khān appointed one Atta Muhammad in September, 1874, to the vazirship. He was sent to Las to make certain inquiries there, to recover property, or its equivalent, plundered from caravans, and to imprison the perpetrators of these outrages. This certainly appeared as if the Khān were desirous of atoning for his past neglect; but events showed that he had in no degree altered his *rôle* of dogged obstructiveness, for on the return to Kalāt of the new vazir, he was at once disgraced and removed from his appointment for evidently too faithfully performing his master's orders, which, as now appeared, were never intended to be carried out.

The regular troops of the Khān are at present presumed to number about 3000 men of all arms, but they are, as a rule, in great arrears of pay, and those of them stationed in Kachhi in 1875 were much disaffected, and had not received any pay for six months. Disturbances on this account with one or other of the Khān's regiments are constantly occurring. Bribery among the Khān's officials is reported to be very rife, and there is at present neither good nor safe government in Kalāti Balochistan. To render matters still worse, the Khān, at the commencement of 1876, caused Nuradin Minghal, of Wadd, who had been moved to suspend his measures against the Khān, to be slaughtered with a number of his followers, and this after the Sardār had been induced to pay his respects to him, on the Khān's guaranteeing his safety by pledging his oath on the Kurān. This step the Khān palliated by stating that both Nuradin Minghal and

Atta Muhammad were plotting his own destruction; but this, as they were then situated, was a simple absurdity. Such a treacherous act on the part of the Khān has tended still more to widen the breach already existing between him and his Sardārs, and it may in the end lead to greater and more difficult complications—to such complications, indeed, as will, it is believed, compel the Indian Government to adopt the very sensible suggestions of strong and vigorous action made to it in 1874 by Sir W. Merewether. In this proposed expedition it was never intended that any annexation of country should take place, but that some town or station, such, for instance, as Quetta, might have to be *occupied* by British troops—a contingency fully provided for, and in perfect consonance with the treaty of 1854.

The occupation of Quetta had been recommended as far back as 1866 by a former political superintendent of the Sindh frontier, the present Sir H. R. Green, whose proposals to the Bombay Government on this subject were thus referred to by him a year or two since:—"I suggested that the three regiments of Sindh Horse should be raised to 600 sabres each, that two of these regiments, with the Rifle Corps and Mountain Train, should be pushed on to Dādar, at the southern entrance of the Bolān pass; that one regiment should remain at Jacobabad, and that the civil duties of the frontier district should be made over to the Shikārpur Collectorate. Further, that about 300 of the best known amongst the Marri and Bughti robbers should be taken into British pay to act as police, and to keep open the postal communication between Dādar and the British frontier, a distance of about 80 miles over a perfectly level country. That, in addition, we should subsidize some of the principal Brahui chiefs with their followers, located in and about the Bolān pass. The duties of the troops stationed at Dādar would have been to patrol the pass between Dādar and Quetta during the summer months, or until the snow in the northern part closed it. No better training ground than the above for soldiers could be found in India. It was also my idea that the valley of Quetta should be thoroughly surveyed by competent engineer officers, and its most defensible positions marked; that a light line of rail should be gradually pushed forward, connecting Sakhar on the river Indus with Dādar, so that, with other uses, it might enable camels laden with merchandise from above the passes to unload after debouching into the plains, and which merchandise might be conveyed direct on board steamers at Sakhar for transmission to Karāchi until the completion of the Indus Valley Railway. The above, in a few words, was the substance of my views. I had thoroughly thought them out, and discussed many points with H.H. the Khān of Kalāt and his principal chiefs, and I feel confident, had not what has been aptly styled by a late writer upon Indian subjects, '*masterly inactivity*' prevailed, I could at that time, with the assistance of the excellent officers associated with me in the Sindh Frontier field force, and with the aid of the chiefs of Balochistan, have carried them out, and before relinquishing my frontier command have consolidated the British power up to Quetta, and at a far less cost than will be now incurred in re-establishing our *prestige* in those parts. The great evil to be avoided was interfering in any way with the social and political *status* of the chiefs and people of Balochistan, and my intimate acquaintance with their institutions, habits, and customs, would, I trust, have prevented me from doing so. I have never advocated a move one step beyond Quetta, but, should events compel such a course, a march onwards from such a position, by a force acclimatized and used to the people of the country, would possess great advantages over one starting from the Valley of the Indus."

In reviewing the modern history of Kalāti Balochistan under the present dynasty, extending from about the commencement of the 18th century, when Abdula Khān was ruler, down to the present time, a period of, say, nearly 180 years, there is not much to call for remark. Undoubtedly the Augustan age of Balochistan was the reign of the first Nasir Khān, the Great Nasir, as he is to this day called by the Balochis. Of his predecessors little seems to be known; they were indeed simply successful robbers on a large scale, with but few traces of any enlightened policy to gild over a long succession of deeds of lawlessness, rapine, and bloodshed. It was different, certainly, with Nasir Khān I., who at an early period of his long reign of 40 years displayed an astuteness and aptitude to govern which would have been deemed praiseworthy in a far more civilized community than that over which the Brahui Khān was called upon to rule. He plainly saw the necessity for a strong bond of union among the many Baloch tribes, and he without doubt most sincerely desired the "unification" of Balochistan.

Had his successors been of the same stamp and metal as himself, the Kalāti kingdom of to-day would not perhaps show that anarchy and confusion which are now its most striking characteristics. The history of the reigns of Muhammad Khān, of the unfortunate Mehrāb, and his son, Nasir Khān II., as also of the present Khān, Mir Khudadād, at once shows how inferior each and all were to Nasir Khān in the threefold character of prince, statesman, and soldier. One alone of these, Nasir Khān II., might, had he lived, have done good service to his country, which at the time sorely needed a vigorous ruler. Under a judicious course of training he might have learnt how best to curb and control with tact and address the unruly chiefs that had given his unfortunate father so much trouble and uneasiness. Cut off suddenly at an early age by poison, it is generally believed, for showing tendencies of too English a nature, his country lost in him a sovereign who promised to imitate the worthy deeds and virtues of his great namesake. The misfortune was but too truly a national one, more especially so when the character of his successor, the present ruler, Khudadād Khān, and his acts during a reign which has already extended to nineteen years, are taken into account.

The latest accounts (August, 1876) relative to Balochistan seem to imply that the negotiations entered into with the Khān of Kalāt and his Sardārs, under orders from the Government of India, by a Panjāb officer (Major Sandeman), who in this duty was accompanied by a strong military escort, have been attended with the most marked success. Up to the end of July, 1876, everything was said to have been satisfactorily arranged between the contending parties; but this most probably, as with other previous pacifications, will hold good only so long as the British troops remain in the country. Should they be withdrawn, the old animosities would, it is feared, burst forth again with redoubled fury; and all the more so from the forced restraint which the late peace negotiations had imposed on the tribes and their ruler. Glib speeches and demands, however courteously urged, if unaccompanied by the power to compel obedience, are utterly unsuited to a savage race like the Baloch. They will only be amenable to reason when they perceive and understand that the paramount power which seeks by fair means to pacify their country, long torn to pieces by intestine discord, is fully prepared to enforce, if need be, its well-meant intentions.

APPENDIX A.

GENEALOGICAL TABLE OF THE KHĀNS OF KALĀT.

- KAMBAR KHĀN.
  - SAMBAR.
    - MUHAMMAD KHĀN.
      - ABDULA KHĀN.
        - MOHBAT KHĀN, reigned some time at Kalāt; superseded by his brother, Nasir Khān, and died a hostage at Kandahār.
          - HĀJI KHĀN, died a hostage at Kandahār.
            - BAHRAM KHĀN, originally a hostage at Kandahār, unsuccessfully asserted his claims to the government with Nasir Khān and his son, Māhmud Khān. Died at Kalāt.
              - AHMAD YAR KHĀN, slain by Mehrab Khān the second year after his accession.
                - SHĀH NAWĀZ KHĀN, temporarily placed in power by the British. Abdicated in favour of Nasir Khān.
                - FATI KHĀN.
        - ELTARZ KHĀN, slain accidentally by his brother, Nasir Khān, when both were hostages at Kandahār; from him descend the Eltarzai families of Baghwāna and Kotri.
        - NASIR KHĀN, originally a hostage at Kandahār, superseded his brother, Mohbat Khān, and ruled about forty years.
          - MĀHMUD KHĀN, ruled at Kalāt.
            - MEHRAB KHĀN, slain on the capture of his capital by the British.
              - HĀSSAN KHĀN, with the assumed name of Mir Nasir Khān, supposed to have been poisoned.
              - KHUDADĀD KHĀN, the present chief of Kalāt.
            - AZEM KHĀN.
          - MUHAMMAD REHIM KHĀN, slain by the sister of Mastapha Khān.
          - MASTAPHA KHĀN, slain by his brother, Muhammad Rehim Khān.
            - SARAFRĀZ KHĀN, slain by Mehrab Khān at the same time with Ahmad Yar Khān.

APPENDIX B.

A SHORT VOCABULARY OF THE BALOCH (HILL BALOCH AND MAKRĀNI BALOCH) AND BRAHUIKI (OR KURGALLI) DIALECTS.

HILL BALOCH.

Ankle	*kar*
Ant	*muri*
Armpit	*bagal*
Ass	*har*
Bad	*gandag*
Belly	*lāp*
Black	*siah*
Blood	*hon*
Blue	*nil*
Bone	*had*
Boots	*muzag*
Boy	*chuka*
Branch	*shāgh*
Bread	*naghan*
Breast	*ghwen-sina*
Buffalo	*gha-mesh*
Bull	*ghanghar*
Bullet	*tir*
Butt (of a gun)	*kundak*
Calf (of leg)	*hush-padag*
Cap	*toph*
Camel	*ushtar* or *hushtar*
Cat	*pishi*
Cock	*nerak*
Cold	*guwar*
Comb	*shak*
Copper	*mis*
Cotton	*karpas*
Cow	*guk madak*
Cup	*tās*
Date (fruit)	*hormag*
Date (tree)	*match*
Day	*roch*
Dish	*tāl*
Dog	*kaochak*
Door	*dari*
Earth	*dāgar*
Elephant	*pil*
Eye	*chhain*
Fire	*ora*
Father	*phis*
Fish	*mahi*
Flea	*kak*
Flesh	*ghust*
Flower	*pūl*
Fly	*makish*
Foot	*panjak*
Fort	*kalāt*
Fruit	*bar*
Frying-pan	*kallind*
Girl	*jane-chuk, kasāne-chuk*
Goat	*buz*
God	*khudā*
Gold	*tila*
Good	*sher*
Green	*saoz*
Hand (palm of)	*dast-dil*
Heat	*garmı*
Heavy	*gāran*
Heel	*punzig*

Hen	*madak*
Horse	*hasp*
Hot	*garm*
House	*lok*
Iron	*asin*
Knee	*padi khund*
Kine	*guk*
Knife	*kārch*
Ladder	*pādi-ānk*
Large	*massān*
Leaf	*tāg*
Leather	*drohal*
Leg	*pād*
Light (adj.)	*subak*
Lip	*lunt*
Louse	*būr*
Man	*mardam*
Marriage	*sang*
Matchlock	*tofak*
Moon	*mah*
Mother	*mās*
Mountain	*koh*
Mud	*liggitch*
Nail (of the hand)	*nahun*
Navel	*napag*
Night	*chhap*
Paper	*kaggīz*
Pen	*kalam*
Powder (gun)	*shuru*
Rain	*hor*
Ramrod	*ter-koh*
Rat	*mushk*
Red	*sur*
Rice	*dān*
River	*dariya*
Rope	*chilik*
Root	*rotag*
Scarlet	*reto*
Screw	*hazarnar*
Sea	*daryā*
Sea-shell	*ghur*
Shawl (for waist)	*sirinband*
Shawl (for head)	*fogh*
Sheep	*mesh*
Shield	*hisfar*
Ship	*buji*
Shirt	*jāma*
Shoes	*kosh*
Silver	*nukra*
Sister	*gohār*
Sky	*āsmān*

Small	*kassān*
Son	*bachh*
Spear	*bal, nizzar*
Star	*yistār*
Stem	*dar*
Stone	*sing*
Sun	*roch*
Sword	*zaham*
Tent	*tambu*
Thick	*baz*
Thigh	*pādi baz ghust*
Thin	*tannak*
Toes	*murdanag*
Tree	*derāch*
Trousers	*shelwar*
Trousers-band	*pai-in-jag*
Uncle	*nakho*
Vein	*ragh*
Water	*hāp*
Water-melon	*kotig*
Well	*chās*
Wheat	*gandam*
White	*sifet*
Wife	*jan*
Wind	*ghwāt*
Wind (north)	*gorich*
Wind (south)	*zir-ghwāt*
Wind (north-west)	*jil-ghwāt*
Wind (south-east)	*sir-ghwāt*
Window	*darwāzā*
Woman	*janē*
Wood	*dar*
Yellow	*zard*
To do	*kartan*
To be	*shutan*
To speak	*gwāshtan*
To burn	*sutan*
To fall	*koftan*
To stand	*pādātan*
To give	*dātan*
To throw	*durdātan*
To carry	*burtan*
To flee	*gistan*
To eat	*wartan*
To bring	*hartan*
To wash	*shūstan*
To sit	*nishtan*
To write	*nawishtan*
To kill	*kūshtan*
To walk	*gashtan*

English	Baloch
To fear	*tārsitan*
To laugh ...	*handitan*
To measure	*gaz kastan*
To break ...	*proshtan*
To see	*dishtan*
To sew	*dotan*
To scrape	*trāshtan*
To reckon ...	*issāb kastan*
To do well ...	*shar kastan*
To open ...	*patch kastan*
To tie	*bastan*
To come	*hahtan*
To read	*wāntan*
To sleep	*waftan*
To awake	*nashtan*
To dry ...	*kusk kastan*
To rub	*lutartan*
To pay ...	*pirmātan*
To fly (as a bird) ...	*bāl kastan*
To plunder	*lutitan*
To milk	*doshtan*
To fight ...	*jang kastan*
To boil	*grastan*
To receive	*rasitan*
To pick up	*chitan*
To kiss ...	*chuk kitan*
To kick ...	*laggat jittan*
To bite ...	*gat girtan*
To blind ...	*cham kushtan*
To flog ...	*chabak jittan*
To beat	*lat jittan*
To wound ...	*zaham jittan*
To fire (a gun) ...	*tofak jittan*
To hit	*laggitan*

MAKRĀNI BALOCH.

English	Baloch
Air	*gwāt*
Ankle	*much*
Ant	*mor*
Apple	*sorob*
Armpit	*bagal*
Ashes	*pur*
Ass	*har*
Axe	*towār*
Bābul (tree) ...	*chish, tish*
Barley	*o*
Bee	*benaga, makask*
Belly	*lāp*
Black	*siyah*
Blue	*nil*
Blood	*hūn*
Bone	*had*
Boot	*kaush*
Boy	*bachak*
Brass	*brinj*
Bread	*nān, nagan*
Breast	*gwar*
Brother	*brās, brāt*
Buffalo	*gamish*
Bullet	*tir*
Butter	*nemag*
Calf	*gwask*
Camel ...	*hushtera*
Cap	*top*
Cat	*pushi*
Clothes	*poshāk*
Cock ...	*koras, kurus, bāngū*
Cold	*sard*
Comb	*shak*
Copper	*rod*
Cotton	*karpās*
Cow ...	*mādagin gok*
Crow	*gurag*
Date (ripe)	*nā*
Date-tree ...	*mach, machī*
Day	*roch*
Deer	*āsk, au*
Den	*namb*
Doctor	*tabib*
Dog	*kuchak*
Donkey	*har*
Duck	*bat*
Dust	*hāk*
Earth	*dunya*
Elephant	*pil*
Eye	*cham*
Face	*dem*
Father	*pis, pit*
Field	*dagār*
Finger ...	*lankuk, lankuh*
Fire	*āch, ās*
Fish	*māhi*
Fisherman	*mēd*
Flea	*kak*
Flesh	*gosht*
Flower	*pūl*

Fly	*makask*
Foot	*pād*
Fort	*kot, kilāt*
Fowl	*kukur*
Fox	*robā*
Fruit	*niwag*
Girl	*janik*
Goat	*siyāhin pas*
God	*hudā, allā*
Gold	*tila*
Good	*shar*
Green	*sabz*
Greyhound	*tāzi*
Gun	*tupāk*
Hair	*mud, nud*
Hand	*dast*
Hare	*kargoshk*
Heat	*garmāg*
Heavy	*girān*
Heel	*pinz*
Hog	*hik*
Horse	*hāps, hāsp*
Hot	*garm*
House	*log, metag*
Husband	*mard*
Infant	*bachak*
Iron	*āhin*
Jackal	*tolag*
Knee	*kund, zān*
Knife	*kārch*
Ladder	*padiānk*
Large	*mazan*
Lead (metal)	*surup*
Leaf	*pan, tāk*
Leather	*post*
Leg	*pād*
Light (adj.)	*subuk*
Light	*roshāni*
Lip	*lunt*
Locust	*madag*
Louse	*bot, but*
Man	*mardum*
Mare	*mādiān*
Marriage	*sir*
Master	*waja*
Melon, water	*kutap, kitag*
Melon, musk	*tejag*
Mouth	*māh*
Moon	*mā*
Mother	*mās*
Mountain	*koh*
Mud	*men, gil*
Nail (of the hand)	*nākun, nāhun*
Navel	*nāfag*
Night	*shap*
North	*kutub*
Nose	*poz*
Oil	*tel, ropan*
Paper	*kāgad*
Path	*rā, kishk*
Pen	*kalam*
Plough	*nangār*
Powder (gun)	*shuro*
Rain	*haur*
Rainbow	*drinag, drinuk*
Ramrod	*tirku*
Rat	*mushk*
Red	*sur, sohr*
Rice	*birinj*
River	*kohr*
Rope	*sād, chit*
Rust	*zang*
Salt	*wād, sūr*
Sand	*hāk, rēk*
Sea	*daryā*
Sheep	*mesh, ispetin pas*
Shell	*gurak*
Shirt	*jāmag*
Shoe	*kaush*
Shore	*tiāb*
Silver	*nugra*
Sister	*gwahār*
Sky	*āsmān*
Small	*kasān*
Snake	*mār*
Son	*zāg*
Steel	*pulād*
Storm	*tufān*
Stone	*sing*
Sugar	*shakar*
Sun	*roch*
Sword	*zām, shamshir*
Tamarisk	*gaz*
Tank	*wateg, talamb*
Tent	*tambu*
Thief	*duzd*
Thick	*zand*
Thigh	*leng*
Thunder	*grund, hūrā*
Toe	*lankuk*
Tree	*drāch, drackk*
Trousers	*shalwār*

Turban ... ... *pāg*
Turtle ... ... *kāsib*
Uncle ... ... *nāku*
Vein ... ... *rag*
Water ... ... *āp*
Wax ... ... *mom*
Well (of water) ... ... *chāh*
West ... *roirsht, magrab*
Wheat .. ... *gandin, gala*
White ... ... *ispet*
Wife ... ... *zāl, gis*
Wind ... ... *gwāt*
Winter ... *zimistān*
Wolf ... ... *gwark*
Woman ... ... *janin*
Wool ... ... *pazhm*
Wood ... ... *dār*
Wrist ... ... *dasta much*
Year ... ... *sāl*
Yellow ... ... *zard*
Young ... ... *warnā*

To do ... ... *kanaga*
To go ... ... *roaga*
To speak *gwashapa, habar kanaga*
To burn ... ... *sochaga*
To fall ... ... *kapaga*
To stand still ... *wushtaga*
To give ... ... *deaga*
To throw ... ... *daur deaga*
To catch ... .. *giraga*
To run ... *maidāna roaga*
To eat ... ... *waraga*
To bring ... ... *āraga*
To wash ... ... *shodaga*
To set ... ... *nindaga*
To write ... *nimishta kanaga*

To kill ... ... *kushaga*
To walk ... *pāda roaga*
To fear ... ... *trusaga*
To laugh ... *handaga*
To meet ... *dochār kanaga*
To break ... *prushaga*
To see ... ... *gindaga*
To sew ... ...*dochaga*
To scrape ... ... *mushaga*
To read ... ... *wānaga*
To desire ... ... *lotaga*
To open ... *pach kanaga*
To tie ... ... *bandaga*
To come ... ... *aiaga*
To rise ... ... *pāda aiaga*
To sleep ... ... *wapsaga*
To awake ... ... *pāda aiaga*
To drink ... ... *waraga*
To rub ... ... *mushaga*
To paint ... *rang deaga*
To fly (as a bird) ... *bāl kanaga*
To plunder ... *duzdi kanaga*
To mix ... .. *lur kanaga*
To fight ... *jang kanaga*
To boil ... ... *lahr kanaga*
To receive ... *wadī kanaga*
To pull ... ... *kashaga*
To keep ... ... *dāraga*
To kick ... *lagata janaga*
To begin ... *sūrū kanaga*
To ask ... ...*justo kanaga*
To fold ... *dotal kanaga*
To beat ... ... *janaga*
To weigh ...*shāhima kashaga*
To fire ... ... *janaga*
To hold ... ... *dāraga*

BRAHUIKI

Afraid ... ... *kolik*
Ague ... ... *larza*
All ... ... *khul*
Alum ... ... *fitki*
Angry ... ... *khar*
Ant ... ... *morink*
Antimony ... ... *surma*
Arm ... ... *du*
Arrow ... ... *sum*
Ashes ... ... *hiss*

Ass ... ... *bīsh*
Aunt (paternal) ... *ir-bāwa*
Autumn ... ... *iricha*
Bad ... ... *gandar*
Barley ... ... *sār*
Beard ... ... *rish*
Beautiful ... ... *sher*
Bee ... ... *hilt-shāhid*
Big ... ... *balun*
Bitter ... ... *karen*

English	Brahui
Black	*mohan*
Blood	*dittar*
Blue	*karur*
Bow	*bil*
Boy	*mār*
Brass	*brinj*
Brave	*bahādar*
Bread	*irag*
Breakfast	*nihari*
Broad	*ghwand*
Brother	*īlam*
Bull	*karighar*
Butter	*kassi*
Camel	*huce*
Camomile	*bu-mādaran*
Cap	*top*
Carpet	*gālli*
Cat	*pishis*
Chain	*zamzir*
Charcoal	*pog*
Cheap	*azān*
Cheek	*kallak*
Cheese	*pānir*
Chin	*zanu*
Clarified butter	*si*
Clay	*litchak*
Cloud	*jamma*
Cock	*bangu*
Cold (adj.)	*yakht*
Colour	*rang*
Comb	*iriss*
Copper	*miss*
Coral	*mirjān*
Cord	*chit*
Cornelian	*akik*
Cotton	*pamba*
Cow	*daggi*
Crow	*khāku*
Crystal	*balor*
Darkness	*tār-māh*
Daughter	*masir*
Day	*dē*
Dear (not cheap)	*kuben*
Death	*kask*
Defile	*tang*
Diamond	*almāss*
Disease	*merz*
Distant	*mūr*
Ditch	*kandak*
Dog	*kuchik*
Door	*dargah*
Dry	*bahlum*
Dust	*mish*
Ear	*kaf*
Earth	*dagghar*
East	*dē-tik*
Egg	*baidār*
Emerald	*zamzūd*
Equal	*barobar*
Eye	*kan*
Eyebrow	*burwāk*
Eyelash	*michāch*
Felt	*tappar*
Fever	*khel*
Finger	*or-pindi*
Fire	*khāka*
Fish	*māhi*
Flame	*lamba*
Flint	*istārkal*
Flour	*nūt*
Flower	*pūl*
Fly	*hilt*
Forehead	*kāhtam*
Fort	*kot*
Fountain	*chushmeh*
Fowl	*kokar*
Fruit	*miwar*
Girl	*maser*
Glad	*khūsh*
Gold	*kisūn*
Good	*sher*
Grain	*ghalla*
Grandfather	*pader-bāwa*
Grandmother	*luma-bāwa*
Grape	*hangūr*
Gun	*tufak*
Hail	*tronghūr*
Hair	*puzhar*
Half	*nim*
Hard	*sakht*
Heart	*ust*
Heat	*bāsūni*
Heavy	*kolin*
Heir	*wāris*
Hen	*makiān*
High	*burz*
Hill	*bot*
Honey-comb	*angumen*
Horse	*huli*
Hot	*basūn*
House	*urāh*
Hungry	*bingun*

Husband ... ... *hari*
Inheritance ... *mirās*
Iron ... ... *ahin*
Juār ... ... *juāri*
Kine ... ... *kharāss*
Kiss ... ... *buzhalk*
Knife ... ... *kattār*
Laughter ... ... *makh-khēk*
Lead (metal) ... ... *surf*
Leaf ... ... *berg*
Leather ... ... *chirm*
Left (not right) ... *chap*
Life ... ... *zindeh*
Light (adj.) ... ... *subak*
Lightning ... ... *garūk*
Little ... ... *machi*
Long ... ... *murghun*
Low ... ... *mandar*
Mad ... . *ganūk*
Madder ... ... *rodan*
Man ... *bandak, bandagh*
Marble ... *sang marmar*
Mare ... ... *madiān*
Marriage ... ... *baram*
Matchlock ... ... *tofak*
Meat ... ... *su*
Melon (water) ... ... *kutik*
Melon (musk) ... *kerbuj*
Milk ... ... *pal*
Mine ... ... *kahān*
Mint ... ... *purchink*
Moon ... ... *tuvi*
Month ... ... *tu*
Mother ... ... *luma*
Mountain ... ... *mash*
Mouth ... ... *bar*
Much ... ... *baz*
Moustache ... ... *birut*
Nail ... ... *had*
Naked ... ... *lagghar*
Near ... ... *khurk*
Neck ... ... *lekh*
New ... ... *puskun*
Night ... ... *nan*
Nipple ... ... *kad*
North ... ... *kotab*
Nose ... ... *bamus*
Nostril ... ... *granz*
Oil ... ... *tel*
Old (in age) ... *pir*
Old (not new) ... *wutkun*
Olive-green ... ... *ghwanki*
Painful ... ... *khal*
Peace ... ... *khair*
Pearl ... ... *dur*
Pepper ... ... *filfil*
Plain ... ... *dan*
Poor ... ... *garib*
Quicksilver ... ... *parrà*
Rabbit ... ... *muru*
Rain ... ... *pihar*
Rainbow ... ... *bilasum*
Ram ... ... *khar*
Red ... ... *kisun*
Rice ... ... *brinj*
Right (not left) ... *rāst*
River ... ... *daria*
Rivulet ... ... *nala*
Road ... ... *kassar*
Rope ... ... *rez*
Ruby ... ... *lāl yakut*
Saddle ... ... *zen*
Salt ... ... *bi*
Sand ... ... *regh*
Scissors ... ... *kaichi*
She-goat ... ... *het*
Sheep ... ... *mehl*
Shield ... ... *hisper*
Ship ... ... *beri*
Shirt ... ... *khuss*
Shoes ... ... *muchari*
Silver ... ... *pihun*
Sister ... ... *ir*
Sky ... ... *asmān*
Slain ... ... *kassīfi*
Slow ... ... *karar*
Small ... ... *chunak*
Smoke ... ... *mult*
Snake ... ... *dushar*
Snow ... ... *barf*
Soft ... ... *kulbun*
Son ... ... *mahal*
Sour ... ... *sur*
South ... ... *sohēl*
Spear ... ... *nizzar*
Spider ... ... *moro*
Spring (season) ... ... *hatam*
Star ... ... *istar*
Stallion ... ... *nariān*
Steel ... ... *polād*
Stick ... ... *lat*
Stone ... ... *khal*

English	Equivalent
Sun	*dē*
Sugar	*kand*
Sulphur	*gogard*
Summer	*tir-māh*
Swift	*zaft*
Sweet	*hanēn*
Sword	*zāhgam*
Tempest	*tofan*
Temple (of body)	*kush*
Thunder	*hura*
Tin	*kallahi*
Tongue	*dari*
Tooth	*dandān*
Tower	*tul*
Tree	*darakht*
Trousers	*shelwār*
True	*rāsht*
Turquoise	*ferozeh*
Ugly	*gandar*
Valley	*dara*
Vigilant	*hushiār*
Waist	*mukh*
War	*jang*
Water	*dir*
Wax	*mum*
Wealthy	*dolatman*
Weary	*damdaruk*
Weeping	*hoyikh*
Well	*dūn*
West	*kebila*
Wet	*pahlum*
Wheat	*kolum*
White	*pihun*
Wife	*harvat*
Wind	*thau*
Winter	*sehl*
Wood	*pat*
Woman	*zaifa*
Wool	*pashm*
Year	*sāl*
Yellow	*poshkun*
Young	*warnar*
To give	*tenning*
To grind	*nusing*
To see	*khanning*
To sleep	*kaching*
To go	*inning*
To come	*banning*
To cut	*terring*
To hear	*benning*
To laugh	*makhing*
To sit	*tuling*
To know	*shāhing*
To burn	*hushing*
To fall	*taming*
To stand	*selling*
To throw	*shāhghing*
To build	*jur-kanning*
To flee	*nerring*
To sew	*muching*
To carry	*danning*
To eat	*kuning*
To bring	*atning*
To do	*kanning*
To strike	*kalling*
To weep	*okhing*
To want	*alling*
To wash	*selling*
To break	*perghing*
To bind	*taffing*
To sow	*dassing*
To pass over	*illing*
To write	*nawishta-kanning*
To kill	*kasfing*
To find	*khanning*
To seize	*halling*
To read	*khwanning*
To repose	*damdanning*
To fly	*bāll-kanning*
To approve	*pasand-kanning*
To call	*khwāst-kanning*
To milk	*biring*
To taste	*chakking*
To fight	*jang-kanning*
To boil	*jush-kanning*
To pull	*pashing*
To kiss	*pad-kanning*
To scrape	*hāshing*
To trust	*peching*
To die	*kahing*
To bite	*bahshāhghing*
To open	*ithing*
To measure	*dahghing*
To drop (as rain)	*chakking*
To kick	*laggat-kalling*
To tear	*parrah-kanning*
To shade	*saikar-kanning*
To sit (in the sun)	*dē-i-tuling*
To speak false	*dqrogh paning*
To weigh	*tul kanning*
To swim	*tar kanning*

To sink ...	*gark manning*
To count ...	*yar-tilling*
To fear	*khuling*
To rest	*karar kanning*
To forgive	*bashking*
To ask	*arfing*
To reap (grain) ...	*ruting*
To tremble ...	*larzing*
To gather	*arraffing*
To sweep ...	*rufing*
To steal ...	*duzi kanning*
To walk ...	*cherring*
To spit ...	*tuf kanning*
To embrace ...	*bagal kanning*
To speak	*paning*
He speaks ...	*payikrri*
I did speak	*parēt*
He did speak	*pāre*
He spoke	*paretni*
He has spoken ...	*pare kanni*
He may have spoken ...	*pare sakni*
He may speak ...	*akhar payikni*
Speak	*pā-kanni*
Let him speak ...	*pā-wanni*

APPENDIX C.

ROAD ROUTES IN PERSIAN AND KALĀTI BALOCHISTAN.

		Length in miles
1.	Banpur to Chāhbār *viâ* the Fanoch Pass (II.)	241
2.	Banpur to Chāhbār *viâ* Geh (III.)	196
3.	Banpur to Gwattar and Gwādar *viâ* Kasrkand (IV.) ...	262
4.	Banpur to Gwādar *viâ* Sarbāz and Pishin (V.) ...	254
5.	Banpur to Bam (VI.)...	230
6.	Bibi-Nāni (in Bolān Pass) to Kalāt *viâ* Rodbar (XII.)...	116
7.	Dādar (in Kachhi) to Quetta (or Shāl-Kōt) *viâ* Bolān Pass (XI.)	90
8.	Dādar to Kandahār (in Afghānistan) *viâ* Quetta (XIII.) ...	232
9.	Gwādar to Karāchi *viâ* Kēj and Bēla (VII.)... ...	431
10.	Jacobabad to Dēra *viâ* Shāhpur (XX.)	109
11.	Jacobabad to Kahan *viâ* Pulaji (XXI.)	121
12.	Jalk to Banpur (I.)	199
13.	Karāchi to Kalāt *viâ* Las Bēla (XVIII.)	392
14.	Karāchi to Shāh Bilāwal (Las) (XIX)	71
15.	Kotri (or Kotra), in Kachhi, to Kalāt *viâ* the Mula Pass (X.)	155
16.	Nushki to Kharān (XVI.)	89
17.	Nushki to Shorāwak (XVII.)	35
18.	Panjgur to Gwādar *viâ* the Talār Pass (VIII.)	233
19.	Panjgur to Gwādar *viâ* Pishin (IX.)	295
20.	Quetta to Mushki *viâ* the Nishpa Pass (XIV.)	93
21.	Quetta to Kalāt *viâ* Mastung (XV.)	112

I.

JALK TO BANPUR.

Halting-place.	Distance in miles.	Water supply.	Food and forage.	Remarks.
Jalk ...	...	Good from Kanāts	Any quantity of dates. A fair amount of wheat, barley, rice, and chopped straw; plenty of sheep and goats.	Jalk consists of a group of villages, each formed by a central fort or tower, with a cluster of mud huts round it, at the mouth of a ravine opening on the desert. The cultivation, which is confined to the ravine, extends for 3 miles, the surface being either cultivated, broken, or swampy. Inhabitants, 3000 to 4000 in number, mostly Arbābis. Jalk is a dependency of Dizak; climate unhealthy.
Laji ...	12	Running stream, very good	Dates, a very little corn and rice; sheep and goats	Leaving the Jalk ravine at once, the road crosses a stony desert for nine miles, when it enters the Kalagān ravine, a little below the village of Laji, near which is a good camping ground on the left bank. Road practicable for field guns throughout.
Kal-i-Baloch	10	Running stream, good but scanty	None; good grazing for camels	Road follows Kalagān ravine past Bālā-Kalāt, Aibi, and Pahura villages for eight miles, when it turns up a ravine to the right, two miles up which is the halting-place. Road good.
Kalpurakan	20.6	Running stream, good and abundant	Dates, perhaps a little corn; plenty of sheep and goats in vicinity, and good grazing for camels	Road follows windings of ravine for 10 miles, where water-parting is reached, 5000 feet above the sea; thence a descent of four-and-a-half miles leads to outlet of the pass, which is called Brinjinan, thence six miles to Kalpurakan, down a gentle slope. Excepting a sharp turn near top of pass, the road is quite passable for guns; governor of Banpur has several times taken 12-pounders over it. An hour's work sufficient to repair road in place mentioned.
Dizak ...	12.8	Good from Kanāts	Plentiful, of all sorts	Level road over plain for nine-and-a-half miles to Ziārat, first village of Dizak, after which road passes through date groves and cultivation to Kaleh-i-Dizak, the principal village and residence of the chief.

JALK TO BANPUR (*continued*).

Halting-place.	Distance in miles.	Water supply.	Food and forage.	Remarks.
Ab-Patān ..	20.3	Running stream, good	None	Two miles across sandy plain to small garden and tower. cross dry bed of a branch of Māshkid river, and up a torrent-bed with pools of water at intervals to the 18th mile, where cross watershed and descend to a group of palms in torrent-bed at a gap in the hills. No village.
Surān ...	6.8	Kanāts; from small river, good	Plentiful, of all sorts	Good road across barren plain, sloping to south-west, to group of three villages, principal of which is called Surān.
Khaur Chaharukan ...	12	Good, obtained by digging shallow wells in torrent-bed	None	After crossing bed of stream, which was running at end of March about one foot deep and 20 yards wide, entered hills at second mile. Two insignificant passes to halting-place in bed of torrent. Camels went by a road about two miles longer, further north, to avoid passes.
Magas ...	15.7	Good from Kanāts	Dates plentiful; grain obtainable in small quantities	At fourth mile a steep descent, passable for guns with drag ropes; at eight miles, Koshān, small tower with date grove on banks of running stream; at 12 miles, Kaimagar date groves. Road good after pass.
Sar-Paharu	13.6	Good from holes in torrent-bed	None	Level road for 10 miles across plain, on through low hills to halting-place in bed of a dry torrent; this is the first place in Paharu, Puhra, or Fahraj, a sub-division of the Banpur district.
Isfidān ...	20.9	From spring 500 yards off, in hills to north	None	At three miles cross water-parting (5000 feet above sea-level) and enter ravine, which soon widens to 100 yards or more, with tamarisk jungle. Road fair.
Aptar ...	25.7	Good from Kanāts	Dates plentiful; grain in small quantities	Road follows torrent-bed, which is from a quarter to one mile wide, and thickly wooded in parts for 17 miles, passing water in two places; it then turns out of torrent-bed to left, and passes through low hills for two miles, when it re-enters torrent-bed, along which guns would have to keep, and follows it, which separates into several ravines to village of Aptar or Haftar, in thick date groves.

JALK TO BANPUR (*continued*).

Halting-place.	Distance in miles.	Water supply.	Food and forage.	Remarks.
Puhra (or Fahraj)...	12.8	Good from Kanāts	Dates plentiful; grain in small quantities	Good road over desert till the cultivation about Puhra is reached. Ground very swampy from watercourses. Camping ground to south of village.
Banpur ...	15.6	Good from Kanāts	Plentiful, of all sorts	Road good throughout, a little sandy in parts; at eight miles Ab-band, a dam across Banpur river, a considerable stream flowing three to four feet deep, between steep banks covered with jungle. Banpur, the capital of Persian Balochistan, is a small fort, with perhaps 200 houses round it, and two walled gardens; to the north a line of sand-hills, on one of which the fort is built, separates the cultivated area, which extends to the river, two to three miles to the south, from the desert. Banpur is 1700 feet above the sea, but the climate is very hot and unhealthy.
Total ...	198.8	miles.		

II.

BANPUR TO CHĀHBĀR *viâ* THE FANOCH PASS (GOLDSMID).

Halting-place.	Distance in miles.	Water supply.	Food and forage.	Remarks.
Kāsimābād	9	Good from Banpur, river or wells	Dates, grain, etc., generally procurable	Kāsimābād, a small Baloch village, with a fort; huts of sun-dried brick, but chiefly of mud, with tamarisk trees and branches and other jungle produce. Inhabitants poor, squalid, and ill-clothed; many dark-complexioned, and of a Sidi or slave caste of features and general appearance. Road amid scattered jungle and occasional cultivation, somewhat heavy from sand.

BANPUR TO CHĀHBĀR (*continued*).

Halting-place.	Distance in miles.	Water supply.	Food and forage.	Remarks.
Balochan Chāh ...	27	From wells, supply uncertain	Sheep procurable from nomads, but provisions generally precarious	Halting-place reached after passing the Gwarpusht sand-hills, the village of Gwarpusht being at some distance to the left, on the road to the Cham pass; at the sand-hills are trees and water. At Balochan Chāh ground harder, and wild vegetation somewhat more abundant, but the whole character of the country sterile.
Maskotu ...	26	From bed of river, precarious	Dates abundant, forage scarce	Poor village, with few inhabitants, situate near a date grove on south bank of a large broad and dry (when passed) *rudkhāna*. Has the ordinary mud fort and a second one in ruins, besides usual Baloch huts. Cause of abandonment, visitation of small-pox and, more recently, cholera.
Fanoch ...	25	From Aimini river, good	Sheep, dates, and grain should all be procurable; forage precarious	A comparatively large and important Baloch village, in plains north of the Makrān hills, and close to a pass bearing the name, which enters Makrān from the Persian district of Banpur; fort in ruins, and seemingly uninhabited. About 100 houses, and probably 500 inhabitants, most of whom said to be slaves. Chākar Khān, a young Baloch chief, of same family as the Nhārnis of Sistān, resided here in 1866. The Balochis of the plains traversed between this and Kāsimābād are Lashāris. Road from Maskotu hard and stony, or sandy and gravelly, intersected with beds of streams and small ravines, and studded here and there with low black rocks and hillocks; at about seven-and-a-half miles met by road from Kalānzas. Aimini river rises in plains after rain, and winds into the Fanoch pass, thence finding its way to the sea, under a new name at Kalig, in western Makrān.

BANPUR TO CHĀHBĀR (*continued*).

Halting-place.	Distance in miles.	Water supply.	Food and forage.	Remarks.
Benth ...	29	From river, amount dependent on rain	Dates, but sheep and grain should be procurable; forage precarious	Benth, a large village at foot of a hill bearing that name, and south of the narrow pass of Fanoch, through which traveller to Makrān proceeds for some distance between nearly perpendicular rocks. Road stony and rugged, and rendered difficult for camels, owing to the water, which at times is very deep, and collects in scarcely fordable pits. At 16 miles defile, which, after gradually improving, widens to open space, with view of distant hills; route then closes and expands as before. At 25 miles Dehan, depopulated a few years ago by cholera, 15 houses only left out of 150, according to local report. Benth suffered on same occasion, but should still have large population, probably 1500 to 2000, all included.
Gonz ...	46	Dependent on rain	No supplies but from nomads	Name of tract; no village. Encamping ground reached after 12 hours' marching on camel-back, of these six spent in following course of Benth river, which changes its name to Korandab, and unites with the Nasfarān. Second half over a wild rugged country, amid bare hills, and with few traces of inhabitants or life of any kind. Halt near tamarisk bushes in sandy soil, and within reach of rain water.
East of Teuk river	28	Dependent on rain	No supplies but from nomads	No village or regular halting-ground, but a position taken up owing to rain rendering road impassable, and after a march along and across the winding bed of the broad Teuk river, entered on two occasions.
Khaur-i-Kir	5	Abundant after rain, otherwise precarious	No supplies but from nomads	As the last, *i.e.*, a position taken up from necessity. The object was to cross the Kir river coming down from Gaih, but the rains had rendered this impracticable, so an encamping ground was chosen on the driest and most eligible spot.

BANPUR TO CHĀHBĀR (*continued*).

Halting-place.	Distance in miles.	Water supply.	Food and forage.	Remarks.
Tiz Hill ...	43	None	None	Again a halt from circumstances, at a place offering neither water, provisions, nor inducement of any kind, but rendered necessary from want of daylight to descend the hill above Chāhbār. Crossing the Khaur-i-Kir at 18 miles, the Khaur-i-Sangam, coming from the hill of Beshimun, is reached and forded; further on at 16 miles are the sand-hills of Paseg, where there are a few huts. Road at one time among low hills and on rocky ground, at another over alluvial or sandy soil, and amid low scattered jungle. From Pareg to the top of Tiz hill, between the villages of Toz and Chāhbār is about nine miles.
Chāhbār ...	3	Wells good and sufficient	Sheep, dates, and other supplies procurable, forage also, but is scarce	Chāhbār is a village on a sand hillock in a small bay of irregular shape, formed by the two points, Ras Tiz north, and Ras Chāhbār south. The fort is remarkable from its contrast to the mat huts around it, but is otherwise an ordinary mud building. There are cocoa-nut and mango trees, with garden and general cultivation, and wells. Sheep obtainable at a short notice, provisions also from constant communication by sea with Maskāt, and larger Baloch villages in the vicinity by land. *Ghi*, cotton, wool, goats' hair, mat-bags, *mung*, and *juār* are brought in from the interior; also rice, dates, and wheat for local consumption. There are, or were, about 225 houses of Bordars, Tizis, Shiris, Mēds, Kējis, Hamālis, Khwājahs and others, with perhaps about 560 inhabitants; the Banyas, or Hindu merchants have only five houses. Chāhbār is too much exposed to the westward, and the anchorage is too shallow near the shore, to be a good resort for shipping, but it is one of the best known, and perhaps the most frequented of the few ports on the Makrān coast.
Total ...	241	miles.		

III.

BANPUR TO CHĀHBĀR *viâ* GEH (GRANT, 1809).

Halting-place.	Distance in miles.	Water supply.	Food and forage	Remarks.
Gizkok ...	13	Brackish water	None	At three miles from Banpur, cross river; no village at Gizkok.
Isfaka ...	25	...	...	Road lies through sand-hills as far as Laskar ravine for about 13 miles, down which it continues for 12 miles to large village of Isfaka. Halted in the ravine two miles south of the village.
Pib ...	15	...	...	At nine miles the small village and port of Sordor-Pib, a large village, the chief place of the Laskar district.
Sarhi ...	13	...	...	At six-and-a-half miles, Oghin, small village with water and palms.
Hichan ...	21	...	...	Steep and difficult road through the Hichan ravine. Hichan, a fine village of 2000 inhabitants, with fort.
Geh ...	14	...	...	Road over hills and through ravines.
Halting-place		...	...	Road leads through the nālā of Geh. At 10 miles the Hichan nālā joins; at 33 miles road leaves nālā, which has water flowing the most of the way, and is in places skirted with palms; two miles more through ravines, then six over plain to a nālā with water.
Parag ...	36	Water from wells	...	For 21 miles through hills and ravines, then plains.
Tiz ...	12	...	...	At seven miles salt creek, called Minkhaur, unfordable at high tide. Tiz, a small village.
Chāhbār ...	6½			
Total ...	196½	miles.		

IV.

BANPUR TO GWATTAR AND GWĀDAR *viâ* KASRKAND (BERESFORD-LOVETT).

Halting-place.	Distance in miles.	Water supply.	Food and forage.	Remarks.
Moien Pisha	24	Scanty ...	Fuel only	At three-and-a-half miles cross Banpur river, about six miles further a small date grove, called Gwarpusht (water procurable), remainder of road quite desert. Halting-place is small ravine to the eastward of road.
Surmij ...	13	From two wells; scanty	Dates and grain in small quantities; fuel and forage	Road skirts hills to south, over steep sandy ridges and ravines. Surmij, a small village with date grove and a little cultivation.
Champ ...	19	Abundant	As above, but plentiful	Gradual ascent to plateau of Champ, a village of 50 houses with date groves. Several other similar villages in the vicinity, three of which are called Suriān, Gwant, and Gwatrak.
Gitan Kushkan, or Kushkan Gitan	7	Abundant from river Kāju	Dates, forage, and fuel only	There are two roads between Champ and Kushkan Gitān, one by Suriān impracticable for artillery, the other following main stream of Kāju river, said to be passable by wheels. One hut only at Kushkan Gitān.
Tang ...	15	do.	do.	Road follows winding of Kāju river along its valley; date groves and cultivation, but no villages. One hut at Tang.
Kwash ...	13	do.	do.	Road as in last march. No villages.
Kasrkand	11	do.	As above, with addition of grain and sheep	Road as in last two marches. Kasrkand, a large village of 1500 souls, with large square fort and extensive date groves. Grain procurable from villagers, and sheep from nomads and neighbourhood.
Gitān ...	23	From small spring in river-bed	None	Route along river-bed as before. Gitān, a halting-place only.
Chirak ...	29	Abundant from wells	Grain, dates, forage, and fuel	Road fair through ravines.
Miri Bazar	23	Abundant from irrigation channels	do.	Road lies through cultivated country, irrigated by numerous watercourses from the Bahu Dashtiyāri river. Villages numerous, camels procurable.

BANPUR TO GWATTAR AND GWĀDAR (*continued*).

Halting-place.	Distance in miles.	Water supply.	Food and forage.	Remarks.
Sisād ...	12	Abundant, from irrigation channels.	Grain, dates, forage, and fuel	Road similar to the last day's march. The crossing of the Bahu river, near Sisād, is dangerous to camels, owing to muddy bottom.
Rimdan ...	14	Precarious, from rain-water in pools	A little forage and fuel only	From Sisād a road leads direct to Gwattar, distant about 30 miles, the half-way halting-place being Sigari. The road to Rimdan leads through more or less cultivation till it emerges on the desert, three miles from Rimdan.
Siroki ...	18	Abundant from Dasht river	Forage and fuel abundant, a little grain, and a few sheep and fowls procurable	Road across a bare alluvial plain to edge of Dasht river, which runs through a belt of jungle, with occasional clearances for cultivation; the river, with but three to four feet of water, and about 50 yards wide. Siroki consists of two groups of mat huts on left bank.
Falari ...	16	Abundant in winter from stream, which dries in summer	Scanty forage and fuel	Good road over desert. Cross low hills just before reaching Falari, which is a halting-place on the bank of a small stream.
Ankora ...	13	Precarious, from rain-water pools	do.	Good road over desert until ravines are reached, in one of which the halting-place of Ankora is situated.
Gwādar ...	12	Good, from wells	Abundant	Leaving Ankora ravine road runs along sea-shore to Gwādar.
Total ...	262	miles.		

V.

BANPUR TO GWĀDAR *via* SARBĀZ AND PISHIN (EVAN SMITH, 1871).

Halting-place.	Distance in miles.	Water supply.	Food and forage.	Remarks.
Sar-i-band	8	Good, from river	Grass and fuel	Good road through acacia jungle. Camping-ground on river bank, near canal dam.
Sirkurān ...	12½	Good and plentiful	...	Road to Puhra, or Fahrej, as in route No. I., on leaving that place, turns abruptly south, and crosses desert plain for about five miles to camping-ground.
Absowarān	17	Good, from spring	...	Road for nine miles over stony desert plain, where enters hills by a ravine, in which it continues for seven miles. Camping-ground on right of road, some distance from ravine.
Pā-Godār	20	Good and abundant	Fuel good and abundant	Road continues in a ravine; at a point called Kāhira, a more direct path leads to Sarbāz, but is impracticable for guns.
Kolani ...	17	do.	do.	A mile-and-a-half from camping-ground, road reaches foot of a ridge which forms the water-parting between the Banpur and Sarbāz rivers, and divides the districts of the same name. After crossing ridge, road enters the bed of the Sarbāz river, which it thenceforward follows.
Sarbāz ...	19	do.	Rice and dates procurable in small quantities	At the 13th mile the direct road to Sarbāz enters the valley, which here widens considerably, and at Sarbāz forms an amphitheatre. Sarbāz, a village of 60 huts, with ruined fort.
Dipkhaur	14	do.	do.	Road through valley as before. Much cultivation and many hamlets.
Pā-rūd ...	12	do.	A moderate supply of provisions obtainable	The road as before follows river valley, which is here wider and less abruptly bounded. Several villages and palm-groves before reaching Pā-rūd, which has a ruined fort and about 180 huts. Camping-ground in stony plateau beyond village.
Rask. ...	14	do.	do.	The road follows river for nine miles, when it crosses a spur from west bank. Rask has 100 huts.

BANPUR TO GWĀDAR (*continued*).

Halting-place.	Distance in miles.	Water supply.	Food and forage.	Remarks.
Bogāni ...	15	Good and abundant	A moderate supply of provisions obtainable	Four miles down the valley, road emerges on plain, stretching to an indefinite distance east and west. Usual camping on south bank of river, which is then unnecessarily crossed in this and the next march.
Pishin ...	10	do.	do.	For four miles over desert plain, then through sparse acacia jungle to Pishin, which has two villages surrounded by date groves, a stone fort in each.
Kastag ...	11	Precarious; rain collected in pools	Forage and fuel only	After crossing small stream from east, road enters hills, and winds among narrow ravines to Kastag; halting-place not far from hamlet of same name.
Ghistān ...	13	do.	do.	Two miles from halting-place road enters wide valley, which it crosses to Ghistān; halting-place near small village of same name.
Kulmarisant	23	do.	do.	Leaving plain, road enters wide gorge between precipitous rocks, and following a torrent-bed for eight miles, passes on to a plain, crossing which for two miles, it descends into a ravine, where is a halting-place called Gwar Mauzil, which marks boundary between Persian and Kalāti Balochistan; further on, for 14 miles, is halting-place of Kulmarisant in a plain covered with low jungle. No village.
Dardān ...	12	Good and abundant	...	Road crosses plain to Dasht river, which is fordable except after heavy rain. Dardān is a village of 100 huts, one mile south of river.
Gurok ...	17	Precarious, from rain-water pools	None	Road crosses low hills and jungly plain for five miles, after which desert to Gurok. No village.
Gwādar ...	20	...	...	Flat plain with brushwood for 14 miles, after which low sand-hills.
Total ...	254½	miles.		

VI.

BANPUR TO BAM.

Halting-place.	Distance in miles.	Water supply.	Food and forage.	Remarks.
Kuchehgar-dān	16	Good, from Banpur river.	Fuel and forage plentiful; a little wheat and barley obtainable	Good road through forest. Kuchegardān small village with little cultivation, irrigated by a channel from the river, which is much diminished in volume compared to its size at Banpur.
Chahsur	21	Bad, from wells	Fuel and forage only	Good road through scattered jungle and narrow plains. Several torrent-beds passed Chahsur, collection of wells with brackish water, scattered over large area; large party should send on men in advance to find best well and clear it out.
Kalanzao...	26	Good wells	do.	Good road two miles through sparse forest, then 20 miles across desert, with occasional trees; last three miles jungle again. No village
Ladi ...	12	do.	Fuel and forage only. Sheep obtainable from nomad Balochis	Good road through sparse jungle or sandy plain. Halting-place in thick jungle, at a well of slightly brackish water.
Khusrin ...	16	Good springs	Fuel and forage only	One mile from Ladi, road leaves jungle, and crosses stony plain. Camping-ground of Khusrin, in bed of torrent, by side of a stream choked with long grass.
Gwān-i-ṭalab Khāni	15	Scanty, from spring	Scanty fuel and forage	Road lies through ravines among low hills of trap and trachyte, passable for guns with little difficulty. Garambigah, a halting-place with water, passed at the 10th mile.
Giran Rig	15	do.	do.	Road very bad and stony, barely passable for guns.
Chāhkambar	23	Fair, from a well	Fuel and forage only. Sheep to be got occasionally from nomads	Bad road up torrent for three miles, when crosses short pass, then a plain, sometimes inundated, called Dag-i-Farhad. Descending from this plain by the Saif-u-din pass, which marks Balochistan frontier, road descends a dry torrent-bed to halting-place.

BANPUR TO BAM (*continued*).

Halting-place.	Distance in miles.	Water supply.	Food and forage.	Remarks.
Konārnai River	15	Good, from river	Fuel and forage only	Good road through marshy torrent-bed to banks of Konārnai river, passing Ab-i-garm, the usual halting-place at 10th mile, when there is water in the Konārnai; its banks are the best halting-place. The whole road on this march, till after passing Ab-i-garm, is much infested by sand-flies, mosquitoes, and gad-flies.
Rigān	16	Good, from water-courses	Of all sorts, plentiful	Fourteen miles across stony plain, two miles through acacia jungle and cultivation. Rigān is the first village in Narmashir; has a small square mud fort; inhabitants Persians.
Būrj-i-Muhammad Khān	16	do.	do.	Good road through alternate cultivation and jungle to village, which is walled.
Jamāli ...	17	do.	do.	Good road through alternate cultivation and jungle. Jamāli, small village among several others, on the south bank of a river running through deep ravine.
Bam ...	22	do.	do.	Road crosses river, and after two miles of desert, skirts a swamp for four more, after which gravelly desert along water-course. At 18 miles, road ascends an abrupt scarp, and passes through rough sandstone hills to Bam.
Total ...	230	miles.		

VII.

GWĀDAR TO KARĀCHI *viâ* KĒJ AND BĒLA (Ross, 1865).

Halting-place.	Distance in miles.	Water supply.	Food and forage.	Remarks.
Tonk ...	25	From wells, scarce and bad	None; forage scanty	Road for 12 miles across level, sandy plain; at eight miles pass patch of cultivation, and some palm trees called Nigore; at 12 miles enter low range of hills; road for two miles stony, but not very steep, remainder level and easy; country barren. Camel food abundant at Tonk, but no water procurable between it and Gwādar.

GWĀDAR TO KARĀCHI (*continued*).

Halting-place.	Distance in miles.	Water supply.	Food and forage.	Remarks.
Belar ...	21	Fair ...	None	From Tonk, road leads more easterly between two ranges of hills, over barren tract; is easy and level all the way; halting-place shady.
Kohak ...	20	...	...	Road leads for six miles over hard barren country to the Talar pass; after passing hills turns north-west to a low hilly range, crossing which by an easy path enters plain called Dasht. Here are fertile patches of cultivation, and a good deal of low wood. Four miles from Kohak pass, Giki, a grove of date trees, and a few huts; water abundant. Cross bed of Dasht Khor close to Kohak; latter part of road good. Kohak is on the north side of the Khor.
Kantadar	12	From Khor, plenty and good	Abundant	Road from Kohak recrosses the bed of the Khor, and leads north-east along the left bank through cotton-fields and jungle. Close to Kantadar it again crosses the Khor; this place, which has 200 houses, being situate on the right bank. Good road all the way, and water readily obtained.
Kālatok (Kēj)	20	Plenty and good	do.	Road recrosses the Khor, and is not seen again until close to Kēj. For first six miles direction is north-easterly to range of hills which are crossed by an easy path, after which direction is more easterly, over barren, stony ground. A few miles west of Kālatok, the Khor (now Kējkhor), is crossed, and a fertile tract entered, abounding in vegetation and groves of trees, and intersected by artificial water-courses. Kālatok has 100 houses, and is situated north of the Khor.
Kala-i-Nao, or Nuki-Kalāt	7	do.	do.	Close to Kālatok, road to Kala-i-Nao crosses the Khor, and skirts the date groves. South of it, road good. Three miles east of Kālatok, passed a place called Sang-i-Kalāt, opposite Kala-i-Nao. North of the Khor stands the Nisri. Road to Turbat good, has 400 houses, and Kala-i-Nao 200 houses. Numerous *karēzes* at Turbat, and many wells. At two miles is a conical hill named Koh Murād, the Zikri shrine.
Turbat ...	2			

GWĀDAR TO KARĀCHI (*continued*).

Halting-place.	Distance in miles.	Water supply.	Food and forage.	Remarks
Sami... ...	20	From Khor and springs, good and plenty	Abundant	Still follow up Khor, which is crossed at Absar the eastern village of Kēj, on a sort of island. Road level, but stony. The valley becomes sterile till at 16 miles to Shohrak (fort and village), where are a grove of date trees and some fields. Four miles further on is Sami, on the north of the Khor, with 500 houses.
Ketok, by the river close to a sarāi	12	From the Khor, good and plenty	None; but grass in abundance	East of Sami, the road, which leads both to Kolwah and Panjgur, lies along the course of the Khor, which is frequently crossed and recrossed. Road everywhere level, though stony in places. Ketok is a name given to one part of the valley, where are several fields under cultivation. From that to Kolwah there is no cultivation in the valley, but sufficient vegetation in most parts to supply food to flocks of goats and sheep, kept by wandering Baloch tribes.
By the riverside of Balgettar	8	From the Khor very little; from a spring good	do	The Kolwah road, which continues east along the valley, was here left, the road to Panjgur branching off and passing through the northern range of hills. Pass is winding for a mile, but not difficult. Springs of water exist among the hills. The usual halting-place is at one of these north of the hills. Forage is scarcely obtainable there.
,,	10	...	None; forage scarce	Across a level plain in general. North of Balgettar is again hilly country. A pond supplied by a spring is the only inducement to halt here.
Balgettar Water	11	Good; from spring plenty	Forage scarce	Across a level and arid plain, in general saltish, but in a few places fertile.
Kil Khor...	12	River ...	None; forage obtainable	A level easy road across Balgettar plain to the hills previously crossed; some groves of trees and plenty of vegetation along the banks of the Khor (here the Kil Khor,) and a running stream of clear water. During the rains it becomes a torrent, and this pass through the hills would be impracticable for baggage animals. The road is for some distance down the river bank, and is difficult at places.

GWĀDAR TO KARĀCHI (*continued*).

Halting-place.	Distance in miles.	Water supply.	Food and forage.	Remarks.
Kil Khor ...	2	River ...	None; forage obtainable	
Pak	12	From wells, plentiful	Scarce	Winding through hills by an easy pass into the same valley before left, road is over stony, barren land, intersected by numerous ravines. Traces of recent cultivation everywhere visible further on. Hills on either side of valley not very lofty, and are about 12 miles apart.
Balor ...	6	do.	Abundant; of all sorts	To Balor, through fields and then jungle, a good road. Balor, which has 20 houses, is close to the southern range of hills.
Chambar ...	20	do.	do.	Along the south side of the valley pass through extensive fields of barley and juār, soil very rich. Half-way is a good halting-place by a well. Chambar has 100 houses.
Fakir's village	10	From ponds, indifferent	None; forage obtainable	Good road through same description of country. Numerous herds and flocks met with; antelope seen.
Grishnak ...	5	From well, plenty	Abundant	Hills trend more northerly than before, their direction being about east-north-east. The rest of the road good. Grishnak fort visible several miles off, being of considerable elevation.
Spring of water	13	Good and plenty	None	Road to Jau leaves Kolwah valley at a short distance east of Grishnak, and enters the southern hills through which it passes for two marches.
Poi Khor (or River)	7	From river	None; forage scarce	No habitations along this route, but springs of water are to be found at convenient intervals, near which forage generally obtainable. Road bad, wet at places; very steep and difficult ascents and descents.
Ziārat ...	12	Spring; uncertain	None; forage obtainable	Road tolerably easy, winding among hills to a fountain in a small valley; the grave of a Pir gives the halting-place the name of Ziārat.
Jao (Jaffir Khān's village)	7	River	Abundant	Three miles from Ziārat the valley of Jao appears. It is about 20 miles long by 10 or 12 broad, bounded on either side by hills, their general direction being east-north-east. Valley in parts thickly wooded and watered by the Jao river. Road through valley good. Cross the river to Jaffir Khān's village, which has only 40 houses.

GWĀDAR TO KARĀCHI (*continued*).

Halting-place.	Distance in miles.	Water supply.	Food and forage.	Remarks.
A nāla ...	15	Scarce, from nāla	None	Leaving the woody fertile portion of the valley, road passes through a dry, barren tract. At six miles a steep, difficult descent of about 200 feet, thence the road is level. A pool of water in a nāla is a favourite halting-place, but grass is very scarce.
Lakshor ...	17	do.	do.	For eight miles road runs easterly through the Arrah valley, which has some fertile soil, affording grass for a few flocks of goats and sheep. Two ranges of hills on either side, which at eight miles converge. From this point the pass through these hills is very difficult, winding along rocky bed of a nālā. Direction then southerly, emerging on Lakshar plain. Halting-place by a nāla containing water in pools.
Kumbi Shirin	10	do.	do.	An easy level road to Kumbi Shirin; lofty hills three miles east, traversed by an exceedingly steep, narrow pass, about a quarter of a mile in length, partly artificial, called here Lak.
Bēla	15	do.	Plentiful	Mountains lofty and of clayey formation. After descending the Lak (or pass), road winds among hills along the bed of a dry nāla, for six miles, when it emerges into the open in the Bēla province, six or seven miles south-west of the capital town.
Liyāri ...	35			
Sonmiāni...	20			
Karāchi ...	45			
Total ...	431	estimated miles.		

VIII.

PANJGUR TO GWĀDAR *viâ* THE TALĀR PASS (LOVETT, 1871).

Halting-place.	Distance in miles.	Water supply.	Food and forage.	Remarks.
Narain ...	25	From a well	None	Leaving the cultivation of Panjgur, road crosses a stony waste for 20 miles. Five miles through low sand-hills brings it to the Dasht plain.
Isaiāb ...	23	In river-bed	Scanty forage only	Proceed across Dasht plain covered with coarse grass and thorn bushes for about 20 miles. Village of Chit passed on right bank, about two miles from Narain. At 20 miles enter the hills, cross water parting, and descend into a ravine leading to the Gazbastan torrent.
In the Gazbastan torrent	17	do.	do.	Road follows general direction of the Gazbastan torrent.
In Shitāb torrent	16	do.	do.	Seven miles along Gazbastan torrent, and nine across hills to Shitāb torrent, which has more water and better forage than the former.
Bolida ...	11	Ample ...	Grain, beans, sheep, and goats in abundance.	Road crosses hills to the valley of the Ghish, in which lies the district of Bolida.
Girok Pass	24	Scanty ...	None	Crossing the Ghish river by a ford, the road lies over a plain to the Girok pass.
Miri	15	Ample ...	Abundant ...	Bad and stony road. From foot of pass to Miri is five miles.
Amulāni ...	22½	Precarious	None	After crossing hills south of Miri, road enters wide plain. Rain-water pools only at Amulāni; when these fail, travellers halt on the Dasht river, a few miles to the westward.
Talār Pass	26	Ample ...	Fuel and forage only	Road level as far as Biri river, after which successive ridges of sandstone to a torrent flowing eastward to the Talār pass, which is impassable for guns.
Kapar ...	21	Brackish and scanty	do.	From the pass to within a few miles of the sea a level plain, after which broken ridges of sandstone.
Gwādar ...	32½	...	...	The road follows the seashore to Gwādar.
Total ...	233	miles		

IX.

PANJGUR TO GWĀDAR *viâ* PISHIN (LOVETT, 1871).

Halting-place.	Distance in miles.	Water supply.	Food and forage.	Remarks.
Burj-i-Souaran	18½	Precarious	Scanty	At two miles from the last village of Panjgur, road passes Kalag hamlet, after which road crosses Rakshān river, and then eight miles of desert to halting-place.
Well	20½	Scanty and bad	Fuel only	Road crosses Gwargo river, which has steep banks 10 feet high; afterwards passes through narrow defiles, at foot of Pampiska peak.
Kalag ...	16	Scanty ...	Scanty	At eight miles pass small ruined fort of Diz. Road over plain. Near Diz fuel plentiful. Some irrigation dams make road heavy after rain.
In bed of Muzdi torrent	25½	Plentiful	Fuel and grass only	After leaving plateau of Diz, a rapid descent to bed of torrent.
Bolida ...	9½	do.	Ample	Through low hills by a very bad road.
Girok Pass	24	Scanty	None	See Route VIII.
Kalato ...	14	Good, from water-courses.	Supplies in moderate quantities	On issuing from Girok pass, road leaves that to Miri (see Route VIII.) on the left, and crosses the valley to Kalato.
Nasirabad	13	Good, from the Nihing river.	do.	Good road through acacia, etc., jungle.
Tump ...	22	do.	Grain, etc., plentiful	Good road; the Nihing river crossed by a ford half-way.
Mand ...	22	do.	do.	Good road through jungle on south side of valley.
Pishin ...	17	do.	do.	do. do.
Kastag ...	11	See Route V.		
Ghistān ...	10			
Kulmarisant	23			
Dardān ...	12			
Gurok ...	17			
Gwādar ...	20			
Total ...	295	miles		

X.

KOTRI (OR KOTRA), IN KACHHI, TO KALĀT *viâ* THE MULA PASS.

Halting-place.	Elevation above sea.	Distance in miles.	Remarks
	ft.		
Pir Chatta	...	8	Mula pass is entered at three miles. Encamping ground among trees.
Kuhan ...	1250	14	Encamping ground on right bank of the Mula river.
Pani-wat	...	8	Cultivation close to this village.
Hatāchi ...	...	9	A small village on the left bank of the river.
Pir Lakka	...	9	Encamping ground near a temple in the bed of the river.
Nar	2850	9	Encamping ground on the plain.
Peshtar Khān	...	8	Encamping ground on side of the pass; the Zidi route to Kalāt branches off from this village.
Guram Bauna	...	8¼	Encamping ground in open space on the south side of the pass.
Pisi-bent	4600	9¼	Slight cultivation on line of road; encamping ground on north side of the pass.
Jangi Jāh	...	14	Village of Basan is the usual halting-place, and is preferable. Encamping ground on a stony plain.
Angira ...	5250	8	Encamping ground is close to a watercourse. A hill road runs from Jangi Jāh to Sohrāb, but is reported bad for laden animals.
Sohrāb ...	...	12	Is the name of a cluster of villages; encamping ground south of Sohrāb, near a small stream of running water.
Surmasingh	...	17	No village; encamping ground close to a watercourse. At 14 miles pass village of Gandagarh, a better halting-place as regards distance, but water supply precarious.
Rodinjo ...	...	9	Encamping ground east of a small village near some watercourses.
Kalāt ...	...	12	Large town; encamping ground east of city among gardens and cultivation.
	Total	155	estimated miles.

XI.

DĀDAR (IN KACHHI) TO QUETTA (OR SHĀL-KŌT) *viâ* THE BOLĀN PASS.

Halting-place.	Elevation above sea.	Distance in miles.	Remarks.
Khundilāni	ft. 965	12	Bolān pass entered at five miles from Dādar, and river Bolān has frequently to be crossed ; ascent slight but road stony ; camel forage scarce and some coarse grass for horses only obtainable. Khundilāni is merely a halting-place.
Kirta ...	1200	14	Road frequently crosses Bolān river, and is very narrow after leaving Khundilāni ; afterwards stony and runs through a valley. Kirta is a small village ; camel and horse forage as in previous stage.
Bibi-Nāni	1695	9	Good road over a plain, afterwards passes through a gorge, thence emerging into the valley of Bibi-Nāni. Forage of all kinds scarce, but water is plentiful. (From this place a hill road runs direct to Kalāt by Baradi, Rodbar, Nurmakh Takht, Johan, and Kishan, an entire distance of 110 miles.)
Ab-i-Gūm	2600	14	Road very fatiguing, being over loose shingle and boulders ; no supplies or forage of any kind, but water is obtainable.
Sir-i-Bolān	4075	6	Is the source of the Bolān river ; ascent gradual though very considerable ; no supplies of any kind obtainable ; water is abundant and good.
Sir-i-āb	...	27	For a distance of 10 miles to top of pass (5800 feet) no water is to be met with. Road to head of pass narrow for about the last three miles, but thence opens out into a narrow valley and afterwards into the Dasht-i-Bidaulat (or plain of poverty). Water abundant at Sir-i-āb, but no supplies procurable.
Quetta ...	5600	8	Road good. Quetta (or Shāl-Kōt), a large town with about 4000 inhabitants ; supplies, forage, and water abundant.
	Total	90	miles.

XII.

BIBI-NĀNI (IN BOLĀN PASS) TO KALĀT *viâ* RODBAR.

Halting-place.	Distance in miles.	Remarks.
Baradi ...	12	For first six miles pass through a plain; road then enters a pass about 150 yards wide. Water from mountain springs. The two villages of Jam and Baradi are off the road on an elevated plateau.
Zer-i-Kotal	20	On leaving Baradi the valley opens out to a breadth of three miles, in which the tamarisk-tree forms a jungle, and water is lost; the pass is then formed again, and the water reappears. At four miles from foot of pass, road is level. There are several ascents and descents till Sar-i-deh is reached. Water is plentiful at Zer-i-Kotal.
Rod Bahar, or Rodbar	18	Water obtainable throughout this march, and small cultivated patches of wheat, rice, and juār met with; peaches, apricots, mulberries, etc., abound in small gardens; the cultivators are Kalhoi Brahuis and others. Fuel plentiful.
Nurmukh	10	At four miles pass Irarmukh, inhabited in summer by Brahui shepherds, to the number of 150 tents; water in three wells, but cultivation is dependent on rain. Nurmukh is on a plain and divided from the Takht plain by a projecting chain of hills.
Takht ...	14	This place is inhabited only in the summer months by wandering shepherds. If rain falls, water will be found at Takht, otherwise precarious.
Johan ...	15	Here is a fort containing some 30 houses. Water obtainable from a running stream; rice and wheat cultivated to some extent, and there are a few gardens.
Kishan ...	12	Water procurable from a running stream; there is some cultivation. Kishan contains only 10 houses.
Kalāt ...	15	The entire road from Bibi-Nāni to Kalāt is passable for cavalry and camels, but not for guns.
Total ...	116	miles.

XIII.

DĀDAR TO KANDAHĀR (IN AFGHĀNISTAN) *via* QUETTA.

Halting-place.	Distance in miles.	Remarks.
Quetta ...	90	See Route XI.
Kuchlak ...	11½	At about three miles pass small village of Abdul Rahim Khān. An ascent and descent in this stage, and the former five stony nālas are crossed. Kuchlak, a small village, with a fort three furlongs beyond it; it is only two or three miles from the base of the lofty Tokātu mountain.
Haidarzai	10	At two miles cross Lora river, 80 yards wide, road now winds a little among low sandy hills on rising ground, but is good; at eight miles again cross Lora river, here only three or four yards broad and twenty inches deep. Haidarzai, a small village, with considerable cultivation.
Haikalzai and Khedazai	11	Road for three-and-a-half miles over a fine open plain, and is good; a few nālas have to be crossed, as also the Sangau river at about eight miles; road then winds along the base of some low sandy hills. Haikalzai, a large walled village; Khedazai, an open one; both places mostly inhabited by Saiyads.
Halting-place	7	Road passes between deep and dangerous nālas, with intervals of good level ground; Lora river crossed before reaching camping-ground. Forage scarce on the plain, but thin grass obtainable in the higher bed of the river.
Aramba ...	7½	In this march two villages, Tukani and Kulāzi, were passed with much cultivation about them; the camp was formed on the Aramba plain, one mile to the right of a fort and village, and with a good stream or canal of running water. Road good. Forage and supplies obtainable.
Near Killa Abdula	6	Camp formed on left bank of river, which is broad and shallow. Forage and supplies obtainable from Killa Abdula, distant about two-and-a-half miles.
Chaman ...	11½	A good road to the Kojak pass, about seven miles, ascent steep near the top, and descent nearly as much so; another steep ascent and descent, after which, at three miles, is Chaman, in the vicinity of which some springs and green grass were found. Camel forage pretty good. (Summit of Kojak pass is 7457 feet high.)
Dand-i-Gollai	15½	Road, on leaving Chaman, for three or four miles over a dry plain; several shallow nālas passed in this march; road then ascends a number of low sand ridges. Forage scarce, and no village near. There is a reservoir of water at Dand-i-Gollai.
Patula Killa	9	Camp formed one-and-a-quarter miles south of the Patula fort. There is another road round the hilly ground, north of Patula.
Mele, or Melamanda	11½	Road ascends very gradually until about four miles north of the fort, when a succession of rough ascents and descents over nālas between the two hills, which approach here to a narrow pass, occur, descending then gradually all the way to the river. The camp was near the remains of several small villages: a small stream in the bed of the river, and some wells.

DĀDAR TO KANDAHĀR (*continued*).

Halting-place.	Distance in miles.	Remarks.
Dori River	14½	Road over undulating, dry, stony ground for 10½ miles, passing at a narrow part between the hills, at six miles on the north-west out of the Melamanda valley, where the road is confined a short way, and more stony. No village near, but a good deal of cultivation along the river. Grass and camel forage about the river, which had four or five yards of water, 18 inches deep.
Deh-i-Hāji	7½	Road from Dori river good, crossing eight nālas, all small, running to a large nāla with high banks. Deh-i-Hāji, a large place, with a good deal of green cultivation around. Large supplies came in here—forage, some short grass, lucerne, and green corn; water from aqueduct.
Khush-āb (camp at aqueduct)	12	Khush-āb, a general name given to the villages in this part of the plain; six or seven large villages in neighbourhood of the camp, and much green cultivation.
Kandahār City	7½	At about two-and-a-quarter miles pass Zankar village, with many gardens and much cultivation; at two-and-three-quarter miles further on the large village of Kurāzi, with gardens and enclosures; afterwards Popalzai on right, and Naudri on left. City of Kandahār nearly rectangular in shape; country outside open on the south and west, but on the north side extensive cemeteries and other inclosures; on west and south-west sides still more inclosed by gardens and villages, which confine the country for between two and three miles.
Total ...	232	miles.

XIV.

QUETTA TO MUSHKI *viâ* THE NISHPA PASS, &c. (1841).

Halting-place.	Distance in miles.	Remarks.
Sir-i-āb ...	8½	Road excellent and level, water from *karēz* abundant; camel and horse forage. Pass some villages on the road where supplies are procurable: none at Sir-i-āb.
Mahbi ..	14½	At three-and-a-half miles pass a small range of hills to left, called Lundai, where road ascends, and at eight miles is broken and stony. It then divides, and leads to westward between two hills to the Nishpa pass, the north entrance of which is 10 miles from Sir-i-āb; it is two miles long, and has lately been cleared. Another road leads over the Kobilikh, a rough and broken pass east of the Nishpa, and is usually taken by horsemen and foot-travellers. Three miles beyond south entrance of Nishpa pass is river, Mahbi, where ground on its banks is open and extensive; water and camel forage abundant. No habitations or supplies at Mahbi.

QUETTA TO MUSHKI (*continued*).

Halting-place.	Distance in miles.	Remarks.
Babbri ...	9¼	Road passes between low hills, and at four-and-a-half miles leaves the made road to Mastung *viâ* Tiri; at eight miles pass village of Dingarb, and thence to Babbri road skirts small range of low hills. Babbri, small village with no supplies, but water good and plentiful from a *karēz.*
Panjpēs ...	13¼	For four miles road passes over open plain, then enters some low hills, after which comes to the Kallan Barak pass through a gorge 120 to 130 yards wide, and 500 yards long; road follows water-course, and is good throughout, offering no obstacles to passage of artillery; descent on western side more abrupt than that on eastern; entire length of pass, two-and-a-quarter miles. At 10¼ miles cross the Sherināb river; Panjpēs is one of the four villages of the Sheri road district, has 120 houses. Supplies very scarce, but corn grown largely in neighbourhood; water abundant from a *karēz.*
Chamani-Singhur	9	For five-and-a-half miles road passes over a level plain, where it enters broken and undulating ground, and so continues to Chamani-Singhur, which is a beautiful green spot in a small valley, 200 to 250 yards wide, and three-quarters of a mile long; has a good supply of water, and excellent forage.
Manu Chakul	8½	Road follows the windings of the river, with a gentle ascent, and is of the same character as before; some small wells of good water passed at intervals. At Manu Chakul fair supply of water with forage for camels and horses; this place is not seen from the road.
Kaisar River	14¾	About half-way between Manu Chakul and the Kaisar river is Jajbad, where there is a small spring of water; two other springs further on are met with at intervals, the last is four miles from the Kaisar river, the road to which is rather rugged and stony; this river has a large stream of water, which rarely dries up. Encamping ground is uneven and stony; forage procurable for camels in the neighbourhood.
Buband ...	12	From Kaisar to Buband the road follows the windings of the river, and is tortuous and very distressing, as this stream has, in a distance of 12 miles, to be crossed *no less than forty-two times.* Encamping ground at Buband open and good, with forage in the neighbourhood.
Nushki ...	3	On leaving Buband the Kaisar river is crossed, road then passes over an open plain, with the termination of the Kuti range on hills on the right hand, distant one-and-a-half miles. Nushki is situate half-a-mile beyond the hill at the southern extremity of a low ridge or spur, 160 feet high, from the Kuti hills, and overhangs the Kaisar river, from which it is watered. It consists of from 90 to 100 *ghedans*, or felt tents; there are *no* houses. No shops or supplies, but camel and horse forage is abundant to the westward, where the plains are extensively cultivated. The Rakshāni tribe occupy Nushki. Encamping ground to the east and west; water abundant from the Kaisar river. The heat between April and September is oppressive in the extreme.
Total ...	93	miles.

XV.

QUETTA TO KALĀT *viâ* MASTUNG (CAMPBELL).

Halting-place.	Distance in miles.	Remarks.
Ispangli ...	5¼	Road good, excepting having to cross a deep nāla about half-way. There is a more direct road to Kalāt from Quetta, but not practicable for guns.
Barg ...	9¾	Road excellent, leading up a valley about eight miles wide; a small running stream and four or five villages on the right, some distance towards the hills.
Kanak ...	12¾	Road as yesterday, leading up the same valley, and equally good; a stream of water on the right of the camp, and the village of Kanak, visible about two miles south-west.
Mastung ...	15¼	Road good as far as Teri, a large village; about 11 miles on the road thence had a deep ravine and several water-courses between it and Mastung. From Teri there is a direct road to Kalāt, leaving Mastung to the left; Mastung is a place with a good many gardens near, but the town seems to be going to decay. The inhabitants are Balochis and Hindus.
Shirin-āb ...	11¾	After leading due west for about eight miles, the road sweeps to the south and enters a valley, the same as from Ispangli to Kanak, and is equally good. No village near the camp but a small river to the right of the halting-place, with ample water in it.
Karēz Dost Muhammad	9½	A small village, with a spring of water from the hills, besides the Shirin-āb river; road excellent, with a slight ascent. The village was almost deserted, as it is the custom of the inhabitants to migrate to Kachhi on the approach of winter.
Zard ...	12½	Two or three small villages, but deserted; a good stream of water, and the road excellent, still continuing up the same valley as before.
Barin Chinar	9½	An aqueduct and much cultivated ground, but the village was deserted; this is near the head of the valley. Mangachar was visible to the left, by which the direct road comes from Kalāt, but is not convenient for troops on account of a scarcity of water.
Girāni ...	17¾	Encamped on a fine stream of water; several villages near, and the road good.
Kalāt ...	8¼	A strong walled town, besides a lofty inner citadel. The suburbs are also very extensive, and there are a good many gardens to the east; this is the residence of the Brahui Khān of Kalāt. The road from the last ground was very good, with hills on both sides until within a mile of Kalāt. A river runs to the east of the suburbs of the town.
Total ...	112¼	miles.

XVI.

NUSHKI TO KHARĀN (1841).

Halting-place	Distance in miles.	Remarks.
Dost Muhammad	12	A plain and open road, south-south-west towards a large detached mountain called Koh-i-Shekh-Husain, about 16 miles from Nushki; it forms a conspicuous object, and is sacred as a *ziārat*.
Tophai ...	18	Road passes over a plain between Koh-i-Shekh-Husain and the main range of mountains to the eastward; water from a water-course which flows from the hills south-east of Nushki, 10 to 12 miles, and joins the Kaisar river some five miles to the westward. Camel and horse forage procurable in small quantities.
Chaki Thal	11	Road good and level, passes up a water-course for six or seven miles, and crosses a small *kand*, not described as difficult. Chaki Thal is situate in a plain where water is scarce; forage from tamarisk bushes in the neighbourhood.
Pat ...	12	Road tolerably good, occasionally passing over level ground, at others in the bed of the Badak river, which flows south from the Shekh-Husain mountain; the inhabitants of this neighbourhood are generally of the tribe of Samalāris. Water found in abundance, and tamarisk as camel forage.
Laipshauki	11¼	The road enters on a plain called Sindh Babul, is good and level, with hills on both sides; a few miles close to Laipshauki the Choringhi and Badu rivers unite; flowing south-west to Kharān they take the name of the Bēl river, running parallel to the road.
Azaad Gaz	7	Road open and follows the course of the river Bēl; hills on each side, those to the westward not lofty. Water from the river, with a little camel forage procurable in the neighbourhood.
Sarawān ...	9	Road open and level, following the course of the river for about a mile, after which crosses a small spur from the hills to the eastward, and enters on the plains of Kharān. Sarawān, a small village; water from wells and *banded* rain-water; large hill, distant six or eight miles to the eastward, to the west it is open to the desert.
Karez Azaad Khān	8	A small village, the favourite residence of Azaad Khān; the *karez* gives a very tolerable supply of water, by means of which and the rain-water, banded-up cultivation is to some extent carried on in the neighbourhood, and generally in the Kharān district. Azaad Khān, like a prudent bandit, has secured to himself an asylum in the fortresses of an isolated hill, called "Kalling," about 20 miles south-west of Kharān, where, in times of danger, he takes refuge with a few chosen followers. The access to this hill is difficult, and only attainable by ropes; the crest of the hill is extensive, and affords shelter for 1500 men, while an abundant supply of water enables the fugitives to cultivate corn, barley, etc; date-trees are also numerous, but there are no buildings of any description on the hill.
Total ...	88¼	miles.

XVII.

NUSHKI TO SHORĀWAK (1841).

Halting-place.	Distance in miles.	Remarks.
Siasingh ...	16	No water; road level but sandy; it skirts the Kuti range of hills, which lie to the eastward from one to four miles. Water usually taken from Nushki, or a long march made to it.
Manduzāi	10	Water from *bandh*, but scarce; road and country as above; *ghedans*, or tents, scattered about; no forage.
Band-i-Mamuk	5	Water from the road, distant two miles, where there is a small spring, but after rain, water is found at the Band-i-Mamuk; road and water as above. Inhabitants are Afghāns of the Manduzai tribe.
Shirāni ...	4	Is the chief town of Shorāwak; it is under Kandahār, being to the north of the river Sohrāb, which is crossed a couple of miles before reaching Shirāni. There is a small enclosure called a fort, but it is deserving of no remark. Supplies of grain, sheep, etc., procurable. Camels and horses are bred extensively in this district; road is level and good, but sandy from the Band-i-Mamuk.
Total ...	35	miles.

XVIII.

KARĀCHI TO KALĀT *viâ* LAS BĒLA (HARRISON).

Halting-place.	Distance in miles.	Remarks.
Habb river	14	Road good; no town; water from river; forage, but no supplies obtainable. (Another road leads to the Habb through Mangah Pir, distant nine miles from Karāchi, thence to Habb, eight miles; road good to Mangah Pir, but beyond is rough in places.)
Lak ...	18	Road good, slight descent towards the sea; no village; sweet water and coarse grass obtainable.
Sonmiāni...	20	Road good; at eight miles pass small hamlet, Nakab, on the Wahir river; at 12 miles village of Arub-Sonmiāni, small sea-port town; forage and supplies procurable in small quantities; water sweet.
Shekh Rāj	18	Road good; town small; no supplies procurable; water from kachha wells but limited in quantity.
Uthal ...	14	Road good, town large, and cultivation extensive; supplies abundant, and sweet water obtainable from wells.
Shekhron-ka-got	22	Jungle on line of road but not obstructive; cultivation large; supplies and sweet water from kachha wells limited.
Bēla ...	24	Road runs through rich alluvial land with *pilu* jungle in parts; at 12 miles pass rain-water tank where kāfilas halt; at 16 miles cross Purali river near Danda village, descent and ascent steep; four or five miles from Bēla road is banded and is distressing to baggage animals. Bēla (once a large town), the residence of the Jambut, is now poorly inhabited. Cultivation extensive and neighbouring village large; supplies procurable; water abundant.

KARĀCHI TO KALĀT (*continued*).

Halting-place.	Distance in miles.	Remarks.
Kishāri ...	14	Road easy, village of Walipat near; cultivation is from the Purali river.
Kaukhāni (or Basin-Khāni)	18	Road in parts bad; sweet water obtainable by digging holes in river-bed; no supplies.
Salās ...	18	Road easy; no supplies.
Rode-Gurāri (or Rode Jamkār)	18	Road rough but practicable; water to be had from the river.
Turk-Bur	19	At nine miles cross the Lak hill, where road is available for baggage mules and camels, but impracticable for artillery; water procurable, but no supplies.
Wadd ...	24	Road good; at 12 miles cultivation once more apparent. Town small and unimportant, but supplies procurable and water to be had from the river.
Wahir ...	20	Road good, and leads through the Wahir valley; drinking water precarious, being dependent on rainfall; no supplies procurable.
Izbotki ...	14	Road good; nearest village Pir Umar. Cultivation scant; no supplies, but water procurable from a hill stream.
Khozdār ...	10	Road good. This place, which is in a fertile valley, has a large fort; supplies abundant, and water procurable from a hill stream.
Bāghwāna	16	Road good, water and supplies obtainable.
Jawir ...	14	Road good, cultivation scant; spring water obtainable, but no supplies.
Angira ...	20	Road at first rough and broken, but practicable; water and supplies limited.
Sohrāb ...	14	Road, which runs through a valley studded with small villages, is easy; water and supplies procurable.
Surmasingh	16	Road good; no supplies, and water brackish.
Rodenjo ...	13	Road good; cultivation, but supplies limited; water abundant.
Kalāt ...	14	Road good; large town, where supplies of all kinds are abundant; water from hill streams.
Total ...	392	miles.

XIX.

KARĀCHI TO SHĀH BILĀWAL (IN LAS).

Halting-place.	Distance in miles.	Remarks.
Mangah Pir	9	Dharamsāla; water from hot springs; no supplies.
Chakura Nālā	11½	Halting-place at the nāla; water obtainable from pools, but no supplies.
Habb river	5½	Water obtainable, but no supplies.
Babura river	15	Water scanty and brackish; no supplies.
Virab-ji-got	8	Road bad and rocky among hills; water abundant, but supplies scanty.

KARĀCHI TO SHĀH BILĀWAL (*continued*).

Halting-place.	Distance in miles.	Remarks.
Junction of the Virab and Amri rivers	11¼	Road very bad; water scanty, and supplies none.
Shāh Bilāwal	11¼	Road very bad and hardly passable for camels; water abundant from a fine spring, but no supplies. Many fruit and bābul trees here, as also a mosque of much sanctity with a cemetery attached to it.
Total ...	71½	miles.

XX.

JACOBABAD TO DERA IN THE BUGHTI HILLS *viâ* SHAHPŪR.

Halting-place.	Distance in miles.	Remarks.
Minoti ...	20½	Road open, level, hard and good; country quite level and chiefly desert; supplies scanty, but horse and camel forage plentiful; water, good but scanty, is found in numerous pits in a nāla to the south.
Shahpūr ...	14	Road open and level, but latter part very heavy and sandy. Shāhpur, an open town on the north side of the sand-hills bounding the desert; encamping ground near the water-pits in the river, whence a good and plentiful supply is obtainable. No supplies procurable here.
Uch ...	11½	The first three miles and the two last very heavy, rest good. Uch is a deserted village; brackish water from a running stream; no supplies obtainable; coarse forage abundant.
Suri Kushta	21	Road heavy and difficult in many parts, running along the dry beds of sandy nālas and across precipitous ravines. No village here; water obtainable from the bed of a hill stream by digging from 13 to 15 feet; coarse forage abundant.
Zurāni ...	10	Road generally good; water and forage as above.
Zin-ka-Kumb	7	Road runs through the Lalli pass, three miles from which it meets the main range forming the southern boundary of the Bughti hills, and then ascends gradually for two miles to the Zin-ka-Kumb pass, through which guns must be unlimbered and drawn up by manual labour. Water procurable from a cleft in the rock 480 yards east of Zin-ka-Kumb; forage as above.
Kumbi	10	Road at first crosses a table-land between two and three miles broad, after which it gradually descends to Kumbi, on the north side.
Dēra ...	15	Six miles from Kumbi the Dēra plain is entered. Dēra is the chief town of the Bughti tribe, and possesses a fort. It is 1250 feet above sea-level, and is bounded on the north by a precipice 1500 feet high. The stream can be turned by those who hold the pass whence the spring issues. Water abundant from a canal fed by a spring in the gorge of the hills two miles north-east of the town; supplies moderate, but forage abundant.
Total ...	109	miles.

XXI.

JACOBABAD TO KAHAN IN THE MARRI COUNTRY *viâ* PULAJI (1840).

Halting-place.	Distance in miles.	Remarks.
Shahpūr ...	34½	See Route No. XX.
Chatta ...	11¾	First seven miles over a grassy plain, sandy and heavy; the remainder good and hard over cultivation. At six miles cross Jywāgh river, in which water is always procurable by digging a few feet. Chatta a large village; water good and abundant from several deep wells; supplies and horse forage abundant.
Pulaji ...	9¼	At four miles pass Thar-ka-got, small village; road through cultivation, good and hard. Pulaji, large village surrounded by rich cultivation, about five miles from the hills; water good and plentiful from wells 90 feet deep; supplies and forage abundant.
Gogri Valley	14	At three miles from Pulaji enter hills, and at six miles cross Tywāgh river. Thence five miles through a valley, after which enter Gogri valley, one and a half miles long by six furlongs broad, bounded on all sides by precipitous sandstone cliffs; water good and abundant but no supplies; grass and camel forage abundant.
Marawar Valley	8	Road very confined along the bed of a river in a narrow ravine. At five miles pass an opening by which a road leads to Dēra; water and forage as above.
Suri Valley	11	Road runs through a succession of ravines and valleys. For one and a half miles pass up the Marawar plain, afterwards through another narrow pass, thence along the valley for a mile and a half through low hills to Suri; water scanty, but grass and camel forage abundant.
Chikargi Valley	9	Road runs through narrow ravines and over steep passes; water abundant from a fine stream, and grass and camel forage abundant.
Sartaff Range (foot of the)	9	Pass two miles through the Chikargi valley, parallel with river, to where the routes from Pulaji to Dēra and Kahan separate. Road then ascends northward to slightly elevated stony plain, and afterwards enters a range of low hills for two miles—is very trying for camels' feet—then descends into the dry pebbly bed of a mountain stream which is crossed to reach the camping-place, a level spot at the foot of the Sartaff range; water to be had from some extensive pools, and camel forage abundant.
Naffusk Range (foot of the)	9	At one mile ascend the Sartaff range (1500 feet high); face of mountain forms a regular slope up which the route winds; guns have to be dragged up by manual labour; no water on summit, afterwards road leads over level country with some wheat cultivation. A small supply of water was found at the bottom of a fissure in the mountain.
Kahan ...	6	Ascend Naffusk pass—range is about 1000 feet in elevation, but more precipitous than that of Sartaff, and only accessible at one point, where a rough road has been formed by traverses at a spot rendered practicable by a slip of the rock. Kahan a walled town, and the capital of the Marri tribe, is about 2000 feet above sea-level, and has much wheat cultivation in the neighbourhood; water is abundant from pools in the bed of a river, and supplies plentiful.
Total ...	121½	miles.

INDEX.

B.

F.

G.

K.

L.

S.

THE END.

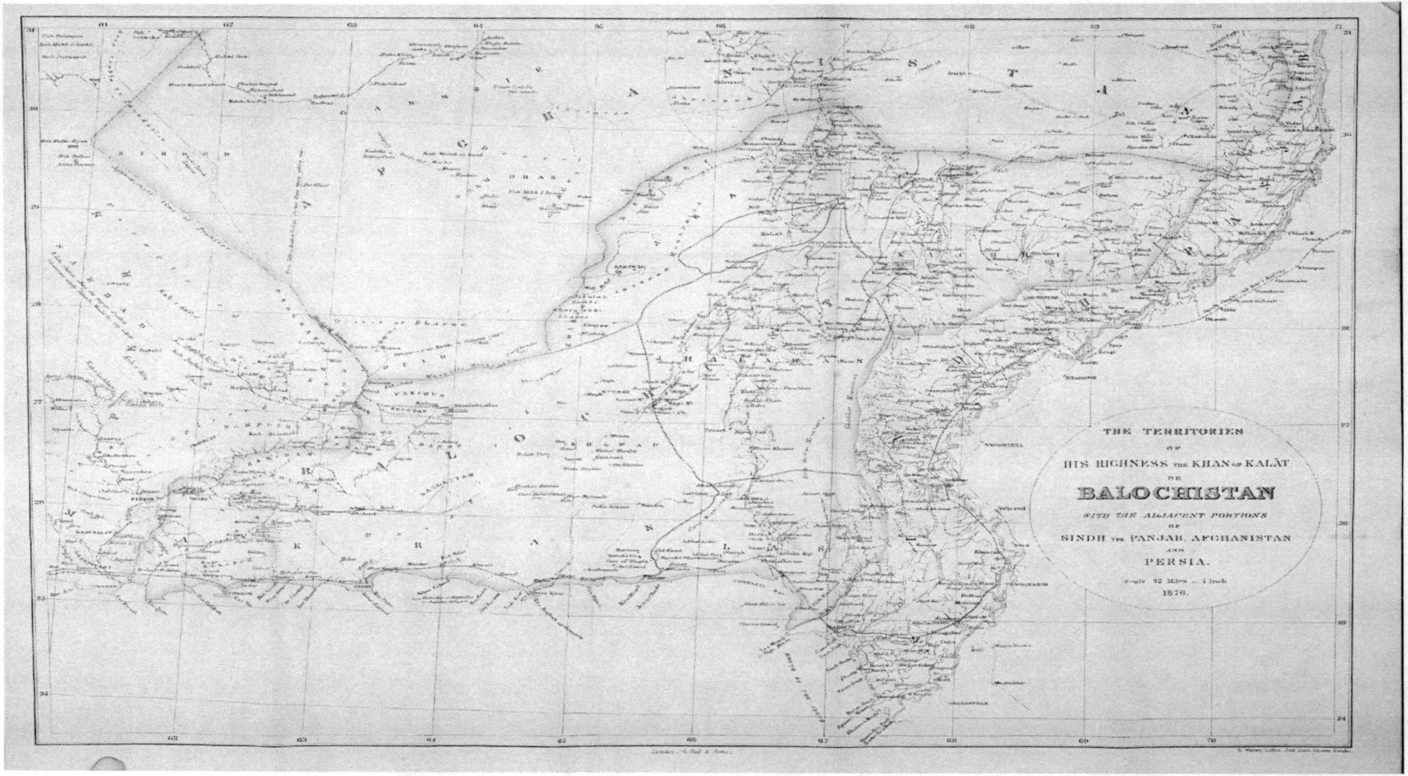
THE TERRITORIES
OF
HIS HIGHNESS THE KHAN OF KALĀT
OR
BALOCHISTAN
WITH THE ADJACENT PORTIONS
OF
SINDH THE PANJAB, AFGHANISTAN
AND
PERSIA.
1876.